THE BOOK OF LISTS FOR TEENS

Books by Sandra Choron

1,001 Tips for Caregivers (with Sasha Carr)

The All-New Book of Lists for Kids (with Harry Choron)

Elvis: The Last Word (with Bob Oskam)

The Book of Lists for Kids (with Harry Choron)

The Big Book of Kids' Lists

Rocktopicon (with Dave Marsh and Debbie Geller)

Everybody's Investment Book (with Edward Malca)

National Lampoon's Class Reunion

The
BOOK
of
LISTS
for
TEENS

Sandra
and
Harry Choron

 Houghton Mifflin Company · Boston · New York · 2002

Visit our Web site: www.houghtonmifflinbooks.com.

Library of Congress Cataloging-in-Publication Data is available.
ISBN 0-618-17907-0

Book design by Melissa Lotfy

Printed in the United States of America

QUM 10 9 8 7 6 5 4 3 2 1

For Kristen Ann Carr,
who graduated with honor

Acknowledgments

There are angels all around us, and we're grateful to them all: Brandy Vickers, our talented editor, understands more about patience than anyone we know; we thank her for her tenacity and enthusiasm. Amy Wuhl contributed her talent and skill as a young journalist who seems to know something about everything. Katie Leeds, Sophie Leeds, Tammy Hull Awtry, and Grace Yang are the best cheerleaders in the world. Dave Marsh, Tony Goldmark, Shannon Garrahan, Shirley Glickman, and Lee Ballinger contributed their kind support and valuable professional opinions. Casey Choron helped by inspiring us always to be as interesting and as funny as he is.

Grace Townley single-handedly organized her army of teens to make sure this book reflects the real opinions of real people. We thank them—

Myanh Hoang   Liz Kinder
Andrew Satterlee   Eric Lorenzen
K. B. Vickers   Dan Peeresechini
Abby Buchheit   Callie Shroeder
Linda Waterborg   Jane Gregory
Danny Akright   Christine Kim
Sara Jordan   Brian McCandless
Ryan Heiling   Matt Wilson
Emi Suenaga   Graham Ryan
Jessica Campbell   Christina Smith

We also gratefully acknowledge the help of about.com and its generosity in allowing us to reprint information from its excellent Web site.

CONTENTS

INTRODUCTION

6 Reasons We Wrote This Book

1. Now that the world is completely wired, there are more choices and opportunities—and information—available to almost everyone. Making lists is a way of organizing information, a skill everyone needs in order to participate in today's action-packed world.

2. We wanted you to read about the lives of other people in the hope that this will make you sensitive to their experiences—and their cultures. So we're hoping that when you read this book, you'll pay special attention to the lists that don't apply to you. You may not have a fear of public speaking, but some people do. Read the list called "14 Tips if You're Nervous About Public Speaking" on page 177 to find out what life is like for them. Maybe it will change how you behave during lectures and speeches.

3. Our previous book, *The Book of Lists for Kids,* which was first published in 1985 and reissued in 1995 and 2002, has been a popular book for kids from 9 to 12. This book addresses the next group up—teens—and covers subjects that are more relevant to the many new experiences that await you.

4. We believe that Truth and Fun are central in our lives. So we've included plenty of both.

5. We know that, as a teen, you are busy and stressed. Yet there's so much you need to remember to cope with it all. This book dispenses with the lectures and tells you only the stuff you need to know.

6. For the money—although it's hard to believe that we got paid to have this much fun!

1.
ME,
MYSELF,
and I

40 Ways to Simplify Your Life

1. Buy all your clothes in colors that work together. That doesn't mean you need to dress in black. Just make up your mind about which colors you like best—pastels? primary colors? hot colors? black, white, and gray?—and try to buy things that can be mixed and matched.

2. Create a filing system and *use* it. If you don't have a file drawer, you can put the files in a box. Label a file for every subject you can think of—school subjects, report cards, birthday cards, memorabilia, letters, shopping receipts—and always file those items as soon as you get them. You'll avoid a cluttered room and the trouble it takes to find something like the receipt for your stereo when it suddenly breaks down two days before the warranty is up. At least once every year, go through the files and get rid of stuff you don't want to keep anymore.

3. Get an address book and keep it up to date. Get one that's a little bigger than what you think you need so you have room to "grow." Or create a file on your computer.

4. Get a calendar with big boxes for each day or a day-by-day date book and use it for everything—school assignments, upcoming events, birthdays, sports events. Having everything in one book makes it easier to keep track of the information. Just don't lose the book. (Write your name and phone number in it.)

5. Always tell the truth. Lying is complicated, time-consuming, and wrong.

6. If you do tell a lie, confess as soon as possible.

7. Confront problems as soon as they develop. That way you won't ever have to feel overwhelmed by what seems like a truckful of trouble.

8. Make lists. Keep track of your goals so you'll always know where you're headed. Make a Monday list: every Monday make a list of all the things you want to accomplish before the weekend.

9. Create a study ritual that triggers your brain into letting you know that it's time for schoolwork—and nothing else. The ritual can consist of a snack, five minutes (no more!) at a computer game, or even a few minutes of clearing your workspace of distractions. This should satisfy the part of you that's always tempting you with distractions while you study—at least for a while.

10. Keep a reading diary. Write down the title and author of every book you read and note the date you finished it. Write just a few sentences about the book that will help you recall it if you need to. You'll save yourself the time of rereading books that are assigned in different classes.

11. Don't wear makeup regularly. You'll avoid having to take it with you wherever you go, you'll save money, and you won't feel weird when you have to go without it. There will be *plenty* of time for makeup!

12. Don't get anything pierced or tattooed.

13. Don't do anything to yourself that will require a regular commitment you might not be ready for. Hair coloring, for instance, might look like fun now, but will you have the money for another treatment once the roots start growing out?

14. Deal with each piece of paper in your life as few times as possible. For instance, if you get a letter from a friend, put it in your file once you've read it. If you leave it lying around, it will probably become part of a mess of clutter that then needs to be dealt with. Get these things out of your way as quickly as they come up.

15. Don't be a prima donna. Use the same shampoo (and toothpaste and breakfast cereal) as the rest of the family.

16. Read a book about etiquette. Know what to do and what to say on certain occasions like the death of a friend, meeting someone really important, or dealing with an awkward situation. There are rules for this stuff, and you don't want to spend half your life wondering what they are.

17. Set priorities. When you have 37 things to do and you don't know where to begin, list them and give them each a number from 1 to 3. The 1s are the most important; the 3s can wait. Start with the 1s. (Hint: Always do the hardest stuff first so it's then out of the way.)

18. Use sunscreen.

19. Don't put your name on mailing lists because you think it's fun to fill out forms and get mail. You're wasting trees, money, and a lot of time. When you have to give your name and address to someone in order to make a purchase, ask them not to put your name on any mailing lists.

20. Learn to travel light, so you can get up and go when opportunity knocks. You can sleep in your T-shirt and borrow shampoo from whomever you're visiting. Another reason not to wear makeup, ladies.

21. Play a sport that doesn't require elaborate equipment, planning, or expense. The same goes for any physical fitness activity. Do stuff you can do anywhere.

22. Enjoy TV, but don't get so addicted to any one show that you start to live your life around its schedule. Think of it as traveling light—through life.

23. Be realistic about donating your time to various causes. Don't make commitments you can't keep. If you want to get involved and aren't sure how things will work out, start out with a trial period.

24. Keep a box in your closet for "junk." When you have to clear the clutter, just throw it into the box. When the box is full, empty it and get rid of anything you don't really need. Put everything else in its proper place. If it doesn't have a proper place, there's a good chance you don't need this thing.

25. Color-code your school supplies by subject so, for instance, everything that has to do with math (the notebook, the textbook cover) is blue, all your stuff for history is red, etc.

26. Try not to have to carry *all* your books home every day. Can you get a second copy of a book out of the library to keep at home for reference? If you study with a friend, can you share your books?

27. Learn to cook easy stuff: pasta, eggs, pancakes, hamburgers. The more self-sufficient you are, the easier it will be to get through hectic times.

28. Learn to iron a shirt, do simple laundry, and sew on a button.

29. Listen to the music before you buy CDs. Use the listening devices at the record store, go online for samples, or try to catch it on the radio. Most CD collections are filled with stuff that's only been listened to once.

30. Budget yourself. Don't spend more money than you have. At the beginning of each month, make a list of your special expenses—birthdays gifts, new handlebars for your bike, club expenses—so that you're prepared for them as they come up.

31. Learn to enjoy something without having to own it. Don't clutter your life with objects that require storage space or maintenance (even if it's just dusting) unless you're sure you really want them and that they will benefit you for a long time. You can admire things from afar.

32. Meditate. Get into the habit of spending a few moments each day thinking about your goals for that day. What will you accomplish? Who do you want to spend time with? What problem will you have to solve? Clear your mind, take a deep breath, start your day. Wherever you're going, you can get there a lot faster with a map.

33. Get to know the librarian. Ask him or her to let you know when books by your favorite writers are acquired by the library.

34. Don't answer every e-mail you get. You don't need to e-mail 37 e-pals on a daily basis. Pick just a few. Let others know you have commitments that keep you offline most of the day.

35. Form a study group so you can share research, resources, and expertise.

36. Create a message chain among your friends so if you need to tell someone something, you don't have to call everyone on the list. You call one person, he calls the next, and so on.

37. Have a scrapbook and paste your memorabilia in it. You'll love looking through it in later years, and it's a way to keep all those little notes you don't know what to do with from cluttering your space. Use one volume for each year of your life.

38. Don't lend or borrow money.

39. Take vitamins.

40. Be a good person. Good karma will benefit you in the long run.

100 Things to Do When There's Nothing to Do
(All Alone and by Yourself)

1. Take lots of deep breaths and listen to the sound of your own breathing.

2. Play music.

3. Rearrange the furniture in your room.

4. Reread your favorite book.

5. Look at the stars.

6. Exercise.
7. Clean something.
8. Make a list of all the things that stress you out.
9. Rent a movie.
10. Make up stories (in your head) about strangers.
11. Say a prayer.
12. Record a funny message on your answering machine.
13. Write a poem.
14. Sing a song.
15. Learn to do something new.
16. Burn incense.
17. Light a candle for someone you miss.
18. Plan a party.
19. Take a nap.
20. Paint a picture.
21. Teach your pet a trick.
22. Plant something.
23. Bake brownies.
24. Cry.
25. Take a bath with your clothes on.
26. Beat up your pillow.
27. Meditate.
28. Look at old photographs.
29. Go into a sealed room and scream.
30. Restyle your hair.
31. Make funny faces in the mirror.
32. Play a sport.
33. Drink a cup of tea.
34. Drink a cup of hot chocolate with marshmallows.
35. Fix something.
36. Go swimming.
37. Take a hike.
38. Give yourself a good talking to.
39. Don't talk for a whole day.
40. Climb a tree.
41. Write a letter to someone you're mad at (but don't send it!).
42. Dance.
43. Plan a trip, even if you can't really take it.
44. Eat something for the first time.
45. Learn to do one new thing on your computer.

46. Practice belching.
47. Eat something yummy.
48. Buy new underwear.
49. Try role playing.
50. Practice kissing — on your own hand.
51. Wear something you never wear.
52. Smell flowers.
53. Daydream.
54. Walk in the rain.
55. Try to figure out how many grains there are in a quart of sand.
56. Read a story out loud.
57. Go to a movie.
58. Work on your collection of whatever it is you collect.
59. Throw out something you don't need anymore.
60. Go to a museum.
61. Make a comic book.
62. Make a tape of your favorite song.
63. Learn to play the harmonica.
64. Learn some words in a foreign language.
65. Memorize the phone numbers you call most often.
66. Whistle.
67. Do tomorrow's homework.
68. Learn to juggle.
69. Practice telling jokes.
70. Learn something about your ancestors.
71. Stand on your head.
72. Visit a playground and go on the swings.
73. Write a love letter.
74. Watch a ball game.
75. Practice writing with your other hand.
76. Make animal noises.
77. Skate.
78. Visualize your perfect place.
79. Blow bubbles.
80. Go to the library.
81. Take a ride on a bus.
82. Line your drawers with weird wrapping paper.
83. Write a letter to your congressperson expressing a political opinion.

84. Read about a religion you know very little about.

85. Go through your baby things and reminisce.

86. Update your address book.

87. Explore the jungle under your bed.

88. Ride your bike.

89. Read the newspaper.

90. Ponder the universe.

91. Play solitaire.

92. Fly a kite.

93. Make a collage.

94. Go jogging.

95. Make a list of all the great things about yourself. If you can't think of any, make them up!

96. Play Scrabble and be all the players.

97. Write a letter to the children you might have one day and tell them about yourself.

98. Enter a contest.

99. Teach yourself sign language.

100. Just be.

4 Ways to Redecorate Your Room — Instantly and for Free

If you're tired of staring at the same four walls and there's just no money to pay for redecorating, try some of these instant makeovers.

1. Get rid of all the little items in your room that clutter the place: the science project you were so proud of in the fifth grade, the action figures left over from a previous life, the cute little party favors you've received over the years that you just can't seem to throw out. Put them in a box if you really want to keep them; throw out everything else (or pass it on to someone who will appreciate it). Now you're ready to decorate your room with new junk!

2. Rearrange the furniture. Go to the library and get a book on *feng shui* (pronounced *foong shway* or *fung shoy*), the ancient Chinese art of managing luck. You'll learn how to place furniture for the best possible flow of energy around you, and you'll learn how to use color for the best possible effects. If you can't move all the furniture, try just changing the position of your bed. A different view of the room can make it seem new.

3. **Take everything off the walls.** This doesn't mean you have to give up your passion for your favorite band or that poster with all the cute puppies you've had up since you were 7. Pack them away safely—you might put them up again when you get tired of the new stuff. As for new stuff, you can get free posters from a variety of sources. Three are on the Web: www.p-rposters.com, www.webfreebees.com, and www.successcertificates.com, where you can print out anything from a certificate congratulating yourself on terrific grades to an award for having finally cleaned your room. Free posters are also available from travel agents, or you can arrange pictures from your photo album into an interesting collage. A word of advice: live with bare walls for a few days before you cover them with new stuff. You might get a completely different idea of what you want to do.

4. **Have a painting party.** If anyone in your neighborhood is painting their house, ask if you can have any leftover paint. Hardware stores sometimes have extra cans of paint colors that have been discontinued. Ask your friends to come over and help you get the job done. Each one has to bring a brush; you supply the music.

How to Make It Appear as Though You Have Cleaned Your Room in Only 26 Minutes — No Matter How Messy It Is

First admit that the reason your room looks like something out of the last few scenes of *Die Hard* is because you don't take a little time each day to curb the mess. So now you're stuck at home, cleaning up this disaster, when all your friends are at the movies watching *I Really Still Absolutely Positively Know What You Did Last Summer*. Poor you!

If you use a timer for each of these steps, you can turn it

into a game. Reward yourself when it's all over by cleaning out a few drawers (not!). And hey, if you hurry, you might still make the movie!

1. Start by getting a few large trash bags. The first thing you want to do is get in there and toss out all the garbage—the plastic wrapping from the last six CDs you bought, the movie ticket stubs, the party favors you got that you know are junk, the "free" stuff you sent away for that wasn't even worth the $1 you included for postage and handling. *Time allowed: 8 minutes.*

2. Throw dirty clothes in the hamper and put clean clothes back where they belong. For now, just throw most of them in the closet—*but you're going to have to clean out your closet at some point! Time allowed: 3 minutes.*

3. Now you're ready to sort stuff into the following piles, which you will *without fail* tackle—one pile at a time—in the next two days:
- stuff that belongs outside your room (the books you borrowed, the letters that need to be mailed)
- school stuff
- computer and music disks, electronic game cartridges
- pencils, pens, and other writing and drawing tools (stick them in an empty jar)
- loose change
- everything else

Make neat piles and keep them out of the way of traffic. If you can sort the stuff into boxes or bags and then store them in the closet, even better. *Time allowed: 12 minutes.*

4. Make the bed. *Time allowed: 2 minutes.*

5. Open a window to air out the place. *Time allowed: 1 minute.*

6. For extra credit, vacuum the room.

The 9 Most Common Social Fears

According to TeenOutReach.com—a great Web site that covers everything from advice, homework help, and games to health, self-help, and trivia—these are the top causes of sweaty palms among teens from 13 to 17.

1. Being the center of attention
2. Having to speak or perform in front of an audience
3. Being teased
4. Being introduced to strangers
5. Making eye contact
6. Eating in front of other people, especially when it's something messy
7. Being stared at
8. Talking with an "important" or famous adult
9. Being in any unfamiliar social situation

10 Childhood Habits That Are Hard to Outgrow

Even though you're older now, you may be having trouble letting go of some of the trappings of childhood. Guess what? You're not alone. Here are some things that a lot of little kids — and plenty of big ones — tend to hold on to.

1. Nail biting
2. Hair twirling
3. Thumb sucking
4. Sleeping with a stuffed animal
5. Arguing incessantly with your parents
6. Talking with a lisp
7. Playing with your food
8. Whining
9. Throwing temper tantrums
10. Nightlights

The 7 Most Common Recurring Teen Dreams and What They Mean

Your subconscious holds the key to your hopes and dreams, your fears and fantasies. When you sleep, it takes over, and that's when you dream. Paying attention to your dreams can help you solve your problems. If you're a vivid dreamer, keep a pencil and paper near your bed and write down your dreams as soon as you wake up. Dreams "disappear" quickly, so write them down before you even get out of bed. Try to figure out why you had the dream and what problem it might be pointing to. Keep a dream diary! The following are all common dreams. They do not mean that you've finally lost it.

1. Being naked. This dream represents feelings of being exposed in some embarrassing way, not the fear that you will forget to wear clothes one day. Finding yourself naked in a classroom may mean that you aren't prepared for a test or project at school.

2. Falling. You may be afraid of failing at something. Or it could mean that you feel you can't keep up with your friends or that you don't measure up. Falling dreams can also mean that you have a sense of failure about a specific situation.

3. Teeth falling out. These dreams can mean that you're concerned about your appearance and that gorgeous smile of yours. But it can also mean that you're worried about what your friends and teachers think of you.

4. Taking an exam. If you dream that you can't complete an exam in the allowed time, if you are late for the exam, or if your pencil keeps breaking during a test, you are feeling insecure and worried that you are letting others down.

5. Being chased. If you are running away, hiding, or trying to outwit your pursuer, it may mean that you're afraid of dealing with fears, stress, or problems in your life. Instead of confronting the situation, you're avoiding it.

6. Flying. Many people have found flying dreams an exhilarating, joyful, and liberating experience. It may mean that you are prepared and on top of a given situation or that you have gained a different viewpoint on things. You feel undefeatable, and nobody can tell you what you cannot do and accomplish. You have a sense of freedom.

7. Weird dreams that make no sense. If you dream, for example, that a large blue shoe is sitting next to you in a spaceship made of marshmallows, your mind is probably searching for a solution to a specific problem.

What Your Favorite Ice Cream Flavor Says About You

Ever hear the saying "You are what you eat"? Alan J. Hirsch, M.D., of the Smell and Taste Treatment and Research Foundation in Chicago, conducts many fascinating tests about how our senses operate. Here are his latest scientific findings.

1. Banana cream pie. You're a well-adjusted person who is easy to get along with.

2. Butter pecan. You're serious, competitive, and a perfectionist. You hold high standards for yourself and you have a fear of hurting others.

3. Chocolate chip. You're competitive, ambitious, generous, and imaginative.

4. Coffee. Lively, dramatic, and flirtatious, coffee lovers often throw themselves into everything they do and then become overcommitted. You're easily bored and so must always surround yourself with interesting people.

5. Double chocolate chunk. You like attention and excitement. You're creative, enthusiastic, and charming. You are easily bored.

6. Mint chocolate chip. You're ambitious and confident. You can also be very argumentative. You'd make a great attorney.

7. Rocky road. You are charming, aggressive, and goal-oriented. You're generally relaxed and secure, but you do have a temper. You sometimes inadvertently hurt the feelings of those around you.

8. Strawberry. You are thoughtful, logical, and intuitive. You have strong opinions, you're generally introverted, and you pay attention to details. You're generally shy.

9. Vanilla. You're impulsive, you take risks, and you have high expectations. Close relationships are important to you; chances are you come from a close family. You often display your affection for people publicly.

What Your Favorite Snack Food Says About You

1. **Cheese curls.** Formal, proper, and conscientious, you have strong principles and morals. You plan for the future, taking into account any obstacles you're likely to encounter, and you take care of details. You are extremely neat and clean. Cheese curl lovers make good psychiatrists and movie producers.

2. **Meat snacks.** Meat snack lovers are at their best in large groups. You talk a lot, love to socialize, and do incredible things just to please others. You are a loyal, true friend and you can always be trusted. You'd make a great bartender or dentist.

3. **Nuts.** You are easygoing and understanding. When confronted with chaos and emotion, you can be counted on to create peace. Your even temper allows you to handle emergency situations with skill. You'd make a good politician, architect, plumber, or sanitation worker.

4. **Potato chips.** You are an ambitious high achiever, programmed to be a winner. No one wants to compete in sports with a potato chip lover. You are furious when something stands in your way, however, and have no patience for standing in lines, for instance. Potato chip lovers are success-oriented: you make great lawyers and police officers.

5. **Pretzels.** Lively and energetic, you become bored by routine. You love challenges, whether in sports, in school, or at home. You're the first to pick up new trends (how many Beanie Babies have you collected?), but you tend to initiate projects that don't always get completed. Your most likely avocation would be journalism, fire fighting, or medicine.

6. **Snack crackers.** You are shy and introspective, thoughtful and logical, rather than emotional. You avoid confrontation because you hate the idea of hurting other people. Your private time is very important to you. You may become a stock broker or race car driver.

7. **Tortilla chips.** You're a perfectionist with high expectations of yourself. You're not satisfied with an *A*. For you, only an *A+* will do. You are concerned about the injustices of society. You are always on time for everything. You'd be a good news anchor, farmer, or travel agent.

Oreo Psychology (What How You Eat an Oreo Says About You)

This has been a favorite subject of serious scientists for many decades.

1. **You eat the whole thing at once** . . . You are fun, reckless, and carefree. Consequently, you cannot be trusted.

2. **One bite at a time** . . . You're in the majority—that's how most people eat them. Which means you are ordinary and boring.

3. **Slow and methodical nibbles, examining the results of each bite afterward** . . . You follow the rules. You're tidy and orderly. You pay great attention to details. No one likes you.

4. **Dunked in milk** . . . Everyone likes you because you are always upbeat. You can turn a rainy day into fun and always look for the good things in people. You are in complete denial about life.

5. **Twisted apart, the creme inside, then the cookie** . . . You have a highly curious nature and enjoy taking things apart to find out exactly how they work. Unfortunately, you don't have the slightest clue about putting them back together. Consequently, you are rarely invited to other people's homes.

6. **Twisted apart, the creme inside, and toss the cookie** . . . You know what you want and you go straight for it. This is also known as being greedy and self-centered.

7. **Just the cookie, not the creme inside** . . . Get help.

The Top 10 Signs You'll Make a Great Lawyer Someday

1. You've replaced your trapper keeper with a briefcase.

2. You've complained to your parents that your curfew curtails your civil rights.

3. When your teacher asks you where your homework is, you plead the Fifth Amendment.

4. When you're punished, you appeal.

5. They're not goldfish—they're miniature sharks!

6. When your friends ask you for advice, you bill them.

7. You threatened to sue because your teacher didn't read you your Miranda rights before sending you to the principal's office.

8. Your favorite sport is jogging behind speeding ambulances.

9. You refer to your stepbrother as "the party of the first part."

10. You love the idea of getting paid to lie.

10 Ways to Tell if You're a Nerd

In the 1984 movie *Revenge of the Nerds*, the geeks win in the end — they get the girls, they get respect, and they have way more fun than the "normal" kids. Unfortunately, that's not how it always works in the real world.

1. You go to school dressed in business attire — the only one who does.

2. You use a TI 83 Plus programmable, graphing calculator.

3. Your broken glasses are held together with tape, and you don't feel at all self-conscious about it.

4. You continually find yourself trying to enter your password on the microwave.

5. You haven't communicated with your parents in six months because they don't have an e-mail address.

6. You think Macs are stupid.

7. You own every video game in addition to the original versions of Pong and Asteroids, you hacked your Win95 registry, and you want to be a borg.

8. You use an OS that no one else ever even heard of.

9. You yell things at the screen when you watch *Star Trek*, which you would never miss, and you have memorized at least three episodes.

10. You once got a grade lower than an *A*, but you're trying to get over it.

5 Reasons That Geeks Rule

1. They're always there when you need them.

2. They're smart.

3. You don't have to compete for their attention.
4. They can fix things.
5. Your parents will love them.

Teens' 30 Most Embarrassing Moments

1. Farting in public.

2. Laughing so hard while you're drinking that the drink comes out of your nose.

3. Sitting on something wet, then getting up to realize that you look like you peed in your pants.

4. Having people laugh at you and not knowing why.

5. Not being allowed to go out with your friends or having to go home early when everyone else is allowed to stay.

6. Opening a sandwich in the lunchroom and having everyone around you yell, "Phew!" "Gross!"

7. Dressing up and then finding out that everyone else is wearing jeans (or vice versa).

8. Being put down or yelled at in front of friends.

9. Singing an extra word in a choral concert when everyone else is silent.

10. Getting caught sending a note in class and having it read aloud to everyone by your teacher.

11. Not understanding a joke that everyone around you finds hysterically funny.

12. Getting caught kissing your girlfriend or boyfriend.

13. Being caught in a lie.

14. Having your teacher read the test grades aloud to the class when you failed or got one of the lowest marks.

15. Throwing up in public.

16. Getting a really bad haircut.

17. Realizing your gift isn't as nice as the others when someone's opening the presents at a birthday party.

18. When someone gives you a present and you didn't think to get anything for them.

19. When a family member kisses you and calls you by a pet name in front of your friends.

20. Accidentally breaking something at a friend's house when you were "just touching" it.

21. When your friends come to visit and your parents are walking around in their underwear or look really bad.

22. Accidentally walking in on your parents when they are doing it.

23. Having your most private secrets, like you still sleep with your teddy bear, spread around the school by your brother/sister/ex–best friend.

24. When you get a private itch in a public place.

25. When a guy has a sexual fantasy in class and is then called to stand up and answer a question.

26. Waving at somebody who you thought was waving at you and then realizing he or she was waving at someone else.

27. When you're in a pool and the water blows up your swim trunks and makes them look like a balloon.

28. When you forget to lock the door in a public bathroom and someone walks in on you.

29. Forgetting your lines when you have to speak or perform in front of an audience.

30. When your parents try to act cool.

10 Ways to Handle Embarrassing Moments

You're not the first person on the planet to be embarrassed—by anything. Somehow, the millions of people who have been in your position managed to survive. You will, too.

1. Make a joke out of it. Laugh! The moment wouldn't be embarrassing if it wasn't funny in some way, even if the joke's on you.

2. Quietly ask the person who is embarrassing you to stop.

3. Get angry—privately.

4. Leave the room.

5. If someone is teasing you, tease them back in a friendly way.

6. Write down your feelings.

7. Talk to your parents or a friend for support.

8. Write down what happened and send it to one of the many teen magazines that publish these stories. They print tons of them.

9. Lay low for a day or two if everyone is laughing at you. In a very short time, they will forget about your episode and find something else to laugh about. No kidding.

10. Read the list called "Teens' 30 Most Embarrassing Moments" (page 17) and be thankful that all those things didn't happen to you!

7 Tips for Controlling Your Temper

1. If you're too angry to think rationally, leave the room or remove yourself from the situation in another way.

2. Think of something relaxing while you're trying to get control of yourself. Imagine yourself in this situation reacting calmly.

3. Take a lot of deep breaths. Put some cold water on your face and on your wrists.

4. Plan a new approach. Think about apologizing for your role in the mess.

5. If you have repeated problems with one person, let him or her know and try to talk out the problem before the next conflict occurs.

6. Make a list of the things you enjoy doing that relax you and make it a point to do them often.

7. Talk to your parents, your teacher, or a friend about dealing with a problem.

6 Ways to Tell Right from Wrong

Too bad being a teen doesn't come with an instruction manual; sometimes things get confusing. Black seems white, and suddenly you find yourself considering actions that you would never have dreamed of last week. Here are some ways to make up your mind about whether something is right or wrong for you.

1. Forget what everyone else is saying. Does the thing make sense to *you*?

2. Will doing this thing be good for *everyone* involved?

3. What are the consequences of this action? Will it lead you to a place you might not want to go?

4. Will you be proud of yourself when it's over?

5. Would the person you most admire in the world encourage you to do this?

6. If everyone in your family found out that you did this thing, would they be proud of you?

10 Signs of Depression

If you are sad because of something that happened—say, your dog died—that's appropriate sadness. But if, months later, you still burst into tears when you see a dog on TV, it's probably something more serious. Fact is, we all experience versions of these symptoms at one time or another. Losing your temper or having a bad night doesn't mean you're depressed. It's when these things happen repeatedly—and they interfere with your ability to live life normally—that we suspect depression. That's a serious problem. Depression is a medical condition, and there are many treatments for it, from exercise and a balanced diet to therapy and appropriate medications. Talk to your parents, and ask them to get you professional help.

1. You feel sad or cry very often, and the sadness doesn't seem to go away.

2. You feel guilty for no real reason; you've lost self-confidence or have no feelings of self-esteem.

3. You feel that nothing good is ever going to happen again.

4. You have a negative attitude a lot of the time or no feelings at all.

5. You lose your temper easily and get irritable often.

6. You want to be left alone most of the time and don't enjoy being around others and having fun.

7. You start sleeping a lot more or may have problems falling asleep at night.

8. You feel restless or tired most of the time.

9. You may lose your appetite or start eating a great deal more than usual.

10. You think about death and suicide a lot.

17 Causes of Low Self-Esteem

If you have ever felt that you don't fit in or are not as good as your friends, you're not alone. Everyone at some time in their life has had doubts about their own abilities, how they fit in socially, or how other people feel about them. Here are some of the leading causes of low self-esteem:

1. Being constantly criticized

2. Not getting enough affection, support, respect, or encouragement

3. Being repeatedly teased, picked on, or laughed at

4. Being the target of verbal, physical, sexual, or emotional abuse

5. Receiving too strict, cruel, or improper punishment

6. Being ridiculed for your ideas, opinions, or performance

7. Being neglected because your parents are too busy or can't deal with your emotions

8. Having your feelings be consistently ignored and rejected

9. Being negatively compared to your siblings

10. Being threatened with abandonment

11. Being abandoned or feeling unwanted

12. Not being allowed to participate in school activities, play with neighbors and friends, or do normal things that other kids do

13. Being blamed for your parents' current problems

14. Being told "You were a mistake!"

15. Not having appropriate social skills

16. Not being encouraged in school and personal interests

17. Being sick and unable to participate in normal activities

9 Ways to Feel Better About Yourself — Instantly!

Your dog hates you, you just lost your best friend, and even your reflection in the mirror doesn't want anything to do with you. The bad news is that this is something you will experience many times in your life. The good news is that you don't

She just threw away a great friendship so she wouldn't get hurt and ended up hurting everyone else

have to take it lying down. Any one of the following is bound to lift your spirits—we guarantee it.

1. Write down what is happening to you in the third person —as though it's happening to someone else. Refer to yourself as "she" or "he" and try to write as objectively as you can. When you finish describing the problem, describe a solution —as though it's happening to the person in your story. Give the story a happy ending.

2. Seek out the people who make you feel good about yourself and hang out with them. If your grandmother always makes you feel like you are the best kid in the whole world and deserve nothing more than love and good fortune, go visit or call her. Our real friends remind us, in the way they treat us, that we are important to them. Go find them now for a refresher course in exactly what your good qualities are.

3. Create things. Express yourself. Tell the world how you really feel by describing your thoughts in a work of art. Or write a poem about them. Or collect pictures of all the things that are making you feel bad and organize them into a collage. Post your work somewhere so that your friends and family can learn more about what you're going through. Maybe someone out there feels the same way.

4. Help someone who is even worse off than you. If you can't think of anyone, you're not thinking hard enough. Someone somewhere needs your help. Go to their aid, and you will suddenly feel better. Why? Because when you give something away, it reminds you that you had something to give. It makes you feel rich!

5. Get outside. Go to the beach and try to count the grains of sand. Or look at the sky at night and contemplate the stars. Or stare up into a tree and try to imagine how old it is and how many leaves it has. You'll see that the world is much, much bigger than you and your problem. You will be reminded that the earth has been here for a very long time and that the chances of you being the first person to experience your particular problem is pretty slim. Somehow the planet has managed to survive; so will you.

6. Pray. You can say religious prayers or you can make up poems with all your wishes in them and recite them every day.

Prayers are wishes we make with our hearts. They are very powerful.

7. Read a book you love. Read one that reminds you of the world you wish you lived in. Know that when you open the covers of a book, you open your heart. Read a book that your heart will love.

8. Make music. You needn't write a song, sing one, or even hum it. You can get in touch with your primal side by making rhythmic noises that express how you feel, even if your "song" comes from using pot covers for cymbals. Or scream. Think about the "music" you are creating. What is it about?

9. Face up to what's making you feel terrible. Make a list. Then name all the things you need to do to solve your problem. Then do just *one thing* on the list.

9 Excellent Self-Help Books

1. *Chicken Soup for the Teenage Soul,* vol. 1–3, by Jack Canfield, editor, et al. These books contain inspirational stories, poems, and cartoons about the specific troubles that all teenagers experience. Stories deal with dating, friendships, and school. But larger issues are also addressed, with essays on topics such as dying young, suicide, and drunk driving.

2. *Closing the Gap: A Strategy for Bringing Parents and Teens Together,* by Jay McGraw. This book provides rules that teens and adults can use to strengthen their relationships with each other. It demonstrates how the bond between teens and their friends and relatives can be accomplished through love and good communication.

3. *Don't Sweat the Small Stuff for Teens,* by Richard Carlson, Ph.D. These 100 motivational and insightful short chapters suggest ways to deal with everyday stresses and how to become a positive thinker. Using sports, theater, literature, video games, teachers, and parents in the stories makes these examples accessible to teens interested in many different things. Carlson sounds like an older family friend who manages to advise teens while demonstrating a level of coolness that they can appreciate.

4. *IF . . . Questions for Teens,* by Evelyn McFarlane and James

Saywell. This book poses questions on all facets of teen life. Teens will have fun asking and answering these questions of one another, leading to some lively discussions. Questions may involve friendships, movies, school, dating, music, peer pressure, cliques, parties, gossip, parents, food, hair, videos, shopping, sports, cards, and the future.

5. *If High School Is a Game, Here's How to Break the Rules: A Cutting Edge Guide to Becoming Yourself,* by Cherie Carter-Scott. Real anecdotes that teens can identify with and learn from. There are also motivational quotes from popular personalities. This book gives teens the tools they need to help them play according to their own rules.

6. *Life Strategies for Teens,* by Jay McGraw. Using the techniques from Dr. Phillip C. McGraw's book (below), his son Jay provides teens with the Ten Laws of Life, which make the journey to adulthood easier and more fulfilling.

7. *The 7 Habits of Highly Effective Teens,* by Sean Covey. A step-by-step guide that enable teens to improve their self-image, build lasting friendships, resist peer pressure, achieve their own goals, and get along with their parents.

8. *Self Matters: Creating Your Life from the Inside Out,* by Philip C. McGraw, Ph.D. This book will help you rediscover the person you have always wanted to be but were too distracted, busy, or scared to become. It shows you how to be your true self instead of who you believe you're supposed to be, the person people tell you you are.

9. *What Teens Need to Succeed: Proven, Practical Ways to Shape Your Own Future,* by Peter L. Benson, Pamela Espeland, Judy Galbraith. Proven, practical ideas presented with an emphasis on a positive approach to developing into strong, caring, and well-adjusted teens.

19 Useful Hotlines

Alcohol Treatment Referral Hotlines

1. **Al-Anon/Alateen Family Group Headquarters.** Helps families and friends of alcoholics recover from the effects of living with someone who has a drinking problem. Similarly,

Alateen is a recovery program for young people sponsored by Al-Anon members.

> 800-344-2666 (U.S.)
> 800-443-4525 (Canada)
> www.al-anon.alateen.org

2. **Alcoholics Anonymous World Services.** Provides information about AA and worldwide referrals to local meetings.

> 212-870-3400
> www.alcoholics-anonymous.org

Drug Abuse

3. **Teen Challenge International Network.** Substance abuse treatment centers for adolescents and adults.

> 800-814-5729
> www.teenchallenge.com

4. **The National Clearinghouse for Alcohol and Drug Information (NCADI).** Provides help and information for those who are practicing a potentially life-threatening practice called "huffing."

> 800-729-6686
> www.health.org

Rape and Abuse

5. **The Rape, Abuse & Incest National Network (RAINN).** A nonprofit organization based in Washington, D.C., it operates America's only national hotline for victims of sexual assault.

> 800-656-HOPE
> www.rainn.org

6. **National Child Abuse Hotline.** Dedicated to the prevention of child abuse. Serving the U.S., Canada, the U.S. Virgin Islands, Puerto Rico, and Guam, the hotline is staffed 24 hours daily.

> 800-4-A-CHILD
> www.childhelpusa.org

Domestic Violence

7. **National Domestic Violence Hotline.** Detailed information on domestic violence shelters, other emergency shelters,

legal advocacy and assistance programs, and social service programs.

800-799-7233
www.ndvh.org

Pregnancy

8. **Teen Pregnancy Hotline**
800-522-5006
www.smhp.psych.ucla.edu/hotline

Legal Aid

9. **Children's Defense Fund (CDF).** Provides a strong, effective voice for all the children of America who cannot vote, lobby, or speak for themselves. It pays particular attention to the needs of poor and minority children and those with disabilities.
202-628-8787
www.childrensdefense.org

Psychological Help Hotlines

10. **Cult Hotline and Clinic.** Offers a variety of services including a speakers' bureau, workshops, literature, and guidance to educators, clergy, and other health care professionals. Also addresses problems of teens who have become involved in religious and political cults.
212-632-4640
www.jbfcs.org/conn/families/cult

11. **The National Suicide Prevention Directory (NSPD).** Provides the public with a central source of contact information for suicide prevention organizations that provide educational and counseling programs aimed at long-term suicide prevention.

A call to 800-SUICIDE will automatically be routed to your nearest crisis line or mental health center.
www.angelfire.com/biz/mereproject/nspdmain

Health Hotlines

12. **The CDC (Centers for Disease Control) National AIDS Hotline.** Provides information and education and answers

questions about the disease, testing facilities, and medications used for treatment 24 hours a day.

800-342-AIDS

www.cdc.gov

13. **National Sexually Transmitted Disease Hotline.** Provides accurate basic information, referrals, and educational materials about a wide variety of sexually transmitted diseases.

800-227-8922

www.cdc.gov/nchstp/dstd/dstdp

Eating Disorders

14. **National Association of Anorexia Nervosa and Associated Disorders.** Call the national hotline for a list of support groups and referrals in your area.

847-831-3438

www.anad.org

15. **Eating Disorders Awareness and Prevention.** The nation's largest nonprofit organization devoted to the awareness and prevention of eating disorders.

206-382-3587

www.geocities.com/southbeach/boardwalk/6384/hotlines

Runaway Hotlines

16. **National Runaway 24-Hour Switchboard.** Confidential and free. Whether you are in a crisis or have a friend who is in trouble.

800-621-4000

www.nrscrisis.org/about_nrs.asp

17. **National Youth Crisis Hotline for ages 17 and under.**

800-448-4663 or 800-Hit Home

Others

18. **Grief Recovery Institute.** Seeks to ease the isolation of those suffering from a loss and assists them in coping with their grief. Offers information, handbooks, resources, and news.

P.O. Box 6061-382
Sherman Oaks, CA 91413
800-445-4808 (8 A.M.–5 P.M.)
www.griefrecovery.com

19. **Shoplifters Anonymous**. Provides information and help to those with this compulsive disorder.

800-848-9595
www.shopliftersanonymous.com

12 Ways Hormones Wreak Havoc on the Teen Body

Welcome to puberty: a wonderful time of life when your hormones start flowing like crazy, your body begins to change and develop, you hardly recognize the person in the mirror, and you and your parents suddenly can't agree on simple things like the color of the sky. Everyone goes through their own special version of puberty, and everyone does it at a different pace. Here are some of the surprises that await you:

1. You experience a growth spurt. You may grow as much as 4 or more inches in a single year.

2. Hair will begin to grow where it didn't grow before. Guys and girls both begin to grow hair under their arms and in their pubic areas (on and around the genitals). Eventually, guys also start to grow hair on their faces.

3. A lot of teens notice that they have a new smell under their arms and elsewhere on their bodies. That's normal body odor, and it's why deodorant was invented.

4. You'll gain weight, and as your body becomes heavier, you'll start to notice changes in your overall shape.

5. Guys' shoulders will grow wider, and their bodies will become more muscular.

6. Girls' bodies usually become curvier. They gain weight on their hips, and their breasts develop.

7. Girls will notice an increase in body fat and occasional soreness under the nipples as the breasts start to enlarge.

8. Usually about $^1/_2$ to 2 years after girls' breasts start to develop, they experience their first menstrual period.

9. Guys' voices will become deeper and sometimes will "crack."

10. Guys will have a lengthening and widening of the penis and an enlargement of the testicles.

11. Guys will begin to get erections (the penis fills with blood and becomes hard), sometimes as they fantasize about sex or sometimes for no reason at all. They may experience nocturnal emissions (or "wet dreams").

12. Say hello to acne and pimples.

19 Things You Should Know About Zits and Acne

A zit attack! Just about every teenager gets one. It can seem a fate worse than death if a pimply breakout comes at prom time or on that first date. If you've tried over-the-counter remedies like benzoyl peroxide or salicylic acid and still have a persistent problem with zits, you need to speak with a doctor.

1. Zits and acne will continue well into adulthood—get used to it now.

2. Zits are most commonly caused by normal hormonal fluctuations in your body. You don't get zits from eating greasy food or too many sweets.

3. Zits are not only found on the face but also can appear on the back, scalp, and neck.

4. Zits are uncomfortable and sometimes hurt, but if you don't let them disappear on their own you can end up with scars.

5. Popping, picking at, drying out, or otherwise irritating zits makes things worse and can cause even more to sprout up.

6. The sex hormone testosterone is the primary cause of zits among guys.

7. Acne in girls becomes worse before their periods, due to changes in their hormone levels at this stage in the menstrual cycle.

8. Poor hygiene alone doesn't cause zits, but it does aggravate the situation.

9. Overwashing can actually make acne worse—by drying the skin and making it sore.

10. Zits don't make you ugly or gross.

11. Acne that consists of four or more zits at one time—along with redness, discomfort, and slow healing cycles—should be checked out by a doctor.

12. Acne can flare up when you sweat a lot.

13. A humid atmosphere makes acne worse.

14. Certain medicines make acne worse. Check the side effects of any prescription drug you are taking. Ask your doctor about your medications if you have a persistent problem.

15. Some cosmetics cause blackheads. Suntan oils can also make acne worse.

16. Stress doesn't cause acne but can make it worse.

17. Birth control pills do not cause acne.

18. You don't have to live with acne or "wait until you outgrow it." Safe and effective remedies are available.

19. Everyone gets zits!

4 Ways in Which Barbie Almost Ruined the Life of Stacey Handler

If you think teenage girls have a tough time competing with the unrealistic images of women on TV and in magazines, imagine how Stacey Handler felt. Her grandparents founded the Mattel toy company in 1940, and her grandmother invented Barbie. It almost ruined Stacey's life. Today, Stacey (for whom the Stacie doll was named) has worked out her problems and is a successful businesswoman who knows that, although there are many things in this world we can't change, we *can* change how we react to them. "I am ultimately responsible for the way I feel about my own body," she writes. "If you focus only on your body, you forget everything else that's great about you. Do you really want to live your life worrying about your appearance?"

1. Stacey competed with Barbie. "I always thought of Barbie as my flawless sister: the girl with the right clothes, the perfect figure, and endless talent." But growing up feeling like a failure made her withdraw. She kept to herself a lot and wouldn't let other people see her. She allowed people to treat her badly because she didn't think she deserved better. Barbie was winning the battle.

2. Due to health problems, including diabetes, Stacey has struggled with a weight problem for most of her life. She starved herself so she could look like Barbie, who seemed to be everyone's idea of the perfect woman. Of course, she never looked anything like Barbie—no one does. "Losing weight doesn't change who you are inside," she says. "I eventually gained it all back because I was trying to change for the wrong reasons."

3. Barbie wrecked her relationship with her grandmother; Stacey imagined she cared more about Barbie than she did her own granddaughter. "Barbie was Grandma's greatest success, and I felt like her biggest failure." Later in life, Stacey learned that her grandmother's mean comments were really meant to help her, and her grandmother was able to accept that all they did was hurt her more.

4. Stacey was confused about the real world and how it worked. Watching Barbie transformed from a stewardess to a teacher to a dream date—all with a simple change of clothes—Stacey imagined that she, too, could be anything she wanted to be—just as long as she had the right outfit and looked good in it. As Stacey matured, she learned that the world didn't work that way. But she had been so busy trying to look good that she hadn't spent much time developing her best qualities.

8 Things to Consider Before You Have a Body Part Pierced

1. You're taking a serious health risk if you decide to get pierced. Body piercing is not regulated in most U.S. states and is even illegal in some. This means there are no rules about how safe or clean the place has to be.

2. Most places that do piercing don't use any form of anesthesia. Ouch!

3. The side effects of piercing may include pain, swelling, infection, and (in the case of tongue piercing) increased salivary flow. Healing takes four to six weeks if there are no complications.

4. If you choose to have a body part pierced, you run the risks of chronic infection, prolonged bleeding, scarring, getting hepatitis B and C (which can be fatal), a permanent hole in your nostril or eyebrow, choking (from mouth jewelry), and a speech impediment.

5. The American Dental Association opposes oral (tongue, lip, or cheek) piercing, calling it "a public health hazard."

6. The American Academy of Dermatology is against all forms of body piercing with one exception: the earlobe.

7. Piercing procedures can transmit dangerous blood-borne diseases. Because of this, neither the U.S. nor the Canadian Red Cross will accept blood donations from anyone who has had a body piercing within the previous year.

8. Self-piercing can result in mutilation, infection, and serious complications. Don't even think about it.

7 Things to Consider When Having an Earlobe Pierced

Because earlobes consist of fatty tissue and have a good blood supply, they heal rather quickly and with few complications, which make them relatively safe to pierce. If you are interested in having an ear pierced, here are some guidelines to follow:

1. Make sure the place that will do the piercing looks clean —floors, walls, countertops, etc.

2. The piercer should wear fresh, disposable rubber gloves and a face mask when he or she works on you.

3. An autoclave should be on the premises. This is a sterilization device that is used in hospitals and doctors' offices to kill all harmful bacteria. You should ask if they use one.

4. Piercing guns should be avoided because they usually aren't sterile.

5. Be sure that needles are used only once and that they're disposed of in a sterile container.

6. Once your ear has been pierced, you should care for the piercing site at home by cleaning it with soap and water. Avoid picking or tugging at it.

7. Don't try it yourself; don't have a friend do it for you. It's not as easy as it looks.

12 Ways to Control Your Weight Without Going on a Diet

To control your weight over the long term (meaning for the rest of your life), think about practicing good habits that can be broken from time to time. You can enjoy a burger without the cheese and bacon. Here are some other tips for maintaining a healthy weight:

1. Keep eating. Your body needs fuel. If you stop eating, your metabolism will slow down, and ultimately you'll achieve nothing except a whole new level of hunger. Eat three times a day; don't skip breakfast.

2. Watch your portions. Do you really need the supersize fries, the 86-ounce soda? Just eat half the sandwich, half the french fries. Don't eat the whole burger bun. Cut your soft drink consumption by half. Forget what they told you about the starving children in Africa.

3. Drink eight 8-ounce glasses of water every day.

4. Don't tell yourself you can never have your favorite food again. You can—it will be there when you need a special treat. But you just can't be pigging out on the stuff all the time.

5. Control yourself. When you get a craving for something, wait. Write it down and have it—after you've asked yourself if you really need it. It's not leaving the planet, after all. Do you respond to every craving your body has? Of course not. If you did, you'd be taking naps during math and peeing in your pants four times a day. Neither do you have to respond to every food thought that pops into your head.

6. Learn what's in the foods you eat. Eating a small cookie may not seem like a crime, but if the ones you live on are loaded with butter or animal fat, give it up. Read labels. They're fascinating.

7. Learn to cook for yourself and be responsible for what you eat.

8. Work out for 20 minutes a day. Walk, climb steps, jump rope, dance to your fave tunes, swim, play a sport—anything! Just do it.

9. Get a buddy who has the same fitness goals you do and work out together. Share your best tips.

10. Don't get discouraged if you're not immediately success-ful. Healthy habits may take some time to yield results, but they'll pay off in the long run. Once you're halfway to your fit-ness goal, your confidence will kick in. Be proud of whatever progress you make.

11. Don't weigh yourself every 12 minutes. (Once a week is best.) Since you are still growing, you may lose inches but not pounds, and you'll become discouraged needlessly if the scale doesn't show the progress you're hoping for (and may actually be achieving). To find out how you're really doing, check your measurements.

12. Be realistic. If you're 5 feet 7 inches tall, there's no way you're going to weigh 100 pounds and still be healthy. Check a weight chart to find out your proper weight range.

15 Tips for Dressing Thin

1. Stick with outfits of one color or shades of one color, preferably a dark color. Wearing a yellow shirt with red pants, for instance, draws more attention to your size. Different shades of blue combined in one outfit, though, or a rust-colored shirt with brown jeans gives you a more tailored appearance.

2. Stick with vertical rather than horizontal stripes. Even horizontal stripes—and busy patterns of any kind—should be avoided on pants, skirts, and stockings.

3. Dress proportionately. An oversized jacket on an over-sized person just makes him or her look—oversized! There's nothing wrong with a baggy top that hides last month's Twinkie binge, but don't try to cover up a big problem with an even bigger problem.

4. The right underwear can make a big difference. Girls, there are lots of special undergarments for all sorts of body im-perfections, and knowing which ones work for you can make a huge difference. Visit the lingerie counter of a fine department store and ask an experienced salesperson to help you. If you're maturing quickly, a good bra, fitted by an expert (leave your modesty at home), is invaluable. Buy two or three of anything that really works for you. If you're too shy for words, order several items from a catalog, try them on in the privacy of your room, and return the stuff that doesn't fit.

5. Forget about belts and styles that bunch at the waist, like pleated pants and skirts, or styles with lots of trimmings, like ruffles or fringes. These styles tend to "cut" your body in half as opposed to presenting one taller (and therefore slimmer) shape.

6. Avoid anything with tight sleeves.

7. Wear your true size. If your clothes seem to be getting smaller and smaller, maybe it's because you're getting bigger and bigger. This is a bad time for denial. Trying to stuff your 34-inch waist into 32-inch pants is going to draw attention to the fact that you're too big to fit in those pants. Don't wear stuff that doesn't fit. Anything that's too small is just going to make you look bigger.

8. Avoid stiff, shiny, bulky fabrics like patent leather, plastics, and anything that glows.

9. Stick with solid colors and small repeat patterns, like small checks or thin stripes. Large patterns make you look larger than you are.

10. Find clothes that work for you and stick with them. Fads are fun, but you don't have to participate in every one that comes up. Good basic clothing, like a pair of jeans that really fit or a jacket that covers you in all the right places might cost a little more. But if you budget yourself by avoiding impulse purchases (which you tend to wear once and then regret having bought), you'll have more money for the things that work for you and that will last longer.

11. Keep your closet organized so you always know what's available. Keep the stuff that doesn't fit in the back of the closet so you're not racked with guilt every time you open the door.

12. Shop alone—and only when you're in a good mood. Trying on bathing suits the day after you learn you are failing Spanish and being grounded for it is probably not going to cheer you up. You need to be able to focus on making the best possible purchase for yourself. The most important thing about any piece of clothing is how it makes you feel. A friend might tell you that dress makes you look exactly like Reese Witherspoon, but if it makes you feel more like Miss Reese's Pieces, take a pass. So when you're at the mall with friends, arrange to separate for a short time so you can concentrate on shopping for yourself. (It's never a good idea to go to a mall alone.) If shopping is a problem for you and you always lose patience, swallow your pride and ask an adult to go with you.

13. Don't shop for occasions at the last minute. You'll drive yourself nuts if you don't find what you need, and even if you do, there won't be time for any special alterations.

14. If you find salespeople who are especially helpful, ask them to drop you a postcard when they get shipments of things that work for you. Let them know how grateful you are for their help. Remember their names.

15. Stand up straight! You've heard this your whole life for a lot of reasons. Here's a special one for you: good posture can easily take 5 pounds off your appearance!

10 Ways to Tell if Someone Has an Eating Disorder

If you are a teenage girl, it is natural for you to be concerned about your appearance. Talking about food and your body and striving to lose weight to fit into that bathing suit or prom dress is normal. But if you have a friend who begins to do things that are physically and emotionally dangerous, she might have a problem. Other than drastic weight loss, some signs that your friend may have an eating disorder are:

1. She has an obsession with weight and food, and it seems as though she never talks about anything else.

2. She knows the calorie and fat content of all the foods she eats.

3. She works out all the time, even when she's sick or exhausted.

4. She avoids eating with friends.

5. She wears big or baggy clothes to conceal her weight loss.

6. She goes on severe diets, cuts food into tiny pieces, or moves food around on the plate instead of eating it.

7. She goes to the bathroom a lot, especially right after meals, or you've heard her vomiting after a meal.

8. She always talks about how fat she is, even though she's not.

9. She takes laxatives, steroids, or diet pills.

10. She has a tendency to faint, bruises easily, is very pale, or often complains of being cold.

8 Ways to Help Someone with an Eating Disorder

People who have eating disorders often have trouble admitting it, even to themselves. Trying to help a friend who doesn't think she needs it can be an uphill battle. Eating disorders are serious, and they can cause permanent health problems or even death. If your friend shows symptoms of an eating disorder, here are some things you can do:

1. Tell her, in the gentlest way, that you're concerned about her.

2. Try to be a supportive listener. Don't tell her she has an eating disorder — that's the job of a doctor, who can tell what's going on.

3. Encourage her to get medical attention.

4. Don't force her to eat.

5. Do not try to solve the problem for her. Your goal is to encourage her to get help from people who understand eating disorders.

6. Offer to go with her to talk to a counselor or doctor. Or give her the number of a hotline where she can get help (see page 27).

7. If she doesn't admit she has a problem, you'll need to get help from either her parents, your parents, a teacher, or a counselor.

8. Be as supportive and caring as you can, and let your friend know you care about her no matter what.

7 Makeup Tips for Girls Who Don't Wear Makeup

1. Petroleum jelly is your best friend. Use it on your eyebrows and eyelashes to make them shine, gloss your lips with it, and dab a drop on each cheek for a healthy glow.

2. Comb or brush your eyebrows with a small comb that is sold just for this purpose. It will make them neater.

3. If you have very bushy eyebrows or hair on your face where you don't want it, consider waxing or other hair removal techniques.

4. You can even out your skin tone or hide blemishes by using a light-textured foundation.

5. An eyelash curler will accent your lashes.

6. If you're tired and need to get the red out of your eyes, apply any of the following to your eyes (while they're closed) for 10 minutes while you lie down: an ice pack, slices of cold cucumber, or cold, wet teabags.

7. The cleaner you are, the better you look. They haven't yet been able to invent makeup that can compete with the healthy glow of really clean skin.

9 Reasons to Keep a Journal

Keeping a journal is easy. You can use anything from a cheap notebook to a fancy leather volume that comes with a key you wear around your neck for safekeeping. Regardless, you need only follow three rules. Write freely and honestly, and don't worry if your entry doesn't make sense. Make it a habit to write something *every single day*, even if you think nothing happened that day. Finally, make sure it's kept as private as you want it to be, so you always feel safe saying *anything*.

1. Your journal won't talk back to you, criticize, or get bored with anything you say. It doesn't forget your birthday, lose your phone number, or invite you to the mall and then decide to go to a movie instead. It's always there for you, and it's always on your side. Keeping a journal lets you express your feelings without having anyone judge you.

2. Even if your life may not seem very exciting now, you'll love having a record of it later on, when you've forgotten so many details that you now take for granted. Imagine your grandchildren, 50 years from now, reading about what it's like to go to a movie. (Do you think we'll have movie theaters in 50 years?) A journal is a living part of history.

3. If you write honestly, you'll be able to go back and read entries that will help you learn from your mistakes. At troublesome times you can look back and see what went wrong. Do the kids you want to hang out with ignore you? If your journal has entries in which you've bad-mouthed these people, maybe you don't really want them for friends. If everything you write about seems sad and negative, maybe you have an attitude problem you should think about. You can use your journal to solve problems.

4. Your journal will be a record of your best memories, and you will always have access to events that may seem unforgettable now but that do fade with time. It will be fun to look back one day and relive your first date, your graduation, or how it felt to see your pet for the first time.

5. You will learn things about yourself. If you write down everything—your dreams, your problems and their solutions, even gifts you've given and received—you will be able to use your journal to see patterns in your behavior. If you always seem to be troubled around school vacations, maybe you need to plan ahead and think about how you really want to spend that time. If you find repeated nasty comments about someone who's supposed to be your friend, there are probably some issues you need to talk about together. And if all your entries seem general and boring, maybe you're not paying attention to everything that's going on around you.

6. Write about your favorite people. Talk about their special qualities and what you learn from them. What's your grandfather really like? What is it about Aunt Jane that makes you so happy when you know she's coming to visit? These people may not always be in your life. Your journal entries will keep their memories alive.

7. A shared journal is one that you and a friend write together—you take turns making entries. It can be an exciting way to explore a relationship. It's easiest to do online in a file you can both call up, but if that's not possible, passing a book back and forth and making copies of the pages from time to time so you both have complete sets also works.

8. A journal allows you to experiment. Have you ever thought of expressing yourself in poetry? You can try it in your journal, and if you think it's a complete failure, no one but you ever has to know about it. Try sketching some of your thoughts or even writing them in another language.

9. You can use it to give people messages. If you're dying for a new computer but are afraid to ask your parents, leave your diary open to the page where you talk about all the great educational benefits of having it. This can also work if you want your little brother to know how you really feel about his geeky behavior. Of course, you can't guarantee that they won't also read the stuff about you and you-know-who!

7 Ways to Make Sure Your Private Journal Stays That Way — Private!

1. Disguise your diary as something else. A bright pink leatherbound book with DIARY emblazoned in gold is going to attract attention. A simple notebook like the one you use for school won't.

2. Don't make journal entries when other people are around. Write in private so you don't arouse curiosity.

3. Don't leave it lying around and then complain when your brother posts your secrets on the Internet. Even if everyone in your family is trustworthy, your journal should remain between you and yourself.

4. If you hide the book, don't always hide it in the same spot. Switch hiding places from time to time.

5. Get a book that has a lock and wear the key around your neck.

6. Keep your journal on your computer in a specially protected file.

7. Respect the privacy of others, and ask for the same consideration in return.

26 Thought-Provoking Questions

Think about them by yourself, try them on a friend, or do them in a big group. You'll learn plenty about your friends and yourself.

1. If you could own any single object that you don't have now, what would it be?

2. If you could have one superpower, what would it be?

3. If you could meet anyone in history, who would you choose and what would you ask them?

4. If you could add one person to your family, who would it be?

5. If you could be best friends with anyone in the world, who would you pick?

6. If you could change anything about your face, what would it be?

7. If you could change anything about your parents, what would it be?

8. If you could fast-forward your life, how old would you want to be and why?

9. What is the one object you own that matters more to you than anything else?

10. What is the one thing in the world you are most afraid of?

11. If you could go to school in a foreign country, which country would you pick?

12. If you had the power to drop any course from your curriculum, what would it be?

13. If you caught your best friend stealing from you, what would you do?

14. If you had a chance to spend a million dollars on anything but yourself, how would you spend it?

15. If you could look like anyone you wanted, who would that be?

16. If you were a member of the opposite sex, who would you want to look like?

17. If you could change your first name, what name would you choose?

18. What's the best thing about being a teen?

19. What's the worst?

20. If someone you like asked you on a date but your best friend had a crush on this person, what would you do?

21. What is the worst day of the week?

22. If you had to change places with one of your friends, who would you choose?

23. If you could be any sports hero, who would you like to be?

24. What's the one thing you've done in your life that you wish you could do over differently?

25. What would you do if you found a dollar in the street? What if you found $100? $10,000?

26. If you had a chance to star in any movie, who would you like as a costar?

30 Things to Paste in Your Scrapbook

1. Postcards
2. Report cards
3. Ticket stubs
4. Invitations
5. Autographs
6. Pressed flowers
7. Hospital bracelets
8. Candy wrappers
9. Photographs
10. Drawings
11. Maps
12. Movie reviews
13. Fabric samples
14. Menus
15. Locks of hair
16. School notices
17. I.D. cards
18. Recipes
19. Toy parts
20. Travel brochures
21. Stickers
22. Stamps
23. Fake money
24. Newspaper clippings
25. Ads
26. E-mail printouts
27. Wrapping paper remnants
28. Orphaned jewelry parts
29. TV listings of favorite programs
30. Photos of mementos that are too big to fit in the book

2.
The WORLD OUT THERE

20 Really Dirty Words

1. Anti-Semitism. A hatred of Jews, based on negative ideas about Jewish religious beliefs and practices or on negative stereotypes.

2. Bias. A preconceived notion about an individual or group that interferes with impartial judgment.

3. Bigotry. A prejudice against members of a particular group based on negative views of their beliefs and practices or on negative stereotypes.

4. Discrimination. Based on prejudicial thinking, it is the denial of justice and fair treatment in such areas as employment, housing, and political rights.

5. Dogmatism. A viewpoint or system of ideas that does not take all the facts or any other ideas into account.

6. Fascism. A governing system led by a dictator who has complete power and control over his country and people and uses force against anyone that opposes his ideas. Such a system often encourages racism.

7. Homelessness. The situation of a people who have no place they consider a home. Every night about 700,000 people in the U.S. are homeless.

8. Homophobia. The fear of homosexuals or of anyone thought to be lesbian, gay, or bisexual.

9. Hunger. The lack of sufficient food to sustain a healthy body. About 31 million Americans live on small meals or skip meals every day.

10. Nazism. A short term for the National Socialist German Workers Party, led by Adolf Hitler. Its ideology was strongly anti-Communist, anti-Semitic, racist, and nationalistic. Nazism, fascism, and extreme nationalism are today at their highest level since the end of World War II, in 1945. Today, all over the world, fascists and extreme nationalists win millions of votes in support of their simple, racist solutions to the very complex problems of every society.

11. Prejudice. Prejudging, making a decision about a person or group of people without sufficient knowledge. Prejudicial thinking is based on stereotypes.

12. Racial profiling. A method used when people are targeted for investigation on the basis of their race, national origin, or ethnicity.

13. **Racism.** Prejudice and/or discrimination based on race. Racists believe that some groups are born superior to others, and, in the name of protecting their own race from "contamination," they justify the domination and destruction of the races they consider inferior.

14. **Scapegoating.** Blaming an individual or group for something when, in reality, there is no one person or group responsible. It means blaming another person or group for complex problems in society because of that person's group identity. Prejudicial thinking and discriminatory acts can lead to scapegoating. Members of the disliked group are denied employment, housing, political rights, social privileges, or a combination of these rights. Scapegoating often leads to verbal and physical violence.

15. **Sexism.** Prejudice or discrimination based on a person's sex.

16. **Sexual harassment.** When someone who has more power (or seniority or experience) tries to coerce another into having sex or doing something sexual. For instance, your boss tells you that it's okay for him to pat you on the butt because he's the boss and if you don't like it you can get another job.

17. **Slur.** An insulting or disparaging remark or suggestion.

18. **Stereotype.** An oversimplified generalization about an entire group of people without regard for individual differences. Even positive stereotypes, such as "Asians are good at math and computers," can have a negative impact.

19. **Supremacists.** Fascist groups that blame the cultural and ethnic minorities for the problems in a society. These individuals and their leaders are a threat to our democracy—and to everything that is decent.

20. **Terrorism.** The use of violence and threats to intimidate or coerce others, especially for political purposes. It produces a state of fear and submission in those affected.

13 National Organizations You May Want to Support

1. **The American Red Cross**, which was chartered by Congress in 1905, is a private nonprofit humanitarian organization. It is also the largest disaster and emergency relief organization in the nation. Its Web site provides links to volunteer leadership opportunities both at headquarters and at chapters around the country.

> 431 18th St., NW
> Washington, DC 20006
> 202-737-8300
> www.redcross.org/donate/volunteer

2. **The American Society for the Prevention of Cruelty to Animals (ASPCA)** promotes humane principles, prevents cruelty, and alleviates fear, pain, and suffering in animals. Contact the national headquarters for a shelter near you or check the phone book.

> ASPCA National Headquarters
> 424 E. 92nd St.
> New York, NY 10128
> 212-876-7700
> www.aspca.org.

3. **AmeriCorps**, the domestic Peace Corps, engages more than 50,000 Americans in intensive service each year. They teach children to read, make neighborhoods safer, build affordable homes, and respond to natural disasters through more than 1,000 projects annually. Most AmeriCorps members are selected by and serve with projects such as Habitat for Humanity, the American Red Cross, Boys and Girls Clubs, and many local and national organizations.

> Corporation for National and Community Service
> 1201 New York Ave., NW
> Washington, DC 20525
> 202-606-5000
> www.americorps.org

4. **The Congressional Youth Leadership Council** is a nonprofit organization that focuses on leadership development for outstanding high school juniors and seniors. Students world-

wide come to Washington, D.C., and New York City to participate in educational programs that inspire them to assume
greater leadership roles locally, nationally, and internationally.

1110 Vermont Ave., NW, Suite 320
Washington, DC 20005
202-638-0008
www.cylc.org

5. **The Council for Exceptional Children (CEC)** is the largest
international professional organization dedicated to improving
the education of exceptional individuals, students with disabilities, and/or the gifted. CEC advocates for appropriate government policies, sets professional standards, provides continual
professional development, and helps professionals obtain the
resources necessary for effective professional practice.

1110 N. Glebe Rd., Suite 300
Arlington, VA 22201
703-620-3660
www.cec.sped.org

6. **Do Something** is a nationwide network of young people
who know they can make a difference in their communities
and take action to change the world around them. As part of
Do Something, young people are asked what they want to do to
make things better and are then given the resources and support to bring their unique visions to life.

423 W. 55th St., 8th Floor
New York, NY 10019
212-523-1175
www.DoSomething.org

7. **Junior Achievement** develops innovative programs to educate young people about business and economics and help
prepare them for fulfilling careers. It supports 156 local offices, which carry out its mission. Its international affiliate
serves another 100 countries with offices around the world.

National Headquarters and Service Center
One Education Way
Colorado Springs, CO 80906
719-540-8000
www.ja.org

8. **The National Crime Prevention Council** makes it easy to get involved. If you're an artist, you can paint a mural to replace graffiti; if you like sports, you can coach a team in your neighborhood; if you're a listener or a problem solver, you can volunteer at a teen hotline or be a peer mediator.

> 1000 Connecticut Ave., NW, 13th Floor
> Washington, DC 20036
> 202-466-6272
> www.ncpc.org

9. **The National Wildlife Federation** is the nation's largest member-supported conservation group, uniting individuals, organizations, businesses and government to protect wildlife, wild places, and the environment.

> 11100 Wildlife Center Dr.
> Reston, VA 20190-5362
> 703-438-6000
> www.nwf.org

10. **SERVEnet**'s users can enter their zip code, city, state, skills, interests, and availability to be matched with organizations needing help.

> YSA
> 1101 15th St., NW, Suite 200
> Washington, DC 20005
> 202-296-2992
> www.servenet.org

11. **Teens for Literacy** encourages inner-city middle school students to become involved in promoting literacy in their own school or communities. Under the direction of committed teachers and counselors, teams of about four or five students at each school design and participate directly in such activities as tutoring, reading aloud, reading contests, and creating displays.

> Allen Berger
> Dept. of Teacher Education
> Miami University
> Oxford, OH 45056
> 513-529-6463
> www.users.muohio.edu/bergera/teensforliteracy

12. **The United Way** is a nationwide network of volunteers and community service agencies whose local chapters raise funds to meet the health and human care needs of millions of Americans every day. Volunteer opportunities can be found easily through the VolunteerMatch Web site. Enter your zip code for the center nearest you.

Alexandria, VA 22314-2045

703-836-7100

www.national.unitedway.org

13. **Youth in Action** exists only as a Web site, where you can learn about different environmental and human rights problems, communicate with others about solutions, and take action to make a positive change. You *can* change the world.

www.teaching.com/act/

12 Ways to Volunteer

If you're the kind of person who can't sit by while others around you are in need of help, this list will give you some ideas about the sorts of things you can do to make their lives and yours better.

1. The Special Olympics is an international program of year-round sports training and athletic competition for children and adults with mental retardation. As a volunteer, you may be able to help train a child for a sports event. Other volunteers plan competitions and fundraising events. Go to www.specialolympics.org for more information.

2. Ronald McDonald Houses can be found in most large U.S. cities. Their mission is to provide aid and assistance to hospitalized children and their families by offering a low-cost "home away from home" for parents and children during treatment. Volunteers help prepare meals, talk to families, and give them emotional as well as financial support. To find out more, go to www.rmhc.com.

3. Every large city across the country has at least one homeless shelter, and each one is more than happy to take on new volunteers. You can help prepare or serve meals or get involved in a food drive to raise money.

4. Food banks collect food and distribute it to those in need. They often work hand in hand with homeless shelters, but they also serve either poor or elderly people in your community (especially around the holidays). Look in the phone book for a local food bank if you are interested.

5. If you are a nature lover and live near a state park, you can join volunteer programs that will enable you to help preserve and maintain the park's beauty and welfare. You can try anything from educational programs to trail construction and maintenance.

6. One of the most amazing ways to help someone and truly change his or her life is by helping that person learn to read. As a literacy volunteer, you'll be able to teach this important skill. To learn more, contact www.ed.gov/offices/OVAE-/adusite.html.

7. Habitat for Humanity, which has been supported by former President Jimmy Carter, builds houses and donates them to poor people all over the nation. You'll be able to help others and at the same time learn a great deal about construction. For information on projects in your area, go to the Habitat for Humanity Web site, www.habitat.org.

8. If you have dreams of becoming a health care professional, what better way is there to prepare than to help patients both inside and outside hospitals. Contact a local hospital to learn more about volunteering in your area.

9. Many senior citizen centers have volunteer programs to provide friendship and community activities to the elderly. If you think you'd like working with seniors, call a senior center in your neighborhood and find out about its volunteer programs.

10. Getting involved with the Sierra Club or another environmental group can be a great adventure. You can help by informing others about conservation issues and by leading hikes or by lending a hand at the chapter office. Contact the local office of an environmental organization near you. Find out more at www.sierraclub.org.

11. If you have computer and design skills and know how to create Web sites, you can create a site for a small charity and perhaps even get funding to pay for the maintenance of the site from local businesses.

12. Many animal shelters are nonprofit or government organizations and welcome volunteers to help take care of the animals and maintain the facilities. Contact your local ASPCA or call a nearby veterinarian.

15 Things You Can Do to End Hunger

Each night, 600 million people go to bed hungry, not just in foreign countries we'll never visit but right here in our own communities. There *is* enough food to go around.

1. Educate yourself. Read about hunger in books, newspapers, and magazines so you really understand the extent of the problem. Talk about what you know with your friends, and include the subject in school projects.

2. Send a chicken to a poor family in a foreign country. It only costs a dollar! The Heifer Project sends animals such as cows, goats, pigs, and even bees to families who must feed themselves. Contact: Heifer Project International, P.O. Box 8085, Little Rock, AR 72203; 800-422-0474; www.heifer.org.

3. Go public. If you're involved in a worthy project, contact the local media and see if they want to do a story about your efforts.

4. Make donations to hunger organizations in honor of your friends and relatives instead of buying them birthday gifts. Write out a card that explains that their friendship has inspired you to help others.

5. Write to your local politicians and ask what they are doing to help solve the problem.

6. Find out what efforts are being made in your community to feed the hungry and volunteer to work for these groups.

7. Many communities have programs enabling restaurants to donate leftovers to hungry people at the end of each day. If there's one in your city, talk to restaurant managers when you go out to eat and encourage them to join the program.

8. Support World Food Day, October 16. Groups all over the country do something special on this day every year to make people aware of the problem of hunger. Contact: U.S. National Committee for World Food Day, 2175 K St., NW, Washington, DC 20437; 202-653-2404; www.reeusda.gov/ree/.

9. Support Oxfam America. Each year, on the Thursday before Thanksgiving, many people skip a meal or fast for the whole day and then donate the money they would have spent to Oxfam America. Contact: 26 West St., Boston, MA 02111; 800-597-FAST; www.oxfamamerica.org.

10. Organize a supermarket food drive. Get your market to urge shoppers to always buy one or two extra items to be donated to local shelters. Talk to the store manager and offer to help by making signs explaining the program. Get your parents to help transport the donated food.

11. Start your own chapter of Youth Ending Hunger (YEH). Contact this group at 15 E. 26th St., New York, NY 10010; 212-251-9100; www.thp.org, to get a starter kit, which will tell you how to organize kids in your area.

12. Hold a CROP WALK. This is a national effort in which people walk for 10 miles (more or less) and get people to donate money for each mile they walk to help local food banks and homeless shelters. People of all ages can participate. To find out more about organizing a walk, contact Church World Service, 475 Riverside Dr., New York, NY 10115; 212-870-2257.

13. Support Africare, which tries to feed people in more than 20 African countries. For $10, you and your friends can provide 100 pounds of fertilizer for crops, feed two people for a month, or buy enough seeds to plant an entire field. Contact: P.O. Box 66415, Houston, TX 77266; 713-521-1420; prores@insync.net.

14. Support the American Jewish World Service, which organizes health and agricultural projects for people of all religions in Africa, Asia, and Latin America. Contact: 989 Ave. of the Americas, New York, NY 10018; 800-889-7146; ajws.org.

15. Help hungry people start projects to end their own hunger. You can find such efforts by contacting IDEX (International Development Exchange), 827 Valencia St., San Francisco, CA 94110; 415-824-8384; idex.org.

29 National Youth Organizations

1. **ABA Center on Children and the Law**
   750 15th St., NW
   Washington, DC 20005
   202-662-1000
   www.abanet.org
   Finds lawyers for kids and offers scholarships for those who want to be lawyers

2. **Al-Anon/Alateen**
   Family Groups
   1600 Corporate Landing Hwy.
   Virginia Beach, VA 23454
   888-4AL-ANON
   wso@al-anon.org
   Helps the family and friends of alcoholics

3. **American Anorexia/Bulimia Association (AABA)**
   165 W. 46th St.
   New York, NY 10036
   212-575-6200
   www.aabainc.org
   Helps kids with eating disorders

4. **American Federation of Riders**
   P.O. Box 53301
   Cincinnati, OH 45253-0301
   513-661-6080
   www.afr1982.org
   Motorcyclists who help kids with education and social issues

5. **Amnesty International Children's Human Rights Network**
   322 8th Ave.
   New York, NY 10001
   212-807-8400
   www.amnesty-usa.org
   Organizes kids in grades 4–8 to write letters to political leaders around the world asking for fair and humane treatment for all human beings

6. **Artists Against Racism**
   P.O. Box 54511
   Toronto, Ont., Canada M5M 4NF

416-410-5631

www.artistsagainstracism.org

Popular artists such as Celine Dion, Mike Myers, Aerosmith, Ani DiFranco, and Raffi work with young people to end racism, homophobia (look it up), and sexism.

7. **Big Brothers/Big Sisters of America**

230 N. 13th St.

Philadelphia, PA 19108

215-567-7000

Hooks up underprivileged kids with adults who can help them

8. **Boys Clubs of America**

1230 W. Peachtree St.

Atlanta, GA 30309

404-487-5700

Tuesday@bgca.org

For kids 7–18, offers organized recreational, athletic, and social activities

9. **Boy Scouts of America**

P.O. Box 152079

Irving, TX 75015-2079

214-580-2000

www.scouting.org

Activities, character development, and citizenship for boys

10. **Camp Fire**

4601 Madison Ave.

Kansas City, MO 64112

816-756-1950

info@campfire.org

Camping skills, responsible citizenship, and self-reliance for boys and girls

11. **Common Sense About Kids and Guns**

418 C St., NE

Washington, DC 20002

877-955-KIDS

www.kidsandguns.org

Educates kids and adults about the dangers of keeping firearms in the home

12. **Childhelp USA**
15757 N. 78th St.
Scottsdale, AZ 85260
480-922-8212
www.childhelpusa.org
Research into and the prevention and treatment of child abuse

13. **Hearts and Minds**
3074 Broadway
New York, NY 10027
212-280-0333
where@heartsandminds.org
Inspires kids and adults to get involved with issues of racism, poverty, and the environment

14. **Cancer Kids**
P.O. Box 2715
Waxahachie, Texas 75168
www.cancerkids.org
Educates kids with questions about cancer

15. **4-H Youth Development**
U.S. Dept. of Agriculture
Washington, DC 20250
202-720-3029
Agricultural, technological, and interpersonal skills for ages 9–19. Camping and international exchange programs

16. **Girls Clubs of America**
30 E. 33rd St.
New York, NY 10016
212-509-2000
Athletic activities and health and education programs, including AIDS awareness and substance abuse prevention for girls

17. **Girl Scouts of the USA**
420 Fifth Ave.
New York, NY 10018
800-478-7248
www.girlscouts.org
Activities, character development, and citizenship for girls; international programs, too

18. **Guardian Angels**
982 E. 89th St.
Brooklyn, NY 11236
718-6649-2607
www.ai.mit.edu/people/ericldab/ga.html
Local programs encourage kids to aid the elderly and others who need their help

19. **National Coalition Against Domestic Violence**
P.O. Box 18749
1201 E. Colfax, Suite 385
Denver, CO 80218-0749
800-343-2823
www.givedirect.org
Gives out free information about organizations that help victims of violence

20. **National Council on Child Abuse and Family Violence**
1155 Connecticut Ave., NW, Suite 400
Washington, DC 20036
202-429-6695
info@NCCAFV.org
Helps people find agencies near them that offer family counseling

21. **National Crime Prevention Council**
1000 Connecticut Ave., NW
Washington, DC 20036
202-466-6272
www.ncpc.org
Offers information about starting crime watch programs in your community to prevent vandalism, robberies, drug-dealing, and other crimes

22. **National Information Center for Children and Youth with Disabilities**
P.O. Box 1492
Washington, DC 20013
800-695-0285
nichy@aed.org
Provides information about support groups, individual disabilities, laws that affect kids with special needs, and helpful state agencies

23. **National Jewish Council for the Disabled**
11 Broadway
New York, NY 10004
212-613-8233
www.ou.org/ncsy/njcd
Provides recreational and informal educational programming for kids with disabilities

24. **The National School Safety Center**
141 Duesenberg Dr.
Westlake Village, CA 91362
805-373-9977
www.nssc1.org
Helps school groups form violence prevention programs

25. **Reading Is Fundamental**
2130 E. First St.
Los Angeles, CA 90033
323-268-8755
info@rifsocal.org
Encourages kids to read by setting up school programs and educating people about illiteracy

26. **SADD (Students Against Drunk Driving)**
P.O. Box 800
Marlboro, MA 01752
508-481-3568
Devoted to spreading the idea that "friends do not let friends drive drunk," with chapters in thousands of schools

27. **Winners on Wheels (WOW)**
7477 E. Dry Creek Pkwy.
Longmont, CO 80503
800-WOW-TALK
wowtalk@earthlink.net
A national learning and social program, similar to scouting, for kids in wheelchairs

28. **Workshop on Nonviolence**
The Martin Luther King, Jr., Center
for Nonviolent Social Change
449 Auburn Ave., NE
Atlanta, GA 30312
404-526-8900

www.thekingcenter.org
Promotes nonviolent solutions to problems, mostly through school programs

29. YMCA of the United States
101 N. Wacker Dr.
Chicago, IL 60606
312-977-0031
800-USA-YMCA (800-872-9622)
www.ymca.net
Local Y's offer a variety of athletic programs, summer camp, and child care facilities. There are national programs, too.

28 Ways to Combat Prejudice

1. Know your roots. Research your ancestors. Draw your family tree. Trace your family's involvement with history.

2. Celebrate holidays with your family. Participate in family traditions that keep your heritage alive.

3. Share your cultural and religious activities with friends who may know little about them. Ask them if you can participate in their customs, too.

4. Watch your language. Avoid remarks based on stereotyping, and challenge others when they disguise racial slurs as "jokes."

5. Know your stuff. If you're confused about certain myths and stereotypes, learn how they got started.

6. Talk about prejudice with members of your family. Find out what their experiences are and use them when you are asked to write essays for school.

7. Visit important landmarks associated with civil and human rights struggles, such as the U.S. Holocaust Memorial Museum in Washington, D.C.

8. Read books that promote understanding between cultures as well as books about cultures you know nothing about.

9. Establish a Diversity Club at school that promotes intercultural fund-raisers (an international potluck supper, dramatic readings of plays that address prejudice). Get other school clubs to join your activities.

10. Invite civil rights leaders to your school to address the student body. Publish an interview with this person in the school paper or on your school's Web site.

11. Form a team of students and teachers who will write Rules for Respect, which can be displayed in classrooms.

12. Designate a bulletin board near the entrance to your school where students can post any ideas, messages, and art—even graffiti, if a wall is available—concerning civil rights issues.

13. Create a calendar with all the important holidays and special events of each of the cultures represented in your school. If it's attractive enough, you can print copies to sell and donate the money to a civil rights effort.

14. Create a speaking program at school for students from different backgrounds to share their experiences. It can be as simple as a five-minute addition to a regular school assembly.

15. Have a "culture bee," where students have to answer questions about various religions and disciplines.

16. Create art with antiprejudice themes.

17. Hold a multicultural film festival at your school. If you're really ambitious, get your local movie theater manager involved. Invite community businesses to sponsor the event.

18. Collect comic books from around the world and ask your librarian to display them.

19. When choosing a school play, pick one that is sensitive to multiculturalism by incorporating a variety of roles and perspectives.

20. Make sure all cultures are represented in all school clubs and committees.

21. Listen to music that promotes respect for all creeds.

22. Research the history of the civil rights movement, from slavery to the present and talk to your friends and family about what you are learning.

23. Talk to your librarian about making sure that all cultures and faiths are represented on the bookshelves.

24. Organize a school arbitration committee that will "referee" racist disputes among students.

25. Plan a community Walk Against Hate and donate the money to an organization that combats prejudice.

26. Suggest that your school paper devote one column per issue to student opinions on prejudice and racism.

27. Ask students to provide recipes that represent their respective cultures and publish them in a booklet to sell in local stores. Donate the proceeds to Amnesty International.

28. Learn the list of "20 Really Dirty Words" on page 44.

37 Ways to Fight Censorship

Censorship is the suppression of ideas and information that certain persons—individuals, groups, or governments— find offensive or dangerous. A censor will say, "Don't let anyone read this book, or buy that magazine, or buy that record, or view that film, because I object to it!" The censor wants to judge materials for everyone and take away your right to make these decisions for yourself. If censorship offends you, here are some things you can do to protect your rights.

1. Speak out against censorship!

2. Send your senators and representatives letters or mailgrams or e-mails expressing your opinions.

3. Support your library, and request that it carries "banned" books.

4. Create art that addresses censorship issues.

5. Speak out about freedom of speech at schools, churches, and to youth groups in your town.

6. Write a letter to your local paper in defense of free speech.

7. Call your radio station's talk show and ask them to publicize your efforts against censorship.

8. Support retailers who fight censorship.

9. Read books about censorship and First Amendment issues.

10. Gather information and news clippings on censorship and organize them in a scrapbook to share with friends and classmates.

11. Buy "banned" records.

12. Write and perform songs about free speech and the dangers of censorship.

13. Contact your local cable outlet to find out if it's being pressured to censor its programming.

14. Join the American Civil Liberties Union (ACLU). Go to www.aclu.org.

15. Join the Freedom to Read Foundation. Go to www.ftrf.org.

16. Support the American Booksellers Association Foundation for Free Expression. Go to www.abffe.org.

17. Get to know censorship groups. Study their literature, and expose them to the public.

18. Write to your favorite artists and entertainers and find out what they're doing to help preserve freedom of expression. Ask them to support your efforts. (When the freedom of one artist is threatened, the freedom of all artists is threatened.)

19. Make an anticensorship home video showing the various benefits of free speech in your community.

20. Write about your positive experiences with art.

21. Write all your book reports about "banned" books, and talk about how you were affected by the issues that some people insist are dangerous.

22. Boycott products made and marketed by companies that fund the censors.

23. Start an organization to fight censorship. Activities can include discussions of banned books and censored art. Invite the creators of the censored art to come talk to your group.

24. Start an anticensorship newsletter.

25. Contact local arts and educational organizations, and persuade them to stage events around the subject of free speech.

26. Use community access cable or community radio to raise everyone's awareness of free speech issues.

27. Stage a mock trial on censorship.

28. Create a public service announcement to be aired over the school radio station.

29. Ask your social studies teacher to talk about free speech in class.

30. Picket the censors.

31. Make the real obscenities — censorship and any other attack on our civil liberties — the issues.

32. If anyone tells you that the censors are trying to protect you, point out that you do not need protection from books like *The Adventures of Huckleberry Finn, The Diary of Anne Frank,* and *Charlie and the Chocolate Factory,* all of which have been banned at one time.

33. Find out which books have been banned from your school and read them.

34. Learn more about censorship by contacting People for the American Way, 1015 18th St., NW, Suite 300, Washington, DC 20036; www.pfaw.org.

35. Talk to your parents about censorship, and urge them to get involved in an anticensorship movement in your community.

36. Get your friends and other members of your community to sign petitions against censorship, and make sure they are delivered into the hands of public officials who can help.

37. Create an anticensorship logo and print it on a T-shirt.

5 Media Myths About Teenagers

TV shows, news reports, commercials—they all seem to be saying such negative things about teens. And you wonder why managers stare at you as if you're a criminal when you walk down the aisle of a store. Teens aren't all violent, reckless, irresponsible punks. In fact, most of you are active, healthy, and responsible people. That's why it's frustrating when adults stereotype you. Here are some of the unfair myths that have been created by the media.

1. Teens are lazy. Ever hear that one? As if all of you just sat around counting the cracks on the ceiling every day! To disprove that myth, a survey in *Hotwired* showed that "teens in America work harder than their counterparts anywhere else in the world." Some 58% hold jobs and 69% do housework regularly. That's more than adults do!

2. Teens are violent and dangerous. News stories often portray teens as perpetrators of crime. They also rarely report when they are victims, especially when they are victims of adult crime. Surprisingly, for every violent or sexual offense committed by a youth under 18 years of age, there are three such crimes committed against a youth by an adult.

3. All teens use drugs. The media loves to portray teens as drug addicts or users. For example, an episode of TV's *Boston Public* showed teens raving in the school basement while one had a seizure from laced drugs. In fact, a study by the U.S. Drug Abuse Warning Network found that 95% of the drug-related deaths in 1994 were adults over the age of 26.

4. Most teens are sexually active, and teen girls are constantly getting pregnant. The media constantly portrays teens as sex hungry and "knocked up." In fact, teen pregnancy rates in the U.S. have been decreasing significantly. Available data for all U.S. states reported declines between 1992 and 1995.

5. Teens love to disrespect adults. In TV shows and commercials, teens are always disruptive or hostile toward adults. But in reality teens are more likely to disrespect peers who disrespect adults. When asked to identify what causes problems in America's schools, 64% of teens said, "Students who don't respect schoolteachers and authorities." When asked what the largest causes of our country's problems were, 56% said, "Selfishness, people not thinking of the rights of others," and 52% said, "People who don't respect the law and authorities."

9 Annoying Things That <u>Some</u> Teens Do at the Mall

The mall is a popular hangout—you can buy stuff, meet your friends, check out new people, and generally chill. You can also completely annoy other shoppers and store personnel by behaving badly. Here are some of the most common mall offenses.

1. Climbing up the escalator the wrong way. When little kids do this, their mommies usually stop them. If you're old enough to go to a mall without a parent, you're old enough to know better. It's dangerous to yourself and others.

2. Shouting to friends on an upper level from below. Trying to catch someone's attention is one thing, but having a full-blown conversation—with the rest of the mall listening—is, well, stupid. Don't do it. And don't yell to your friends sitting five tables away in the food court. Your amusing anecdote isn't nearly as funny to total strangers.

3. Making out at the mall. Kissing, groping, getting hot and heavy in public? Gross. If you want to work up a sweat with your sweetie, do it somewhere private.

4. Running through the mall. Think it's funny to race your friends to the fountain, pushing shoppers out of the way as you go? Think again.

5. Dropping objects from an upper level. This rude but common pastime can hurt someone and get you kicked out of the mall—maybe even permanently.

6. Stealing. Irritating, immature, illegal, and definitely not cool.

7. Staring at people or making fun of them. Do you think these people aren't real because you don't know them personally?

8. "Decorating" the mall with graffiti. It's also against the law.

9. Bumping into people without apologizing. It's called being rude, and doing it gives all teens a bad name. Grow up.

5 Smart (but Fun) Things to Do at the Mall

1. People-watch. This can actually provide hours of fun. Check out the weird outfits. Try to imagine the relationships between the couples you see. Watch the people. Invent a game: see who can spot the weirdest hairdo, the best shoes, the person with the most nose rings. Be discreet, please.

2. Listen to music. The listening booths at most large record stores give you a chance to hear new music for free. Some stores even let you listen to any CD they have in the store.

3. See what's doing at the bookstore. Some have string quartets and jazz bands playing, which makes for a nice free concert. Check out the store schedule for poetry readings, celebrity book signings, and other special events.

4. Eat free food. See how many free food samples you can pick up at the food stands; you might even be able to score a whole meal.

5. Shop. That is, basically, what it's there for.

6 Reasons That Teens Shoplift

Although teens make up only 7% of the U.S. population, they account for almost 50% of all shoplifting. If you think shoplifting is harmless, consider the fact that over $25 million worth of merchandise is stolen every year. If someone you know suddenly seems able to buy expensive gifts and has no explanation for how she or he was able to afford them, this person may have a problem. Offer to help by passing on some resources (see the next list). Whatever you do, don't go shopping with them.

1. **Peer pressure.** If other kids are shoplifting and some kids want to be accepted as part of the crowd, they may do it even though they know it's wrong.

2. **They want to fit in.** They can't afford the same stylish things that other kids have, so they steal them.

3. **To relieve stress or make up for some other loss.** Kids who are mistreated at home sometimes act out by shoplifting treats for themselves. Someone whose parents are getting divorced, for instance, may steal in order to make up for what they think they are losing.

4. **To get attention.** Even negative attention is a welcome change from being totally ignored. Some shoplifters are simply trying to get their parents to notice them.

5. **Revenge.** Kids are angry at their parents and want to embarrass them by letting the whole community know that their children are thieves.

6. **Depression.** When kids shoplift, they get a surge of adrenalin, and this relieves—at least for a short time—the feelings of depression that some people have.

4 Web Sites That Help Shoplifters

1. www.shopliftersanonymous.com
2. www.shopliftersalternative.org
3. www.thefttalk.com
4. www.sharingvillage.com

8 Signs of Stalking

Every year, 120,000 teens believe they are being stalked. This means someone is pursuing them or paying unwanted attention to them—and they won't back off. You are being stalked if you answer yes to any of these questions.

1. Someone knows things about your whereabouts that you don't expect them to know.

2. You get unwanted phone calls.

3. Someone tries to approach you in inappropriate ways.

4. Someone shows up looking for you at school or when you are visiting a friend.

5. Someone repeatedly asks you for personal information, like where you go on vacation, where you are babysitting, or where your parents are, your full name and phone number, or where you go to school.

6. Someone online seems to know more about you than you are comfortable with.

7. Someone you met online insists on meeting you in person, even if you say you're not interested.

8. Someone threatens you or tells you not to tell anyone else that you know them.

8 Steps to Take if You Think You Are Being Stalked

1. Tell someone—your parents, a teacher or guidance counselor, or a security person if you're at a mall or in a store. Even if you think it was your fault because you attracted this attention in the first place, let someone know about it. No matter what you've done, *getting stalked is never the fault of the person being stalked.*

2. Don't try to be nice or polite when you tell the person to leave you alone. Let them know in no uncertain terms that their attention is not welcome.

3. Don't reply to notes, e-mails, or any other messages you get from the person. But hold on to the messages.

4. Find yourself online by entering your name as a search engine keyword to see if there is information about you on the Internet that you didn't know was there.

5. Always let someone (your parents, for instance) know where you are going and where you will be hanging out.

6. Make a note of anything that happens in connection with a stalking incident.

7. Avoid being alone, especially in parking lots, at the mall, or at school after classes are over — especially at night.

8. If you are afraid of one person in particular, tell your friends who that person is in case he or she tries to get information from them.

14 Out-Alone Safety Tips

Going out alone at night should actually be avoided; you are always safer with other people around. But if you have to be out alone (day or night), be aware of your surroundings at all times. Here are some facts you should know and some of the warning signs to help you distinguish between an adult you can trust and someone who could try to harm you.

1. Stay alert.

2. Act calm and confident to send a message that you're in control.

3. If a person or situation makes you feel anxious, get away, even if you think your fear is silly.

4. Carry and use a cell phone.

5. Stick to well-traveled and well-lit streets. Avoid shortcuts through parking lots or alleys.

6. Make sure someone knows where you are going and when to expect you back. Be sure they have your cell phone number.

7. Use automated teller machines (ATMs) only in the daytime. Avoid the machine if you're uneasy about people nearby.

8. Don't wear expensive jewelry or clothing.

9. If you carry a purse, keep it close to your body, not dangling by the straps. Don't keep your wallet in your back pocket; you're better off putting it in a front pants pocket or a zippered jacket pocket.

10. If a stranger asks you for help with a problem, such as finding a lost dog or assisting with packages, tell them to find another adult to help. If the person really has good intentions, they will understand your refusal.

11. If someone wearing a uniform approaches you and tells you to cooperate with them, ask to see some identification. Make sure they're really who they say they are.

12. Never go anywhere with someone you don't know.

13. If you think someone is following you, switch direction or cross the street. Walk toward an open store, restaurant, or lighted house. If you're scared, yell for help.

14. If someone tries to grab you or hurt you in any way or if someone tries to force you to go with them, scream, "FIRE!" at the top of your lungs and do whatever it takes to get away.

7 Safety Tips for Driving Alone

1. Always keep your car doors locked.

2. If your car breaks down, stay inside with the windows up and doors locked. If you have a cell phone, call for help. Otherwise, display a Call Police sign in the back window or wait for someone to stop. Open the window a crack to communicate. If they offer to help, thank them and ask them to contact the police. Wait for the police to arrive before getting out of your car.

3. If someone hits you from behind, pull over but don't get out of the car. When the person confronts you, open the window a crack and tell them to pull into the nearest gas station or variety store parking lot. Be sure to get their license plate number first, but never get out of your car.

4. Try to keep blankets, water, flashlight, flares, and other safety materials in the car in case of emergency.

5. If you think you are being followed, drive to the nearest commercial area or to a police station.

6. Never pick up hitchhikers. *Never* hitchhike.

7. Sign up with your local Automobile Association of America (AAA) center for free road service. Visit www.aaa.com.

17 of the Most Common Driving Mistakes Teens Make

Teenagers get into a lot more accidents than adults do for one simple reason: they have less driving experience, so they are more apt to make the mistakes that adults have already learned to avoid. Here are some of the most common errors teens make:

1. They tend to expect the best outcome of any driving situation rather than the worst. They don't drive defensively, which means they aren't aware that another driver may do something crazy or unexpected.

2. They don't look around often enough and check the positions of the cars around them.

3. They drive with other teens in the car. Music, conversation, and laughter can be distracting. Teens are four times more likely to die in a crash when they are with other teenagers than if they are alone or with an adult.

4. They drive too fast. Doing 35 miles an hour in a 25mph area *is* speeding.

5. They drive too aggressively. They take risks like driving through red lights and tailgating. Impatient teens make terrible drivers, especially if they tend to get angry easily.

6. They don't slow down in difficult conditions.

7. They don't check for cars twice before pulling into an intersection at a stop sign.

8. They fail to look behind them before backing out of a parking place.

9. They don't look both left and right when making a right-hand turn.

10. They don't watch for cars rushing through intersections at the end of a red light.

11. They don't always wear seat belts and don't insist that their passengers use them.

12. They drive like they own the road, not like they own the car.

13. They blast the radio, making it impossible to hear either a siren or other drivers' warning beeps.

14. They drive under the influence of drugs or alcohol.

15. They try to drive even when they know they can't do it safely.

16. They talk on their cell phones while driving.

17. They put on makeup, comb their hair, or eat while driving.

8 Basic Rules of Cyber Safety

You are in the age group most likely to participate in on-line discussions. You are also the most likely group to be victimized by anyone wishing to do harm or misrepresent themselves. If you ever have any reason to believe you are being lured by someone for any illegal purpose, contact the police immediately.

1. Do not give out personal information to strangers. Never tell your computer passwords to anyone in a chat room or in an instant message. Think very carefully before giving out your real name, address, telephone number, school, or any other information that someone could use to hurt you.

2. Never give out your Social Security number. If you are registering for a service that has a legitimate need for it, provide the information through the mail.

3. Know who you are doing business with. If you're making a purchase on the Internet, do it only if you can check the seller's record of transactions. Most sales networks provide a way for customers to rate the person or business with which they've done business. Check these reports and avoid those that don't have a rating.

4. Be very selective about who you give your credit card number to. Some Web sites have set up systems for conducting secure credit card transactions by encrypting your information when you order merchandise. Those are the safest ones to use.

5. Do not download files from anyone you don't know or from obscure Web sites. Most computer viruses come in the form of downloaded files.

6. Think before you post your e-mail address. Otherwise

your computer may end up being a dumping ground for junk mail. If you have already received a large amount of junk mail, try contacting your service provider to change your e-mail name and leave no forwarding address. If this doesn't work, you may need to change your service provider. Then, let only those you wish to communicate with know your new e-mail address.

7. From time to time, search for information about yourself on the Internet by using your name as a keyword on a search engine.

8. Let your parents in on the fun: talk to them about your online activities, and if you are concerned about anything you've clicked onto, discuss it with them.

Netiquette: 19 Rules of Online Courtesy

Congratulations. You are now a citizen of a global village. Be a good neighbor!

No one likes someone who interrupts, hogs the conversation or changes the subject, or is intolerant of other people's opinions or mistakes. So you don't come off looking like a total feeb, here are some expert tips to make yourself e-welcome.

1. **Listen before you leap.** Plunging into a forum discussion is like trying to jump in while your buddies are turning the jump rope. If your timing and rhythm are off, you'll get all tangled up—and no one will have any fun. Take some time just to read a lot of the messages on the message board before sending any of your own. Before joining a live forum discussion, listen in for a while. You'll learn a lot by watching how the "pros" handle themselves.

2. **Get your FAQs straight.** FAQs are "frequently asked questions." Everyone new to the online world has lots of questions. Chances are, you're not the first person to wonder how to download a file or send a message to a pen pal. Before taking up other people's time with a question that's already been asked a squillion times, check to see if the forum's library has a FAQ file that contains answers to basic questions. Read it carefully. Then, if you still don't understand something or if you need more information, feel free to post a message to other members.

3. **Don't send test messages.** There's no need to waste time (and money) sending messages like "Hello! Just testing to see if this works." Better to go ahead and say what you want to say. When you get a response, you'll know the system is functioning—and you won't take up valuable cyberspace in the process. (Sometimes people on forums waste so much time saying "Hi!" and "Hello" to one another that they never say anything important. Some forums even have a rule: "No hi!"

4. **Stay "on topic."** If everybody in the forum is discussing pets, it's impolite to say "Hey, did anybody see that new *Simpsons* episode yesterday?" And post your questions to the appropriate forum. A forum on inline skating is no place to start discussing the way-cool fatalities in the latest war-'n-gore game.

5. **Think twice; post once.** Once you've sent a message, you can't take it back. Before you hit the "Send" button—and experience that twinge of regret or an oh-no second, read over what you've written. If there's a chance it might be misunderstood or that it might hurt someone's feelings or that it might make you look like a dweeb, erase it. After all, that's what the "Del" key is for.

6. **Watch your tone of voice.** If you call your best buddy a doofus, he'll know from your smile or that playful punch in the arm that you're just giving him a hard time. Online, though, you don't have that luxury. Words on a computer screen don't always carry the teasing or joking tone of voice we intended. If your joke might be misinterpreted, you can soften it a little by using a "smiley" :). BTW, use acronyms and emoticons :-) sparingly. They do help to make a message shorter and to the point, but they can be overused. And be careful—some grouchy people really hate those things. :>(

7. **DON'T USE ALL CAPITAL LETTERS WHEN YOU WRITE!** It looks like you're shouting, and that's what people will think you're doing IF YOU WRITE LIKE THIS.

8. **Watch your temper.** There's a great temptation to be real snotty when we're talking to people whose faces we can't see and whose names we don't know. If someone goofs or says something clueless, it's all too easy to say "What an idiot!" (or worse). In computer talk, this is known as "flaming." All too often, forum discussions wind up as insult wars. This is an utter waste of time for everyone. If you *must* respond with a strong comment, do everyone a favor: at least give a little warning by writing "Flame" or "Flame on!" before launching your tirade. Or ask your fellow net-neighbor to continue the discussion privately, via e-mail (or Instant Messages), instead of mucking up the public forum. And you'd better be sure of your facts or you risk getting flamed yourself. Better yet: just chill out. Thumper's mother was right: if you can't say something nice, clam up. Read over your e-mail before you send it, especially if it's an inflammatory message. Once you click on "Send," that's it.

9. **Don't correct people's grammar or spelling.** Nobody's "perfekt." Some forum participants type better than others. Other people are in a hurry to post their comments and will send messages without bothering to clean them up. Remember, too, that online services let you talk with people from all kinds of places and backgrounds. Some may not even be from your country and may not be as adept at using English as you. Be tolerant of other people's errors, and hope that others will be as tolerant of yours!

10. **Do correct your own grammar or spelling.** Try to clean up your own act as much as possible. Nobody likes struggling to read sloppy writing, whether it's on a piece of paper or a computer screen. Do the proofreading. You'll be more likely to receive responses to your postings if you look like a careful and conscientious writer and not some slob.

11. **Don't believe everything you read, and don't forward it to everyone you know.** Some people use the forum to create new identities for themselves. They pretend to be smarter, richer, better looking, older, or younger than they really are. Just because they sign their message "Shaq" or "Chelsea Clinton" doesn't mean that's who they really are. Computer forums are open to everyone—and unfortunately that sometimes means a few creeps and losers will be hanging out. E-mail hoaxes are getting worse because of the gullible users who mindlessly pass on messages without doing any research. If a message contains the line "Send this to everyone you know," don't.

12. Don't be a spoiler. If you're talking about a great movie you saw or a book you read, don't ruin it for others by giving away the surprises. If you just *gotta* say something to make your point, give fair warning: print the word SPOILER! before your comment.

13. Don't assume your e-mail will be kept private. You may think your remarks to another person are no one else's business. But once you've posted a message, you have no control over what might happen to it. If you're using a school's system or your parents' computer service account, your notes might wind up in some unexpected places—like the principal's office or your mom's boss's desk. You may even find your flames included in a Top Online Insults list in the next edition of this book!

14. Share what you know. After a few weeks online, you'll be a pro. If you see messages from people who are struggling to catch up, help them out. Maybe you've discovered some great new way to make your computer dance and do tricks. Tell others! Remember, the info highway is a two-way street.

15. Be as concise as you can. Most people don't want to read long letters. Get to the point. Some people get dozens, if not hundreds, of messages every day.

16. Don't attach large files (over 50KB) to an e-mail message unless the recipient knows that it is coming. Sending a picture of your new skateboard may seem like fun to you, but your recipient may not be amused when they see what a 20-minute download has produced.

17. Don't leave the subject line blank—many people simply delete any message without a subject line. Make it short and descriptive, so the recipient can make a quick decision about the message without having to open it.

18. Use blank lines to separate your paragraphs. Your e-mail will be easier to read.

19. Don't repeatedly send jokes to anyone without getting their permission.

The 4 Basic Rules of Chat Room Safety

The Internet is a wondrous tool that gives you access to a world that didn't even exist a few years ago. It also poses dangers, including mean and dishonest people who roam chat rooms in search of innocent young people. Let your parents know you follow these rules.

1. Keep your identity private. Avoid giving out your full name, mailing address, telephone number, the name of your school, or any other information that could help someone figure out exactly who you are or find you in person. The same applies to your family and friends: never reveal anything about other people either.

2. Never respond to a message that seems inappropriate or in any way makes you uncomfortable. Instead, show it to your parents or a trusted adult to see if you can do anything to make it stop. Sending a response just encourages the sender.

3. Never get together with someone you "meet" online. You never know for certain if people you meet online are who they say they are. If you do think it's appropriate to meet with someone, discuss it with your parents, and *never go to the meeting by yourself.* Arrange to meet in a public place, like a coffee shop or mall that you (not just the other person) are familiar and comfortable with.

4. Talk to your family and friends about the people you chat with. If these relationships are really safe, there should be no need for secrecy.

5 Sobering Statistics About Teens and Alcohol

According to the National Safety Council and Students Against Drink Driving:

1. Over 4 million teenagers in America have serious problems with alcohol.

2. Approximately 30% of boys and 22% of girls classify themselves as drinkers by the age of 12.

3. Some 28% of high school seniors are "binge drinkers," consuming five or more drinks at a time.

4. Every year, over 3,000 teens are killed in crashes that involve drunk driving.

5. Every 26 minutes, someone is killed in an alcohol-related accident.

6 Reasons to Keep Your Mouth Shut When You Are Approached by a Police Officer for Any Reason

These tips apply whether you're guilty or not. In our interview with the Haworth (New Jersey) Police Department, we were told that the biggest problems arise when teens attempt to answer questions before they are even asked. They emphasize that you should always answer truthfully and respond to the officer when he or she questions you. But there are some good reasons to say only what you need to say—nothing more.

1. Wait for an officer to ask you a question before you say anything. You can incriminate yourself by acting guilty. Most teens say, "I didn't do it," before they even know why they were stopped.

2. Acting defensively or belligerently makes you look guilty even if you're not.

3. Giving more information than the officer asks for can get you in trouble, especially if you're nervous. You may say something by mistake, but when you try to correct it, you might appear to be lying.

4. Until he tells you, you cannot know for certain why the officer is approaching you. Some teens 'fess up to something the minute they see a cop, but it turns out that he was going to ask about something else.

5. You'll appear more mature and, therefore, less guilty if you appear to be in control of yourself. Keeping quiet indicates control.

6. Everything you say to an officer becomes part of the record. Find out more about what's going on before you decide how you want to contribute to that record.

10 Reasons Teens Do Drugs or Alcohol

1. Peer pressure.
2. They are trying to escape some sort of pain (fear, sadness, anger).
3. They think it's "cool," that they will fit into the crowd better if they do drugs.
4. Boredom.
5. Curiosity.
6. They're trying to get attention.
7. The idea of taking a risk is appealing.
8. They are too stupid to think of another way to have fun.
9. They don't know how to stop.
10. They didn't know what they took was a drug.

8 Ways to Tell if Your Friend Is Taking Drugs

Don't jump to conclusions about people just because they exhibit some of these characteristics. People can be tired or angry for many reasons. If you suspect some friends are on drugs, the best thing you can do is talk to them and try to get them to help themselves.

1. Constant fatigue.
2. Loss of appetite.
3. She just doesn't behave the way she usually does.
4. Frequent mood changes, from deep sadness to euphoria.
5. He doesn't seem to enjoy hobbies or sports that he once really liked.
6. She seems angry all the time.
7. Petty theft (to get money to buy drugs).
8. Strange odors appear in their room or on their clothing.

7 Ways to Report a Hate Crime

A hate crime is committed when someone attacks a person because of race, religion, national origin, sexual orientation, disability, or gender. Hate crimes are generally committed by kids in their teens or early twenties who are acting out deep

feelings of hatred. They often think that these feelings of hatred are shared by their family, friends, or community, which
makes what they are doing acceptable. But it's not. If you wit-
ness a hate crime, report it to one of the following:

1. Your principal, if the crime was committed at school
2. Your local police department
3. The FBI, Civil Rights Program: 216-522-1400; www.
fbi.gov
4. U.S. Dept. of Education, Office for Civil Rights: 216-522-
4970; www.ed.gov
5. The Anti-Defamation League: 800-821-4058; www.adl.org
6. The Lesbian/Gay Community Service Center: 888-GAY-
8761; www.lgcsc.org
7. The National Conference for Community and Justice:
216-752-3000; www.nccj.org

6 Misconceptions About Fake IDs

It's not like a *real* crime, and nobody gets hurt, right?
Wrong. Here are some other things you should know about
fake IDs.

1. **It's only a misdemeanor.** In some states, the use of a fake
driver's license is now a felony, which can mean jail time, high
fines, and years-long suspension of driving privileges. In the
long term, a felony means you now have a criminal record,
which will make getting a job mighty difficult. It can also affect
your ability to get into college, own a gun, or even vote.
2. **So in states where it's only a misdemeanor offense,
there's no real consequence.** Penalties vary from state to state,
but in many places they can include jail time, fines, community service, and suspension of your (real) driver's license. Bar
and store owners often confiscate suspected IDs and may display them—for everyone to laugh at!
3. **Computer-generated fake IDs are so good, no one can tell
they're fake.** Bar owners and employees have actually become
quite good at spotting fake IDs. They have to—their business
depends on it. They pay stiff fines and face the loss of their operating license if they are caught selling to minors.

4. Some fake IDs come with money-back guarantees! Do you really think that anyone who has so little respect for the law is going to deal fairly with you? Once your money is gone, consider it gone forever.

5. My "fake" ID isn't really fake — it belongs to my older sister, and I look just like her. Laws about fake IDs also apply to IDs being used by someone other than the original owner. And if you borrowed the ID, the person who gave it to you is liable for the same punishment as you.

6. It's a victimless crime. Think again. The person who created the ID has committed a felony. The bar owner who lets you in could face fines, suspension (being forced to close temporarily, which means losing business, which will put a business under if it happens often enough), and outright revocation of his liquor license. Even if the business doesn't go under, employees who sell liquor and cigarettes can be fined and fired for failing to spot a minor. As for you, you've put yourself in a situation you might not really be old enough to handle. Still think there are no victims?

10 Ways to Stay Safe at Concerts

Going to concerts with friends can be great fun, but dangers abound, and for this reason parents will often hold out on this privilege as long as they can. Maybe they'll feel more confident if you let them know you're aware of the following guidelines:

1. Always tell your parents which concert you are going to and who you'll be with. Make sure you have a ticket with an assigned seat.

2. Go with a friend and stay with your friend the whole time. If one of you has to go to the bathroom, you should both go. If the crowd is dense, hold hands so that you can stay together. Choose a place to meet if you get separated.

3. Get to the concert early enough so that you can find your seat while the place is still well lit. But don't get there so early that there's nothing to do for three hours except hang out in the parking lot.

4. If you find yourself in a crowd that begins to surge in one direction, don't resist it, but as soon as you can, find your way out.

5. If you're being harassed or followed or if you've attracted attention you don't want, don't be shy about asking security people for help. If no uniformed personnel are close by, ask a responsible-looking adult to help you.

6. Drink water to keep yourself hydrated. Take a water bottle to the show.

7. If you get hurt, go to the security area and ask them to write a report, even if you think the accident is minor or might have been your fault.

8. Have enough money to pay for a taxi to take you home if your ride fails you. Also take the phone number of a taxi company. Make sure you have change for phone calls or a phone card.

9. Don't accept drinks or refreshments from people you don't know.

10. If you're the only one doing something at a concert (like standing on your seat or singing along), you're probably being annoying. Stop it—it just attracts the kind of negative attention you don't need.

5 Tips on How to Buy Sneakers That Fit

1. It's best to try a shoe on later in the day. Your feet swell as the day goes on, so you don't want to buy shoes that fit only in the morning.

2. Wear socks of the same thickness as those you'll wear during your intended activity. Obviously, if you wear thick socks while trying on your sneakers, you might slip around in them later when you're wearing thinner socks. And vice versa.

3. Check for width. In North American sizing, shoe width is indicated by a letter or letters after the number (B is standard width; D, E, and EEE are extra wide). And don't buy a shoe that's too long in order to make up for its being too narrow. Your feet will eventually pop out from the sides.

4. Lace them up and see how they feel. There should be a half-inch of space between your longest toe and the end of the shoe. Measure the space by pushing on the front of the shoe with your thumb. If you feel pain, you've hit a toe.

5. **Walk around wearing the shoes.** If you don't feel ridiculous, try to even run or jump a little. The sneakers should feel good right away. Don't buy with the notion that you'll break them in eventually. Sneakers are made for comfort, and if they don't feel right, then they're not right for you. (Even if they look really, really cool.)

6 Tips on How to Manage Your Money

1. Keep your money in a place where it is not too easy to get to, such as a bank. This will prevent you from spending it too quickly.

2. Always comparison shop when you are buying something expensive. Compare the prices at two or three different places before you make a decision. And look for sales.

3. Don't buy anything on impulse! Decide if the item you want to buy is something you sort of want or something you really need. Almost 85% of all items bought by teens are impulse buys — stuff they only think they need.

4. Avoid shopping when you are tired, depressed, hungry, or just feeling rushed. This may lead to purchases you'll regret later.

5. Always keep receipts and be aware of the store's return policy.

6. Set a money-saving goal for yourself. If you have a specific goal, you will have the incentive you need to save money. Goals can be short term, intermediate, and long term. A short-term goal might be saving money to go to a movie with your friend on Friday night. An intermediate goal might be saving money for holiday gifts. A long-term goal would be saving money for a summer trip.

7 Consumer Scams Aimed Specially at Teens

1. **Music clubs.** They appear to be a great value, but they can rip you off big time. For instance, if you don't send back the card that comes every month asking if you want the newest selection, they'll send it to you anyway, and you will be billed. You can send it back, but that costs money. Plus they make you buy more selections than you might really want. Sure, the prices are low, but that's only because their shipping and handling charges are outrageous. The simplest way to save yourself from being cheated is to not join in the first place. Many stores offer music at a cost only slightly higher than the music clubs do, and the quality of the recordings will usually be better.

2. Phony designer items. At flea markets and street sales, it's common to see items that sell for hundreds of dollars suddenly reduced to $10. These are "knockoffs"—items made to look like the real thing but not nearly as good. These copies may work for you just fine, but they won't perform as well as the expensive originals, and when they break (they often do), there's no store to complain to.

3. Credit cards. A credit card is a huge responsibility. While it can sometimes get you out of a jam, it is more likely to get you into one. Regardless, you need to be aware of the risks and advantages of a credit card. If you need to carry one, try and use it only in an emergency. If you don't pay your bills on time, you'll be spending a lot more than you thought you would on interest and late charges. Never give out your credit card number to anyone. A thief can use it to order any number of items, which may result in your having to pay a hefty bill. If your credit card is lost or stolen, report it immediately.

4. Pyramid schemes or chain letters. This is when you receive a letter asking you to send money to the person at the top of the list and then add people you know to the bottom and pass the letter along to them. In a perfect world, you would get big bucks in the mail from everyone on the list by the time you're at the top. But by that time, the scam has usually dissolved and you get nothing.

5. Internet scams. The Internet is crawling with ruthless scam artists, and it's especially risky since you almost always have to pay for things before you receive them. You may pay for a product or service that never arrives, and there's a good chance you won't ever hear from the company again. If you must do business online, ask for references and make sure you get everything in writing.

6. **Charitable donations**. Before you donate money or ask your friends to do so, make sure that the charity channels money directly to the people who need it instead of holding on to it for "office expenses." Don't respond to charities that call you on the phone, even if they say they are with a police organization. Tell them to mail you a description of their charitable activities so you can decide if you want to donate. Don't give them your address. If they are reputable, they already have it.

7. **International telephone numbers**. Someone contacts you claiming that you have, for example, won a prize. They then say that you need to call a certain number to speak with a supervisor. Watch out for numbers beginning with 805, 756, 664, and 809, which are not regulated under U.S. laws. You won't be told that there will be a charge for the call. You make the call, and the person on the other end will try to keep you on as long as possible with some sort of mumbo-jumbo. You eventually hang up, receive your phone bill, and find that you have been charged up to $25 a minute!

8 Tips for Teens with Credit Cards

If you're ready for the responsibility of a credit card, you're ready to take these steps to ensure you use it properly.

1. Keep all the receipts for your purchases. When your credit card bill comes, check your receipts against the charges listed to make sure you really bought all those items. If there is a discrepancy of any kind, get in touch with the credit card company.

2. Keep your card and your account number safe. Don't lend it to friends, flash it around to impress them, or use it as a bookmark. It's quite easy to make purchases with a stolen card, so you want to know where yours is at all times. If it's lost or stolen, report it right away, or you could be held responsible for any illegal purchases that are made — proof that life is not always fair. *Never give your credit card number to anyone.*

3. Talk to your parents about the rules that come with the card. Do they expect you to use it only for emergencies? Is glitter nail polish an emergency? Make sure everyone understands who pays for what. Write down the terms of your agreement.

4. Shop around for a credit card with the lowest interest rate (don't even think about getting a credit card until you understand what interest rates are) and the most lenient payment rules. The "bonuses" that often come with some purchases ("earn a ten-dollar credit for every $500 you spend") aren't free —those cards usually carry higher interest rates. To compare your options, go to www.bankrate.com and check out their student credit card survey.

5. Understand the rules of your credit card company. Know how much interest you are being charged. Read the small print. If you don't understand something, ask for help.

6. The card will come with a spending limit, but it's a good idea to set a lower limit of your own. That way, if you go over it, you'll still be within the confines of the credit company rules. Don't be tempted to spend money because it's there.

7. Pay your bills on time, at least a week before the payment is due. If you pay your bill after the due date, you'll be charged a late fee even if you've paid the full amount. To avoid paying interest, you should always try to pay the whole amount that's due, even though only a minimum payment is required. If you can't make the whole payment, stop using the card until you're paid up.

8. Remember that your first credit card will be the first chapter in your credit history. Screw up now, and the mistake may come back and haunt you in a decade or two.

12 Things You Can Sell to Raise Money

Fund-raising is tons of fun, and you can use your imagination to come up with wacky ideas that just may work. If you can't manage a separate event for your sale, take it to the next school game or community picnic, for instance—wherever there are lots of people. Everyone wins—you, your patrons, and the cause you're helping. Even if you don't make a lot of money, your presence will raise awareness of the issues surrounding your cause. Be sure to have literature available for anyone who wants to know more.

1. Baked goods
2. Car washing services
3. Used books
4. Used video games, videotapes, and CDs
5. Babysitting services
6. Used household items
7. Tutoring services
8. Homemade crafts
9. Unwanted Christmas presents (a great idea for a first-day-after-Christmas-break event)
10. Collectibles
11. Any of the drinks listed in "12 Nonalcoholic Cocktails," page 267
12. Slightly irregular or damaged goods donated by local merchants

14 Ways to Kiss Up to Your Employer

1. Be organized.
2. Write down instructions so you don't forget them.
3. Mind your own business.
4. If you can't come to work, let them know ahead of time and try to find a replacement if that's okay with your boss.
5. Contribute ideas and positive thoughts.
6. Help others around you. (You never know who will be the next boss.)
7. Learn to do other people's jobs.
8. Let your employer know what your ultimate goals are.
9. Pay attention. Stand up straight. Dress neatly and appropriately.
10. Speak clearly and confidently.
11. Don't act like you can do the job with one hand tied behind your back; put your whole self into the job.
12. If you make a mistake, admit it and learn from it.
13. Arrive a little early.
14. Leave a little late.

6 Helpful Hints for Teens Buying Cars

You'll want to do this one on your own, now that you're a hot shot with a driver's license, but if you really want the coolest wheels you can afford, get an adult who knows something about cars to help you. This is not a slur on your maturity; inexperienced adults usually enlist the aid of someone who's driven around the block a few times, so to speak.

1. Read everything you can about the car you're thinking of buying, including the labels on the car itself, stickers, and any literature that comes with the car. Check *Consumer Reports* and other publications that compare cars and make recommendations. Talk to people who own the car already and ask them for advice. Keep an open mind. If the car you're in love with gives you six miles to the gallon and parts for it are no longer available, maybe it's not the one for you.

2. Choose a car that will fit your situation. Do you have a place to keep it? Will you be able to afford the upkeep and gas? Will it spend more time in the repair shop than in your life?

3. Get an experienced mechanic to examine the car carefully before you buy it. He'll look at the general condition of the car for signs of heavy use or poor maintenance. The areas that need to be inspected include under the floor mats, inside the trunk, under the hood, in the engine. The mechanic should also check for things like the oil, the coolant, and the transmission levels. And it's a good idea to have the emission equipment tested and the body and frame carefully inspected. If there were any major repairs to the car, find out why.

4. Find out as much as you can about the history of the car. Has it been sold many times? That could be a sign of trouble. Find out who owned the car and how it was used. Don't believe every "little old lady who only drove it on Sundays" story you hear.

5. Don't buy on impulse.

6. Take the time to read the contract before you sign it. Remember, if you are under 18, you can't legally sign a contract; you'll need an adult to cosign for you. Keep copies of all paperwork.

15 Ways to Tell When People Are Lying

1. Look for signs of panic. If they fidget and stutter, they're nervous about something. (On the other hand, practiced liars can also appear unnaturally calm, cool, and rigid.)

2. They won't answer a direct question. Liars usually stall for time so they can think up a good story. They say things like, "Well, that depends on . . ." and "Why would you say that?"

3. When people say, "To be perfectly honest," they're usually not.

4. The person constantly changes the subject when you ask a pointed question.

5. Liars try not to make eye contact with the person they're lying to. They're afraid that if they make eye contact with you, you'll see right through them. So they look around the room for a distraction or cast their eyes downward.

6. Body language tells the truth. Are they suddenly fidgeting or fixing their hair when it doesn't need fixing? Also, look for a jiggling leg and a sudden, maddening itch.

7. Blushing and sweating are obvious signs.

8. How credible is their excuse? Is it *so* outrageous that it *only* could have been dreamed up? Made-up stories tend to include too many details, some of which contradict each other.

9. You have a gut feeling that the person is lying. Trust your instinct, especially if the liar is a stranger.

10. They laugh nervously.

11. They pretend they don't know something that you know they know.

12. Look for tense muscles around the mouth and cheeks of liars. They also bite their lips and raise their eyebrows when they speak.

13. Liars talk fast and in a voice that may be just a little higher than their normal voice. Also, look for fake coughing and clearing of the throat (while they think up a story).

14. Experience is a good teacher. If a person has lied to you many times in the past, you have reason to be suspicious about everything they say. (Never being trusted is one of the high prices liars pay.)

15. If it sounds too good to be true, it probably is.

5 Ways to Complain Effectively

You've finally saved up enough money to buy the new Xbox you've been dying for. You go to an electronics store and make your purchase. You hook it up to your TV, and it doesn't work. What do you do next?

If you've saved the receipt, warranty, and all the product information that came with the system, you're in luck. And if you know the store's return policy, better still. You are now in a position to get your problem solved. Here's how:

1. Go back to the store—or call—immediately. Ask to speak with a customer service representative or store manager. If you state your problem politely, you will have a much better chance of being helped. Most stores have become successful because they try to keep their customers happy. Give them a chance to do the right thing.

2. If this doesn't work, write a formal letter to the manufacturer that clearly states your dissatisfaction. A letter shows you mean to be taken seriously. Address the letter to the company's customer service department. State your problem clearly and briefly. List as many appropriate details as you can, such as the name of the product and its serial and model number. Note the date and place of purchase. Tell them whether you want a refund, repair, or exchange. Enclose copies of any papers like receipts, warranties, canceled checks, etc. It's a good idea to send the letter with a return receipt request. This will prove your letter was received, and it also tells the company you're very serious about your complaint and you won't give up until you get results.

3. If they fail to respond to your letter, send a second one. Mention that you've already sent them a letter but did not get a response. Say that you intend to contact the Better Business Bureau or a consumer protection agency if they don't respond to this letter promptly. Keep copies of everything.

4. If you still don't get results, write to your local Better Business Bureau (check the Yellow Pages) to register your complaint against the company. There are also many consumer hotline services throughout the country. Some of them may try to resolve every consumer complaint while others may get involved only with more serious complaints. Check with your newspapers or libraries to find these services. Your TV or radio news station may also provide help.

5. Your last resort is small claims court (think *Judge Judy*). Generally, small claims courts review only cases that involve disputes about $2,500 or less. Go to your courthouse, and they will give you the papers you need to start the process. You will need the cooperation of an adult.

14 Babysitting Tips

To be a good babysitter, you basically have to like children. If that's in place and you use your common sense at all times, you'll do great. Here are some tips to help you along the way.

1. When you first babysit, start with older kids and work your way down to toddlers and babies.

2. Try to babysit only for families you know or who are recommended by friends. Answering newspaper ads can lead to problems.

3. Before you leave home, make sure someone there knows where you're going and when you'll be back. Make sure you've arranged for an escort home (if you're sitting at night), even if you live just a short distance away.

4. Make sure you understand how the household works — how doors lock, how the phone works, how pets are to be treated, what to do in case of emergency. Before the parents leave, make sure you also know about any health problems the kids may have and what to do in case you have to leave the house for any reason. You should also know when the parents will return and where they can be reached. They should know if you have a curfew.

5. If you're leaving the house with the kids for an outing, make sure you have a key to the house and that you're back when you're expected.

6. If you can, observe how the children and parents interact. It will give you a better idea of how to communicate with the kids.

7. Try to make it a fun night. Ask the kids what they want to do and try to accommodate them. If you're getting paid enough, you might even want to rent a video or video game, but check with the parents first. Remember that you're there to entertain the kids and be a friend. You are not a surrogate parent.

8. Bring your own "bag of tricks"—a shopping bag or box filled with some of your own cool stuff to share with the kids (nothing that's alive, please, unless it's a plant), or with some old toys that you've saved just for this purpose. Got any puppets? Kids love puppets. Maybe you can make some out of socks. You can also fill your bag with magazines, games, dolls, joke books, interesting rocks and bells, coins, photos, and other assorted, cool junk. A book of the kinds of games you play in the car can be a great tool, since kids of all ages can participate and you usually don't need any game pieces or tools.

9. Tell the kids the ground rules up front. If they ask to do something that doesn't seem safe "but Mom lets us do it," stand firm. If all else fails, bribe them.

10. Don't invite your friends over without permission. Generally, it's not a good idea to have visitors. They'll distract you from your job and give the kids the idea that they are not your first priority.

11. Respect the family's space and privacy. If you're not invited to raid the fridge, don't do it.

12. Don't tell anyone who calls that you are alone with the children. Don't open the door for anyone you don't know, even if the children seem to know the person.

13. In any kind of emergency, stay calm. Children will most likely react the same way you do, so if you seem in control and remain in charge, they're less likely to panic.

14. When the parents return, tell them anything that happened that might be out of the ordinary. They have a right to know how the kids behaved, even if you promised them you wouldn't tell.

How Much to Charge for Babysitting

Your fee can depend on a lot of things—the number of kids, how active they're going to be, how late you'll have to stay, whether there's an ample supply of ice cream in the freezer.

Most people leave it up to the parents, assuming they are reasonable. Here are some suggested rates broken down by the age of the babysitter.

Age	Range per Hour
11	$3–$4
12	$4–$5
13	$4–$6
14	$4–$6
15	$6–$8
16	$6–$8
17	$6–$10

The 8 Biggest Mistakes Teens Make During Job Interviews

1. They don't prepare for the interview. They walk in knowing nothing about the company they want to work for or exactly what the job entails. Always do research before an interview to find out more about the company and the job. If there's nothing on the Internet, try talking to other people who have worked there.

2. They get to the interview late and then say they were given the wrong directions, thus letting the interviewer know, right off the bat, that they don't take responsibility for their mistakes. Even if someone at the company did give you the wrong route, it was your responsibility to leave early enough to allow time for getting lost, especially if you're unfamiliar with the area.

3. They either overdress (like wearing a suit when applying for a job as a busboy) or underdress (wearing jeans and sneakers to an interview for an office assistant). Or they show up completely disheveled. Think about what you should wear, and prepare it the day before the interview. Launder anything that needs it.

4. They don't communicate clearly; they slur their words, they talk too softly, or they answer questions with overly simple "yes" and "no" responses. They tell a story by rambling through a series of events. Be direct. Look the interviewer in the eye when you talk and make it clear that your ideas are well thought out.

5. They are too shy about asking important questions, like, "What, exactly does this company do?" "What would my duties be?" or "How much will I get paid?" That last question doesn't have to be the first one you ask, but don't be afraid to bring up the subject if no one else does.

6. They don't talk about themselves enough. A prospective employer wants to know exactly what he or she is getting. Talk about your accomplishments and goals. Let the person know why this job is important to you.

7. They don't ask questions. Even if you have no questions, make some up. Ask why the person who had this job left. Ask how long the company has been in business or how long the interviewer has worked there. Ask how the company got its name. Let the interviewer know that you are a curious person with concerns about how you will be spending your time.

8. They don't follow up. This means calling or writing a note the day after, thanking the interviewer for his time, and then calling again to find out if you got the job. You can even benefit from an interview for a job you don't get by staying in touch with the company and letting them know that you're still interested if a job opens that's more appropriate for you. Remember also that every interview you go on will teach you more about the interview process and make you more comfortable with a skill you will probably need throughout your life.

14 Unusual Summer Camps

Sick and tired of making lanyards on Lake Whosawhatsis? Can't stand fighting off mosquitoes? Had enough sing-alongs to last a lifetime? These days, summer camps are as different as the campers themselves, with their focus ranging from computers and filmmaking to sailing the Caribbean. Some of them cost plenty, though, so these may be places you just want to dream about.

1. **ActionQuest Worldwide Summer Sailing & Scuba Adventures for Teenagers (ages 13–19)**. A three-week live-aboard summer camp offering multilevel water sports training and certification courses in sailing, PADI scuba diving, wakeboarding, water skiing, windsurfing, exploration, and adventure. Programs are available in the Caribbean, Galápagos Islands, Mediterranean Sea, Tahiti, and Australia.

c/o ActionQuest Programs
P.O. Box 5517
Sarasota, FL 34277
800-317-6789
www.actionquest.com

2. Adventure Pursuits (ages 12–21). This camp is internationally recognized for its progressively challenging and fun wilderness adventure camps and expeditions for young people. Kids aged 9–14 join programs in Colorado, while others, 12–21, experience dynamic and exhilarating outdoor adventure trips across the U.S. and Canada.

31160 Broken Talon Trail
Oak Creek, CO 80467
888-651-TEEN
www.apadventures.com

3. Aloha Adventure Photo Camp (ages 12–17). In addition to lessons in photography, the two-week session on Maui includes exploring the ruins of old Hawaii, snorkeling, a trek to the Haleakala Crater (10,023 feet above sea level), a beach barbecue or two, and other photo-worthy events.

3825 McLaughlin Ave., Suite 210
Los Angeles, CA 90066
877-755-2267
www.hawaiicamps.com

4. Astronomy Camp (teens and adults). Campers become astronomers, operating research telescopes, keeping late hours, interacting with leading scientists, and interpreting their own observations. Programs for beginner and advanced teens.

c/o Steward Observatory
The University of Arizona
933 N. Cherry Ave.
Tucson, AZ 85721
520-621-4079
www.ethel.as.arizona.edu/astro_camp

5. **Aviation Challenge (teens).** At Aviation Challenge, you train like a fighter pilot, right down to land and water survival, escape, and evasion maneuvers.

c/o The U.S. Space & Rocket Center
One Tranquility Base
Huntsville, AL 35805-3399
800-637-7223
www.spacecamp.com

6. **Classroom Earth (teens).** Take the helm of a 50-foot sailboat and guide her through the turquoise waters of the tropical Caribbean. Chart a course between the coral heads of the barrier reef. Stand by as the remainder of your team "mans the sails" at your command.

P.O. Box 1544
Riverton, UT 84065-1544
866-797-8995
www.classroom-earth.com

7. **Coach Dom's Warrior Wrestling Camp (teens).** This camp features technique sessions, dual meets at every session, and an individual all-camp tournament. Inexperienced wrestlers will be able to compete at their own level on a separate junior varsity mat. Team unity and technique sessions are emphasized.

c/o Delaware Valley College
Doylestown, PA 18901
570-977-1178 or 908-416-6436
www.warriorcamps.com

8. **The Dick Ritger Bowling Camp (teens).** Professional bowling instruction that will result in a dramatic improvement in your game. They cover all the physical, scientific, and mental phases of bowling by using a proven teaching program.

201 Christopher La.
Ithaca, NY 14850
800-535-0678
www.ritgerbowlingcamp.com

9. **Harvest Moon Community Farm (ages 15–adult).** Teens and adults explore four cultures (Native American, Norwegian, African, and Hmong) and their interests, practices, and beliefs about the arts, agriculture/gardening, and nature/natural resources. Harvest Moon also offers a Farm Animal Sponsorship Program that gives individuals, schools, and organizations an opportunity to help farm animals.

14363 Oren Rd. N.
Scandia, MN 55073
651-433-4358
www.hmcf.org

10. **InternalDrive's high-tech computer camp (ages 8–17).** This computer camp offers programs in gaming and robotics, multimedia, and Web programming, in addition to art and graphic design instruction.

iD Tech Camps
2103 S. Bascom Ave.
Campbell, CA 95008
888-709-TECH
www.petersons.com/summerop/sites/inc

11. **Journey to the Center (teens).** Great fun, cool exhibits, and family adventure offered by the U.S. Space & Rocket Center.

One Tranquility Base
Huntsville, AL 35805-3399
800-637-7223
www.spacecamp.com

12. **New York Film Academy (high school students).** Each participant in this intensive four-week program will write, direct, shoot, and edit short, 16mm films in New York City. The sessions combine classroom instruction on writing, directing, and editing with location training in cinematography, lighting, and production. The academy provides the equipment, editing supplies, and film stock and processing.

100 E. 17th St.
New York, NY 10003
212-674-4300
www.nyfa.com

13. **Space Camp (teens).** Want to train like a real astronaut? At Space Camp you will spend five days flying on a realistic, simulated shuttle mission, and even experience weightlessness.

c/o The U.S. Space & Rocket Center

One Tranquility Base
Huntsville, AL 35805-3399
800-637-7223
www.spacecamp.com

14. **Tahoe Extreme Sports Camp (ages 8–18).** In Lake Tahoe's Squaw Valley Resort, activities include circus flying trapeze, a ropes course, paintball, white-water rafting, extreme mountain biking, bungee jumping, in-line skating, skateboarding, water skiing, extreme mountain biking, indoor rock climbing, and more. The camp provides all the gear.

P.O. Box 3297
Olympic Valley, CA 96161
800-PRO-CAMP
www.tahoeextremesportscamp.com

Summer Camp Packing Checklist

This is a recommended list for a two-week stay at summer camp. Your camp director will send you a more detailed list when you sign up. But it's never too early to start shopping for:

Clothing

- [ ] 8 shirts or T-shirts
- [ ] 5 pairs of quick-dry shorts
- [ ] 4 pair of quick-dry pants or jeans
- [ ] underwear
- [ ] sneakers, flip-flops, or sandals
- [ ] rain boots or waterproof light hiking boots
- [ ] 14 pairs of socks
- [ ] 1 light jacket
- [ ] 3 sweaters or sweatshirts
- [ ] 3 bathing suits
- [ ] 1 poncho or waterproof rain jacket
- [ ] waterproof pants (if required)
- [ ] 2 pairs of pajamas
- [ ] hat, baseball cap, bandanas, whatever

Bedding

- [ ] 1 sleeping bag
- [ ] 1 waterproof stuff sack for sleeping bag
- [ ] 2–3 sets of cot sheets and blankets (fleece or wool)
- [ ] 1 pillow & waterproof pillowcases
- [ ] 1 waterproof mattress pad (required at many camps)

Luggage / Packing Accessories

- [ ] 2 large duffel bags or a footlocker (depending on camp requirement)
- [ ] 1 daypack / backpack
- [ ] stuff sacks — assorted-size Ziploc bags

Personal Care

- [ ] bath towels and washcloths
- [ ] bar soap in a container or a plastic bottle of liquid soap
- [ ] shampoo & conditioner
- [ ] toothbrush & toothpaste
- [ ] deodorant & other items in a toilet case
- [ ] beach towel
- [ ] laundry bag
- [ ] sunscreen
- [ ] whatever you use for zits and acne
- [ ] insect repellant
- [ ] afterbite or itch balm
- [ ] plastic drinking cup
- [ ] tissues
- [ ] all prescription medications in their original bottles and copies of the prescriptions
- [ ] lip balm and protector
- [ ] extra contact lenses, cleaning solution, & glasses
- [ ] sunglasses

Miscellaneous

- [ ] camera and film
- [ ] binoculars
- [ ] flashlight
- [ ] extra batteries

☐ journal
☐ pens
☐ stationery and stamps
☐ address book
☐ games (not electronic)
☐ water bottle / canteen
☐ stuff to read
☐ a copy of this book

9 Things Not to Take to Summer Camp

1. Computers
2. Glass containers
3. Money
4. Valuable possessions, jewelry
5. Hair dryers
6. Radios
7. Knives
8. Intoxicants
9. Electronic games

21 Table Manners That Can Make Your Life Easier

It's always polite, at the end of a meal, to thank your host. In the meantime:

1. No elbows on the table. Duh.
2. Don't reach for anything that isn't right in front of you. Ask someone to pass it to you.
3. Don't blow on your food. If it's too hot, wait for it to cool.
4. If you put something in your mouth that's too hot to swallow, it's polite to take a quick swallow of water as opposed to spitting it out.
5. Don't talk with your mouth full or while you're still chewing.
6. If you're in a restaurant and you spill something, call the waiter and politely ask him to clean it up.
7. Don't sneeze at the table.

8. If you have to remove something from your mouth, place your napkin up to your mouth and spit it into the napkin as inconspicuously as possible.

9. When eating fruits with pits, like cherries, it's okay to remove the pits from your mouth with your fingers.

10. It's okay to eat parsley and other decorations, but you don't have to.

11. If you hate what's being served, take a small portion anyway and nibble at it if you can. Say you had a big lunch.

12. If someone asks you to pass the potatoes and you haven't taken any for yourself yet, pass them first and then request the bowl so that you can serve yourself.

13. Never take the last piece of anything.

14. When you're asked to pass the salt, pass both the salt *and* pepper if they're on the table together.

15. When you're eating spaghetti and are left with all those long strands hanging out of your mouth, it's best to suck them all in rather than bite down, with the ends dropping back onto your plate.

16. In Japanese restaurants, it's okay to drink the soup out of the little soup bowl. Just try not to make slurping noises when you sip.

17. When eating sushi, you're supposed to put the whole thing in your mouth at once. If you can't, you can eat it in bites.

18. If you can't deal with chopsticks, there's nothing wrong with asking for a knife and fork.

19. Don't be the first to start eating after the food has been served. Wait until the head of the house has begun. While you're waiting, you can put salt, pepper, and butter on your food.

20. Don't wear your hat.

21. Don't blow your nose, apply makeup, comb your hair, or groom yourself in any way.

The Real Facts of Life

Robert A. Hall is a dad who didn't have time to write a whole rule book for teens, so he composed what we think is the funniest (and most helpful) guide to teen life we've come across. We're grateful to him for sharing these points with us.

1. There is no "garbage fairy." When you dump soggy corn flakes in the sink, Mom or Dad cleans them out, usually by hand. When you live alone, you are the garbage fairy.

2. The refrigerator does not eat the offerings you leave for it. You must eventually clean them out, even if they are gross. Some refrigerators do not even make their own ice cubes. Then a person must fill the trays with water.

3. Sunlight is free; electricity is not. You must pay a company large amounts of money each month, or the lights, the stereo, and the air conditioner stop working. This is not a small, fixed fee. When you go out and leave electrical devices on, the company quite unfairly charges you even though you're not there.

4. Credit cards are not magic. You must regularly give the company money or they stop working.

5. The trash is not taken away by elves looking for craft materials.

6. Clothes are not self-cleaning. You must wash them, dry them, perhaps even iron them, and put them away yourself.

7. Burger-bashing won't do it. Independent living requires a regular income, health insurance, and sick days. Welcome to the real world.

8. Most real jobs require you to get up before noon. This means you may need to go to bed before midnight, which can seriously interfere with your social life.

9. Many real jobs will require you to dress up, and your boss may have strong, old-fashioned gender expectations about your choice of attire.

10. The person who will decide if you get a real job may be even older than Mom and Dad. Unlike your friends, the boss will not be impressed by baggy clothes, torn jeans, backward ball caps, or your tattoo, even if it is the stick-on kind.

11. If you "cut work" like you cut school, you don't get paid. If you do it often, you get "fired," an adult word that means "hungry."

12. Living on your own means that money for necessities like pizza, cool clothes, and CDs must instead be wasted on rent, heat, and electricity.

13. When you borrow money from a bank, unlike Mom and

Dad, they will make you pay it back. They can be quite nasty and unreasonable about this.

14. If you keep your apartment like your room at home, your landlord probably will evict you. The landlord will know the condition of your apartment because very old people (those over 25) develop another sense, called "smell," by which they detect gases, called "stink," given off by your possessions, called "junk." They will introduce you to something called "the Board of Health," which will be concerned about a problem called "plague."

15. Mom and Dad recognize that you are now an "adult" who has "the right to live your own life." Of course, you don't want to be "treated like a child." To really drive this point home, ask your parents to stop demeaning you by sending you "money."

3.
RELATIONSHIPS

10 Tips for Raising Well-Adjusted Parents

1. Encourage their good behavior. On those rare occasions when they do something right, reward them—offer to stay home and babysit while they stay out way past curfew. Remember that if they get the idea they can't please you, they'll stop trying all together.

2. Don't be overly critical. Parents have feelings too. When you correct their behavior, try to add a compliment about something nice they've done lately. They respond positively to the words "thank you."

3. Try to conceal your disgust. If you must be out in public with them, walking 10 feet behind them will only draw more attention to your plight. Instead, walk with them and show the world how bighearted you really are. Only a truly confident person would allow themselves to be seen with losers.

4. Be consistent. If your style is to talk on the phone for four hours each day after school, don't suddenly decide to do your homework first and use your phone time before you go to bed. This will only confuse them.

5. Don't try to teach them more than one new thing at a time. They are easily overwhelmed and will shut down if you feed them more information than they can process at once.

6. Keep an eye on them. You never really know what they're up to, so it's a good idea to spend time with them now and then just to see what's on their minds. This is also a good time to reinforce any point you have been trying to make lately.

7. Never let them see you sweat. If you lose your cool, you lose your power. Where parents are concerned, indifference is your greatest weapon. If they're having temper tantrums and laying down all sorts of ridiculous rules, don't argue. Don't show any reaction at all. This drives them nuts. When they're finished, calmly suggest that it might be better to have this discussion when they're feeling more rational.

8. Show, don't tell. Parents can be really stupid, and yes, they need everything spelled out for them. So if you want them to think of you as someone other than a 10-year-old, you have to act grown up around them so they *really get the picture*. They need to see you completing your schoolwork, doing your chores, and generally acting like you're in charge of yourself. This is the only way they will "get it."

9. **Make it appear as though they're not really losing the battle.** Make it a win-win situation by giving them a point for every few you win. If they finally caved in and gave you permission to go to the mall, offer to pick up something that they need. Or, once in a while, if they agree to let you stay out past curfew, come home early anyway. Try to give them the impression that being responsible is actually important to you.

10. **Never give up.** Your parents have a very short attention span, so it's important to make your point many times. Letting them see you treat your bratty sister lovingly once isn't going to do the trick; they need to see this behavior many times before they come to understand it. Hang out with them and campaign every chance you get. Talk to them at breakfast, call them from school, show up for dinner. Let them know that the only way they will get rid of you is by giving you what you want.

30 Stupid Things That Parents Do

They don't mean to be annoying. They just are that way because they're, well, parents! If you're particularly troublesome, you might try leaving this book open to this page, with stars and arrows pointing to the parts you want them to notice.

1. They take out their bad moods on you.
2. They don't stick to a punishment.
3. They try to bribe you.
4. They shut you out by keeping secrets from you.
5. They constantly compare you to your brother or sister.
6. They have different rules for you and your siblings.
7. They give you the silent treatment.
8. They think they're spending time with you, but they're really thinking about something else.
9. They tell your secrets to other people.
10. They send you mixed messages.
11. They don't listen!
12. They don't bother telling you when you've done something good.

13. They fight in front of you and tell you to take sides in their argument.

14. They don't tell you about their past or about your ancestors.

15. They try to "fit in" with your friends, like they're part of the crowd.

16. They don't punish you fairly.

17. They make fun of you in front of your friends.

18. They ask you to perform in front of their friends.

19. They expect you to enjoy something just because they did —like listening to the Grateful Dead.

20. They tell you not to do something—like tell lies—when you know that they do it themselves.

21. They try to act like they're perfect.

22. They don't apologize when they're wrong.

23. They're serious all the time.

24. They tell you what your opinions should be.

25. They make fun of your favorite things.

26. They ask your friends too many questions.

27. They blame you for things you didn't do.

28. They don't include you in major family decisions—like where you'll live.

29. They forbid you to do something they don't even understand, like go to a party that's really going to be safe.

30. They act like parents!

5 Ways to Get Your Parents to See You're Not a Baby Anymore

You're almost grown up now, but your parents still keep treating you like a little kid. How do you make them realize that you're mature, you can make your own decisions, and you can stay up later than ten o'clock on a weekend evening? Here are some suggestions.

1. Make some mature decisions on your own. This doesn't mean that you stay up all night because you want a later curfew or you decide to get drunk. The key word here is "mature," and since you're not on your own yet, don't scare your parents with any drastic decisions. When you make responsible choices—such as deciding to stay home and study on a night when everyone else goes to the movies or cleaning your room before it gets to bomb-squad proportions—Mom and Dad can see you thinking for yourself.

2. **Act mature.** When you do something immature, think about what you did and follow it up with something that demonstrates your personal growth. If you've been harassing your kid sister, apologize and take her out for a soda. Offer to help around the house with things that are not necessarily your responsibility. Also, it never hurts to remind your parents of the grownup things that you do to help build their image of you.

3. **Take responsibility for yourself.** If your parents won't let you do certain things like stay out later or go to the mall with friends on your own, show them how responsible you really are. Communicate more with them, do the dishes after dinner, volunteer to babysit—and don't argue! Prove that you can be responsible.

4. **Be honest and open.** If they're afraid of your attending a party because the crowd there might be wild, tell them how you'll protect yourself from drinking or smoking and discuss your opinions on sex and birth control. Whatever they are imagining about the party is probably worse than the truth, so admitting the facts and revealing your thoughts may reduce their anxiety.

5. **Speak of the future.** Assure your parents that you'll still need their help when you're on your own. Talk about things such as how much you look forward to having them over for dinner when you have your own apartment, how you'll need their help when you move to college, or how you can't wait to have them help you think about your future.

7 Tips That Will Help if You Absolutely <u>Have</u> to Travel with Your Parents

A family vacation is really not such a bad deal. The 'rents pick up the tab, and you can count it as quality time. On the other hand, they are parents, which means they're going to get out of hand. Here are some tips for coping.

1. Stay flexible. You never know what they're going to want to do next. Neither do they. The thing is, they spend so much time cooped up in their jobs that when they finally go on vacation, they don't know what to do first. Be patient. They usually wind down by day 3.

2. Try to go to places where nobody knows you, so you don't want to die when your mother shows up in "that sweater." Also, you'll feel more comfortable showing them affection, which will hopefully encourage them to buy you more stuff.

3. If you're staying in a hotel, beg them for your own room. If that's not possible, arrange to spend a little time on your own from time to time. Maybe you can visit the gift shop or explore the hotel. Be sure they have time for a nap. They're less likely to be cranky in the evening if they've had a nap during the day.

4. Pack your own suitcase. Parents have this weird thing about wanting to unpack the second they get to a hotel and checking out the swimming pool later. If you pack your own suitcase, you can unpack quickly and be applying suntan lotion while they're still trying to figure out who gets which closet.

5. If you're bored beyond belief, don't tell them. Act cheerful and say, "This place is great. When can we leave?"

6. At mealtime, encourage them to order their own desserts so they don't wind up eating half of yours because they're "on a diet."

7. If your father appears to get the family lost, do not suggest that you stop and ask for directions. It won't help.

Teens' 15 Most Common Complaints About Parents

1. "I'm not allowed to pick out my own clothes."

2. "They treat me like a baby."

3. "They criticize everything I do."

4. "They're nicer to my siblings than they are to me."

5. "They argue with everything I say and do"

6. "My parents don't know what they're talking about."

7. "My parents are racists."

8. "My parents pressure me to get better grades than I'm capable of."

9. "They don't keep their promises."

10. "My parents give me no privacy."

11. "They don't trust my friends."

12. "They don't trust me."

13. "They want me to become something I don't want to be."

14. "My parents don't have a clue!"

15. "They're always embarrassing me in front of my friends."

13 Ways to Break Really Bad News to Your Parents

1. **Choose your moment.** Don't blurt out the news the second they get home from work, just as they're about to leave for work, or at any other time when you might not have their complete attention. If your older brother announced yesterday that he's leaving home and your little sister was suspended from school today, maybe this isn't the right time.

2. **Avoid Fridays (it'll ruin their weekend) or Mondays (which are generally stressful).**

3. **Talk first to another adult** who's likely to know what your parents' reactions might be so you can plan a strategy.

4. **Describe the problem first as though it happened to someone else,** to give them a chance to digest and formulate an objective response. Then, once you've let the cat out of the bag, gently explain the real deal.

5. **Is there a hotline that addresses your particular problem?** Check out the list of "Hotlines for Teens" on page 24. You might be able to talk to someone who can give you an idea of what your options are before you break the news at home.

6. **Be prepared to take responsibility for the problem.** Start out by letting your parents know you've screwed up and need their help. Even if you think the problem resulted from someone else's actions, tell them up front that you know that this is *your* problem.

7. **Say it with flowers!** That won't solve the problem, but if the trouble has to do with damage that you did, this might be a good way to let them know you plan to make amends.

8. **Use a film or book when you introduce the subject.** "Mom, remember in that movie *Risky Business* where the kid loses all his parents' furniture?" This will remind your parents that you are not the first person to have this problem and that solutions do exist.

9. **Put the problem in perspective.** Check the statistics to find out how common this problem is. While you're at it, look for some solutions as well. Let your parents know you want to work toward a resolution.

10. **Write a letter.** If the problem involves a lot of feelings that may not get expressed in the heat of an argument, try writing it all down first. This won't replace a confrontation, but it will help everyone get an idea of the scope of the problem and where you stand. It will also help you get your story straight in your own mind before you spill the beans.

11. **Just do it.** You know you're going to have to face the music eventually. Sometimes the best approach is to just take a deep breath and make your announcement. Be prepared for the inevitable lecture, anger, punishment, and blame. Know that your parents' first reaction may not be the one they wind up with once they've had a chance to digest the news. Trust them. They are, after all, your parents, and they will want to do the right thing for you.

12. **Once they start reacting to what you've said, let them finish.** Don't interrupt, don't let out sarcastic remarks, and *don't roll your eyes at them,* no matter what. Stay cool. When it's your turn to speak, politely ask for the same consideration.

13. **At the end of the confrontation, agree with your parents on what the next step is.** If there is to be a follow-up discussion, schedule it now.

7 Things You Can Do if Your Parents Are Racists

People tend to adopt the attitudes with which they are raised. But if you feel that your parents' ideas about race are wrong, know that you don't have to follow in their footsteps. We call this progress.

1. Remember that your parents love you, no matter what views they hold. If you do confront them, do it gently. They may be more responsive if you show them the respect that they deserve as parents. It's wrong to disrespect your parents.

2. Tell them racist remarks make you uncomfortable. Explain that you think that the color of a person's skin doesn't reflect their personality and that you wish that they wouldn't make racist remarks while you're around. You might not be able to change their views, but maybe you can get them to be more tolerant.

3. Question them when they make racist comments. Most people will suddenly become very uneasy when questioned — for most of them, it's just a habit, and when they are forced to think about what they are saying, they begin to realize it's wrong. Some parents are slow learners. Be patient.

4. Love them for the part of them that isn't racist. If you don't accept your family because of their views, then you are acting with prejudice. Hating them won't help at all.

5. Know that racism and prejudice have been a problem in every country throughout the world and stem from old-fashioned ideas that go back many generations. They are bad habits that need to be broken. Talk to your parents about racist events in history and tell them how you look at those events.

6. Arrange to bring your parents together with your friends from other cultures at large get-togethers, like school events or community fund-raisers, where they can meet in a relaxed atmosphere and learn more about one another.

7. Talk to your parents about how they came to feel the way they do. Maybe they have some misconceptions that you can set straight.

The 5 Most Common Reasons Siblings Fight (and What You Can Do About Them)

Sibs — can't live with 'em, can't put them up for adoption. Here are some common causes of brother/sister friction and some possible solutions. Note that the closer you are in age, the more intense the problems probably are. That's because you're both trying to occupy the same "territory."

1. One sibling borrows another's clothing, music, or book without asking and/or returns it in bad condition. Try brainstorming and writing down as many ideas as possible on how to solve the problem (without insulting each other). For instance, one of you may write, "Ask me if you want to borrow something at least a day in advance." Or, "If the clothes are not returned the next day on my bed in good condition, you may not borrow anything for two weeks." Then present each idea with its good points and drawbacks. Try to agree on at least one of your solutions.

2. The "bratty" little sister or brother is mean to an older sibling. First, realize that you can't let your younger sister or brother rule your life. If they're calling you names, hitting you, or just intentionally bugging you, you must take control. Besides, your younger siblings look up to you and, believe it or not, they would also like their relationship with you to be positive. So give them some positive attention. If your younger sis calls you an idiot, say, "I'm sorry if you think I'm an idiot because I'd like to be your friend."

3. Siblings fight over TV shows. Make a list of your favorite shows and ask your sibling to make a similar list. Agree that you each get to watch your top three shows. If your favorite shows are on at the same time, alternate so that one gets to pick the show one week and the other gets to pick the show the next. Or channel surf between the two shows. This works with sports events and variety shows.

4. One sibling feels like they have too much responsibility and is jealous of the one who seems to be getting off too lightly. Ideally, this dilemma should be worked out among the whole family. Ask your parents to hold a family meeting and address the issue. If this doesn't work or they don't have time to meet, speak to them calmly and rationally in private until you work out a solution. Show them a list of your chores and talk about the ones you think are unfair.

5. Siblings disagree on just about everything and therefore hate each other. Believe it or not, you won't always feel this way, so if you're going to be mean, at least try not to do or say things that may hurt for a very long time. You may wind up needing each other someday soon. Try to find at least one thing that you both like or agree on. (There must be at least one!) If it's skiing, go on a trip together. If it's someone you both hate, make lists of why you hate that person and then compare the lists.

The 7 Best Things About Being the Oldest in Your Family

Being the firstborn has its advantages. Here are some of the greatest things about being the oldest.

1. You get more privileges and independence.
2. You experience things first so you can tell your siblings what to do and how to handle life's issues.
3. Your siblings and other members of the family look up to you.
4. You have more responsibility, so you have many chances to prove yourself.
5. You don't get stuck with a lot of hand-me-downs.
6. You're the first to experience the world and gain insight.
7. You can pick on your siblings.

The 10 Worst Things About Being the Oldest in Your Family

It's not always easy being the oldest, and here are some reasons why.

1. Your parents expect more of you.
2. You get blamed for everything.
3. You're expected to set an example for your siblings.
4. You have to take care of your siblings when your parents can't, which means babysitting for them or dragging them along when you're going out.
5. You're the family "guinea pig" because your parents practice their parenting on you first.
6. Sometimes you have too much responsibility and get assigned too many chores.

7. Your parents let your siblings do things that you were never allowed to do when you were their age, which makes you mad.

8. When your siblings are younger, you have to clean up their messes.

9. You experience everything first, so you don't have any older siblings to warn you about important situations and issues.

10. Parents are sometimes harder on the oldest sibling in the family. That's because parents are still "new" with the first, and they haven't yet been properly trained.

The 11 Best Things About Being the Youngest in Your Family

Here are some of the coolest things about being the last-born.

1. The "baby" in the family is usually the most spoiled.

2. You're assigned fewer chores.

3. Your parents are more lenient with you because they're more experienced and therefore less nervous.

4. You always have someone's attention.

5. You have an older sibling to give you advice when you need it.

6. You get lots of hand-me-downs, so you always have plenty to wear.

7. If you get into trouble with your parents, an older sibling can stick up for you.

8. You get to check out your older sibling's friends and learn from what they do.

9. You don't have to babysit for anyone.

10. Parents are usually more relaxed with the youngest, which means you can get away with being "the baby in the family," which means you can get away with more.

11. You can blame everything on your older siblings. After all, you're the youngest. You didn't know any better, right?

The 10 Worst Things About Being the Youngest in the Family

Here are a few annoying things about being the youngest.

1. Your parents protect you more because you're their "baby."

2. Your older siblings have more privileges, like a later curfew or a bigger allowance.

3. Your older siblings tease and pick on you.

4. When you're younger, you get jealous of your older siblings because they can do things better or faster than you.

5. People sometimes have less respect for you and value your older sibling's opinions and actions more.

6. Your parents don't take you seriously when you try to be responsible for yourself.

7. Your older siblings boss you around.

8. Your parents don't get as excited over some of your accomplishments because they've already seen it done before by your siblings.

9. You get fewer new things and more hand-me-downs.

10. It seems as if your older siblings are getting all the responsibilities and trust while you're stuck on Saturday night with a ten o'clock curfew. Sound familiar?

The 6 Best Things About Being the Middle Child

What would an Oreo be without the cream?

1. You're on your own more, so you get to make decisions for yourself.

2. Your parents don't bug you as much, because they're usually too busy nagging the oldest and youngest.

3. You get away with more because you're less noticeable.

4. You're the mediator, so when your parents get frustrated with your siblings, they come to you.

5. You have some of the advantages of being an older

child but also some of the advantages of being the youngest.

6. You get advice when you need it from the older sibling, and you appear really wise when you pass it on to the younger one.

The 5 Worst Things About Being the Middle Child

Watch *The Brady Bunch* and you'll understand the "middle-child syndrome." Plain Jan was never the gorgeous Marsha, who got all the guys, nor the cute Cindy, who got all the laughs. Live the life of the middle child and you'll know why it's not always easy. Here are some of the gripes you may face.

1. You don't feel special because you're not the cute baby or the respected older one.

2. You feel ignored or neglected by your parents.

3. You have an older sibling to pick on you and a younger sibling to annoy you at the same time.

4. Life can be confusing: you want to be as smart and respected as your older sibling but you also want to be pampered and protected like the younger one.

5. You're too old to be close to the youngest sibling and too young to be close to the oldest. It can get lonely in the middle.

3 Ways to Find Out if You Were Adopted (if Your Parents Won't Tell You)

If your parents have never talked about the details of your birth, have never told stories of your early childhood, or have never showed you baby pictures of yourself, you might be suspicious. If there is a possibility that your well-intentioned and loving parents have not told you the truth, and talking to them doesn't resolve the matter, here are some steps you can take:

1. Find the name of the hospital where you were born and request your medical records at birth. If they agree to send them to you without any problems, chances are you were not adopted. If you find it difficult to obtain these records, they may be "sealed" for a reason.

2. Ask other members of the family that you are very close to—a cousin, for instance—if you were adopted. They may be more honest with you than your parents have been.

3. You may be entitled to the adoption certificate, which can be obtained from the court that ordered the adoption. This certificate, generally issued by a Youth Court, confirms your status of adoptee and names the birthparents as well as the witnesses. But since the law guarantees confidentiality, you will not be able to initiate contact with your parent until he or she tries to contact you.

21 Ways to Make Life Better for Your Grandparents

1. Take Grandma out for a manicure.

2. If Gramps uses a wheelchair, decorate it for the holidays, birthdays, or just for fun.

3. Visit the library together. See if you can find the books they read when they were your age. Share your favorites by reading aloud.

4. Invite them to a school function, even if most kids aren't inviting grandparents.

5. Find out what dietary issues your grandparents might have and learn to make a dish that they can eat, like a low-fat cake or a creamy soup made with low-fat yogurt instead of cream.

6. Take a fitness class together. Yoga, water aerobics, and swimming are all good candidates for activities you both will enjoy.

7. When you're watching something on TV that you really like, tape it for your grandparents.

8. If your grandparent has trouble communicating, cut out pictures of everyday objects from magazines and paste them on index cards. Ask them to point to the cards to help them communicate. Be patient. Don't finish their sentences for them.

9. When you visit your grandparents, make yourself useful. Is there something that needs to done, like shopping, cleaning an out-of-reach corner, or working in the garden?

10. Call your grandparents often, and try to make the conversations interesting for both of you. Don't just say, "How are you?" Show interest in the details of their lives. Saying, "How did that doctor's appointment go?" or "Is your back still bothering you?" shows them you really care.

11. If your grandparents have a problem that you find embarrassing (they drool when they eat or they're incontinent), try to learn more about the problem so you'll be more comfortable around them. Ask them questions and be patient if they don't explain everything all at once.

12. Allow them to show you off to their friends. It makes them so proud!

13. Teach each other something new. Maybe your grandmother taught you how to make cookies or to ride a bike, but you never learned embroidery or how to speak the language from "the old country." In the meantime, you can teach her something you've recently learned.

14. Ask Grandpa to join you in a new hobby. Learn something new together.

15. Keep them updated on current events. Read the newspaper or watch or listen to the news together *and talk about what's happening*.

16. Take your friends when you go to visit. Everyone will have a better time.

17. Don't repeatedly cancel visits. If your schedule needs to remain flexible, let your grandparents know. Don't set dates and times for visits until you're sure you can follow through. You'll avoid their being disappointed and your feeling guilty,.

18. Don't constantly correct a faulty memory. Ask yourself if it's really important before you do. Maybe the factual details aren't as meaningful as the subject under discussion.

19. Accept limitations. It may be hard to face that your grandparents can't do things the way they used to, but change is inevitable. If Gramps can't play piano anymore, he may still love to attend concerts. Find ways to incorporate old pastimes into new activities.

20. Respect old habits. You may know a faster route to the post office or a more efficient way to organize the bills, but if Gramps can still do it all right on his own, try to let him be.

21. Make a scrapbook of letters, greeting cards, and other artifacts from your grandparents and other relatives. Date everything and add explanatory captions. These books will be enjoyed for generations to come.

13 Ways to Stay Close to Your Family Even if They Are Far Away

They say that absence makes the heart grow fonder. They also say, "out of sight, out of mind." Your family is your family forever. Here are some ways to stay close across the miles.

1. Visit them when you can.

2. Write letters.

3. Send postcards.

4. Call them often. Don't rely on e-mail for communication.

5. Keep an itinerary of where your parents are going to be, if they are traveling, so you always know where you can contact them.

6. When you e-mail them, send photos of yourself and your friends.

7. You can use voice-enabled Instant Messenger services and talk over the Internet for free.

8. Have a family reunion online in a chatroom.

9. Send them a videotape of yourself.

10. Send them your report card.

11. Save their letters and reread them from time to time.

12. Use an encyclopedia, history book, or go online to learn more about the city they are in.

13. Speak to other relatives they may have spoken with or written to.

When Someone in Your Family Has a Serious Disease

When one of your relatives is seriously ill, it affects the whole family. No matter who is suffering, it's natural to worry about how your own future will be affected. Sometimes the hardest part is coming to terms with the fact that you're feeling so many different things—all at once. If you are going through this, be sure to find someone to talk to, preferably someone who has some distance from your family and can therefore focus on you.

1. You hate watching the person in pain and feel like it's wrong for you to feel good about anything while they are suffering.

2. You're depressed and can't think of anything else. You want to cry all the time.

3. You feel like maybe the disease was your fault.

4. You're jealous. This is perfectly normal. The person who is sick is getting everyone's love and attention, but you haven't stopped needing those things just because the other person needs them too. Plus they're getting all kinds of cool gifts. Being sick is starting to look like not such a bad deal after all! It's okay to feel this way. Really.

5. You have mood swings. One minute everything seems fine, and the next you just want to scream at someone for no reason at all. That's because illness disrupts people's lives, and yours doesn't seem predictable anymore. You wish for just one boring day in which nothing at all happened.

6. You're angry all the time.

7. You worry about the treatments the person is going through. You'll feel a whole lot better if you learn about the disease and treatments so that you aren't surrounded by mystery. Maybe you can get more involved with the person's care so you don't feel so helpless.

8. You worry that you'll get the disease next. If it's not handed down genetically, you have no reason to worry. If it is, talk to a doctor about any precautionary and testing measures you should take.

9. You find all this terribly inconvenient! Your mom's no

longer available to drive you to basketball practice, and the person's treatments seem to take all day every day. You still don't have a dress for the prom, and Mom can't schedule a shopping trip. This is so unfair to you!

10. You worry about your future and how this illness will affect the goals you've been working toward so hard.

11. You're scared. You can't imagine losing that person. Know that all the other people in your family feel the same way. Talk to them. They need your love right now just as much as you need theirs.

Are You a Good Friend?

To find out how you rate, ask yourself the following questions. If you need an answer key, you're hopeless.

1. Do I accept the person for exactly who they are without trying to change them?

2. Do I take the time to really understand the person?

3. Am I sincere in everything I say and do?

4. Do I make him laugh?

5. Do I share myself and my things with this person?

6. Am I there for him when he needs me?

7. Do I take her for granted?

8. Can he be open when telling me what's on his mind?

9. Am I a good listener?

10. Do I make this person happy?

11. When he has a problem, do I always give my best advice?

12. Are we happy when we're together?

13. If the person makes a mistake, do I forgive them easily?

14. When I screw up, do I take the time to apologize?

15. Can he trust me to keep secrets?

16. Do I let this person know that I am grateful for our friendship?

17. Do I lie to my friend?

18. Do I get jealous if he spends time with other people?

19. Do I keep my promises?

20. Do I treat him the way I wish he would treat me?

21. When we fight, do I always fight fair?

Teens' 15 Biggest Complaints About Friendships

1. "My two best friends are enemies."
2. "My friend can't keep a secret."
3. "He never wants to talk about important issues."
4. "My friend forgot my birthday."
5. "She flirts with my boyfriend."
6. "She never calls when she says she will."
7. "He doesn't stick up for me."
8. "She always exaggerates."
9. "He says things about me behind my back."
10. "I've lost respect for my 'druggie' friends."
11. "She pressures me to be 'cool.'"
12. "He's into stuff I know is wrong."
13. "She's mean to other kids."
14. "She's always hanging around and won't give me space."
15. "He acts like he's bored with everything I say."

When Bad Things Happen to Good Friendships

During the heat of battle, it's hard to imagine that the two of you will be best friends again tomorrow. Right now you just want to !*##%&!@!!! But if you keep a cool head now, you'll avoid doing and saying things you'll want to take back later. But hurtful words are not easily forgotten. Here are some tips for surviving the rough times that come with any good friendship.

1. Say little. No matter how much you're dying to tell her off, hold it in for now, and give yourself a time-out. Don't talk about the fight to other people, either; the fight may be over in a day, but the story of it may stay alive a lot longer. Promise yourself to wait 24 hours before doing anything.

2. Don't write a letter. It's common to get the urge to put all your grievances down on paper. Forget it. In the first place, writing a letter gives you false courage: you don't have to face the person you're telling off. Also, you never know when that letter will come back to haunt you. If you must write a letter, wait a few days before you send it to make sure the feelings expressed are really the ones you want to communicate.

3. **Fight fair.** No suddenly telling secrets that you swore to keep forever or telling her boyfriend what she was really doing last Tuesday. Stick to the subject of the fight and don't get into areas that will only create another fight after this one's over. (See the list of "15 Ways to Fight Fair," page 124.)

4. **Get over it.** Is this fight more important than the friendship itself? If your friend suddenly moved to another state and you never saw him again, how would you feel? Remember that good friends, like all good things, are worth fighting for.

5. **Ask yourself if having you for a friend is such a bargain.** Do you ever make mistakes? Did you contribute to this fight?

How to Stay Best Friends When One of You Moves Away

Your friendship is going to change, but that doesn't mean you won't still be best friends. But if you really want to maintain this friendship, you have to make it a priority and put in the time and effort it will take to keep you close across the miles.

1. Talk with your friend and make sure you know where each of you will be and how you can be reached.

2. Spend a day with your friend doing all the things you love doing together and take pictures all day long. Make sure you each have a camera or get duplicate prints when your film is developed.

3. Decide together how often you will communicate. Be realistic. If you're going to a new school and facing new challenges, you're not going to have time to write every day. Maybe you could e-mail each other once a week and arrange to have a phone conversation once a month.

4. If your friend doesn't get in touch as often as he or she promised, be patient. Keep writing when you said you would.

5. Don't be afraid to tell your friend about your new friends. Talk about what's really going on in your life.

6. Try to establish new traditions with your friend—like long phone chats on birthdays or an exchange of photos once a year that keeps you both informed of where your lives are taking you.

15 Ways to Fight Fair

1. Don't start an argument when you know the other person can't possibly stop what they're doing to focus on you.

2. Tell the truth.

3. Respect the person you're arguing with. Don't use sarcasm or belittle them. If you overstep and say something you want to take back, say so right away.

4. Stick to the problem. If you're arguing because she borrows too many things, don't bring up the secret she blabbed last summer. Tackle one problem at a time.

5. Don't drag innocent friends into the argument.

6. If you can't control yourself, take a time-out and schedule the discussion for a time when you can both approach the subject calmly.

7. Keep an open mind when you hear the other person out. Give them time to express their point of view. Try to imagine what it's like to feel like they do.

8. Do not use physical violence or threats.

9. Take responsibility for the actions that someone may be challenging. If you're confronted with a lie you told, admit it. Don't make up excuses for things you know you shouldn't have done.

10. Don't try to intimidate someone into accepting your opinion.

11. Don't tell the other person what he or she thinks or feels.

12. Remember that the goal of the argument is for both of you to resolve an issue, which doesn't necessarily mean that you have to agree. You can agree to disagree and still get along.

13. When the other person apologizes, accept the apology, even if you sense that it's not entirely sincere.

14. Try not to say things you don't really mean. Know that words can hurt deeply, and although you can apologize later, they'll be remembered.

15. If you decide that you really can't be friends with this person anymore, don't end the relationship in the heat of the moment. Wait to see if you still feel that way in a few days and then take action.

5 Ways to Forgive Someone

Sometimes it's hard to let go of anger, even if you know that holding on to it is hurting you as well as the person you're angry at. Forgiving someone doesn't mean you have to forget all about the things that happened. It just means that when you think about them, you'll think about them without anger. Here are some steps you can take:

1. Acknowledge that you're feeling bad about what was done to you. Admit that you're angry.

2. Decide that you want to get over it.

3. Decide how much longer you want to stay angry. This is totally up to you.

4. Let the person who hurt you know how you feel.

5. Continually remind yourself that you have made up your mind to get over it.

8 Ways to Stop Tears Before They Start

Crying can be good—a release of frustration and sadness, a unique form of expression. But if the floodgates are about to open and you're going to die of embarrassment if they see you cry, there are some things you can do.

1. Immediately leave the situation that's upsetting you. You'll see things differently right away and "divert" the tears. Don't wait to see if other people are noticing.

2. Get a friend to distract you. Ask her to talk about anything—her lunch, her dream, her acne. Just get your mind onto something else.

3. Don't attract sympathy. If everyone focuses on your problem, you'll definitely start crying.

4. Imagine yourself *not* crying. Visualize a cool you responding to the situation as though you were in complete control.

5. Look up. Rolling your eyes backward really does help.

6. If you get away and have a chance to cry yourself out a bit, don't do it for too long or everyone will know. Be careful—sometimes, once you start to cry, you can't stop.

7. Smile.

8. Shake your head abruptly for a moment and give yourself a chance to "snap" out of it.

9 Things You Can Do About Bullies

Bullies are people who pressure other, more vulnerable people into doing things they don't want to do. Bullies are usually the product of homes in which they themselves are bullied. They have low self-esteem and don't know how to get what they want without demanding it. Here's help.

1. You can report the bully to school or police authorities without giving your name. Tragedies that could have been prevented in recent years have caused people to start taking bullies more seriously than ever before. Don't be shy about making the report.

2. Travel in groups. Try not to be alone at any time after school. Leave with your friends when school lets out. Don't hang around to see what the bully is going to do next.

3. Avoid the bully. Ignoring him will make him feel as though he has no power over you.

4. Can you try to make friends with the bully? Remember, he's got low self-esteem and probably doesn't have many friends. Maybe you can make a friendly connection.

5. Humor the bully: "Okay, okay, you win. Now can we just skip the part where you whip my butt?"

6. Confront the bully. This might work if the bullying is mental or verbal. Let him know how his actions make you feel and that you don't intend to stand for it. (But don't make senseless threats.)

7. Take a self-defense workshop. Hopefully, you won't have to use what you learn, but the classes will make you more confident, and confidence shows. Bullies hate confident people.

8. Stand your ground.

9. File a police report.

9 Drawbacks to Being Popular

Every teen wants to be popular, and one of the biggest pressures in your life will be in meeting the expectations of friends and peers just to stay popular. But popularity can backfire. Read this list, then ask yourself how important popularity really is to you.

1. A lot of teens, in attempting to be popular, often can't be themselves around their friends. They wind up feeling pressured to act a certain way just to be liked. They lose out because in the end, people who can't show others who they really are don't have many real friends.

2. Popular kids often feel like they've got to go along with the crowd to stay popular, so they wind up saying "Sure" when they really mean "No way!" This can get dangerous.

3. In order to maintain their popularity, some teens act tough and encourage others to be the same way. Often, they'll find someone or some group to pick on. This is how a gang mentality develops.

4. Some teens use drugs or alcohol to stay popular.

5. Teens often have sex before they are ready to handle it because "everyone's doing it." In doing so, they're sacrificing their self-esteem and possibly their safety.

6. Popular teens often hide their real emotions and pretend to be happy when they are really sad. They're afraid to express their real emotions because everyone expects them to be happy and in control.

7. Some teen girls develop serious eating disorders because they feel that they must be thin to be popular.

8. Keeping up with the latest fashion trends to be popular can be stressful and expensive.

9. Popular teens often make friends with other teens just because they too are popular. Often they don't really enjoy those people or have real bonds with them.

The Top 10 Cliques

Cliques are groups of kids who have some common traits or interests and exclude others from their group. If you're on the outside looking in, it can hurt to be left out, even if what you're being left out of isn't really worth your time. Here are the most common cliques you're likely to come across.

1. The Popular Group. These are the cool people who have the best clothes, the most privileges, and usually the richest families. Everyone wants to be in this group, even if they don't admit it.

2. The Jocks. Visible and popular, these people are praying for athletic scholarships.

3. The Losers. Their grades are terrible, and they cut classes right and left. They're rarely invited to parties but tend to show up anyway.

4. The Nerds. They're usually brilliant, and even if they have other talents, their brains cause them to get lumped into this category, especially if they dress oddly. Also known as geeks.

5. Hackers (a subset of the Nerds). They're usually intelligent but rebellious. RAM is more important to them than air.

6. The Outcasts. Usually the most artistic kids, they're sometimes morose and try to go unnoticed. You don't have to be especially smart to be in this group. You just have to own a lot of black clothes and be interested in all things goth.

7. The Rappers. Verbally talented, beat-loving, music-worshiping kids sometimes known to bring their own scratch tables to parties.

8. The Skaters. These days, you'll find most skaters on skateboards. They use the word *dude* a lot.

9. The Surfers. *Fast Times at Ridgemont High* is a great movie about this group. It once applied only to people who actually surf but these days can refer to blonds with lousy grades who have spent at least five minutes in California. It's all about the 'tude, dude.

10. The Airheads. In the '80s they were called Valley Girls, and they were made popular by the Frank and Moon Unit Zappa song called "Valley Girl." To belong to this group, you need lots of clothes, a lobotomy, and Daddy's credit card.

12 Ways to Start a Conversation

Avoid questions to which someone might easily respond with a simple yes or no or a one-word answer. And try not to answer questions that way, either. The idea is to let the person know you're interested in learning more about them.

1. Instead of "Did you like the movie?" say, "That was an incredible movie. What did you think of the soundtrack?"

2. Instead of "Did you work hard on that science project?" say, "Your science project was great. How did you get such authentic sound effects?"

3. Instead of "I saw you walking your dog yesterday. Do you like owning a collie?" say, "How did you decide to get a collie?"

4. Instead of "What did you get on the math test?" say, "How did you manage to get an *A* on that test? What books did you use?"

5. Instead of "Did you just move here?" say, "I've lived here my whole life and can't imagine living anywhere else. What was your old neighborhood like?"

6. Instead of "How many brothers and sisters do you have?" say, "What's it like to have seven siblings?"

7. Instead of "Did you like that book?" say, "I liked the book but hated the ending. What did you think of the way the guy saves the world in the end?" (Don't give away the ending if you're not sure the person has read the whole book.)

8. Instead of "Do you think the test will be hard?" say, "What kinds of questions do you think will be on the test?"

9. Instead of "What kind of computer do you have?" say, "What are the advantages of your system?"

10. Instead of "Are you going to the opening of the new library?" say, "What do you think the new library will be like?"

11. Instead of "Are you against censorship?" say, "What kind of experiences have you had with censorship?"

12. Instead of "What book are you reading?" say, "Let me tell you about *The Book of Lists for Teens*."

13 Conversation Stoppers

These weird facts may get you some attention, but we're not sure they'll lead to a conversation that includes you. Don't use them in school reports, either; it's difficult to guarantee their veracity. Find more at www.uselessfacts.net.

1. 0.3% of all road accidents in Canada involve a moose.

2. 1 out of 4 Americans do not know what their astrological sign is.

3. 111,111,111 squared equals 12,345,678,987,654,321.

4. 13 people a year are killed by vending machines falling on them.

5. 2,500 newborn babies will drop in the next month.

6. 25% of U.S. 4th-graders are pressured by friends or class-mates to use drugs or alcohol.

7. 27% of Americans think billboards are beautiful.

8. 27% of U.S. male college students believe that life is a meaningless existential hell.

9. 56% of the video game market is adults.

10. 57% of British school kids think Germany is the most boring country in Europe.

11. 60% of electrocutions occur while talking on the phone during a thunderstorm.

12. 69% of guys say that they would rather break up with a girl in private than in public.

13. 7% of Americans think Elvis is alive. Really!

14 Ways to Cover Up Your Shyness (Even if You're Scared Stiff)

1. Make a commitment to address your problem. Admit that you need to take steps to overcome your shyness. Think hard about the fun you're missing by hiding all the time.

2. Think about when you are most shy and identify one or two things you can do differently in these situations. Take these steps when you have the opportunity, but do only one new thing each time. Small steps will actually get you there faster, and the steps will be easier to take once you get a little practice.

3. Smile. You can be cringing inside and wishing you were home under the covers. Smile anyway.

4. Try to show some interest in the people around you by making eye contact with them, even if you can't think of anything to say. When the cat returns your tongue, ask a question. (See "12 Ways to Start a Conversation," page 129.)

5. Pay attention to what everyone is saying, even if you don't have the courage to join in. Nod a lot.

6. Smile some more.

7. If your voice is shaky, take a short breath, smile, then speak. Your voice sounds shakier to you than it does to the listener.

8. Excuse yourself to go to the bathroom from time to time to dry your hands and to put some cold water on your face, on the back of your neck, and on your wrists.

9. If your hands are sweaty, before you shake someone's hand, casually slip your hand in your pocket to dry it off.

10. Relax. Try to laugh at your own mistakes and learn from them as well.

11. Use people's names when you talk to them.

12. If you're in a difficult conversation, it may not be a good time to take an adversarial position on anything. If you agree with what's being said, nod your head.

13. Have something to hold, like a glass of water or a snack. Girls, bring a purse even if you don't need one; guys, you can always carry a newspaper or a book. These are great security blankets.

14. Smile.

5 Ways to Be Comfortable with a Disabled Friend

Imagine what it would be like if everyone judged you by the zit on your cheek because that's what they saw first when they looked at you. That's what it feels like to have people define you as disabled when, in fact, your disability is only one small part of you. Here are some other tips that will help you overcome shyness with friends who are disabled.

1. Learn more about the disability. Go to the library, research it online, or talk to an organization that deals with the disability.

2. Don't ignore the disability and pretend you don't know it exists. Talking about things openly and honestly is good for any relationship. It's okay to say things like, "I don't understand how the brace helps you," or "Sometimes I don't know how to help you or if I should even try," or "Were you born with this disability? How did it happen?" If your friend doesn't want to answer a specific question, let it go.

3. Don't let the wheelchair or the brace or a special prosthesis or other equipment fool you: disabled people have the same feelings you do.

4. Don't avoid certain subjects just because the disabled person might not be able to do the same things you can do. Talk about the basketball game and the shopping trip and the dance. Your friend will be pleased to share your excitement.

5. Don't be overprotective. Offer to help the person if you see them struggling, but do only as much as they ask you to do. If it seems to take forever to get the wheelchair through the entrance and you think you can make it easier, *don't!* Instead, be patient and pitch in only if asked.

9 Dating Tips for Guys

You're interested in a girl who seems to like you also. You may already know her as a friend or you may have just met her, but you think she's terrific. You want to spend some relaxed time with her and get to know her better. But you're inexperienced and you don't know what to do. Here are some tips to get you off to a good start.

1. Keep it casual. Saying, "Would you like to go out with me?" puts pressure on her, and she may back off right away. A better way to ask her out is to say "Let's get together and do something sometime." No big deal. Friends getting to know each other, not a formal date. And if she does reject you, at least she should be nice about it. If you get a positive response, wait a day or two and then suggest something specific.

2. Don't ask her out for a Friday or Saturday evening. The chances of her being busy are far greater, and asking her out during the weekend makes this date formal, which you may not want to do. Asking her out during the week gives her the impression that you have plans for the weekend, which will imply that you have plans with some other girl. This might make her even more interested in you.

3. If she acts completely uninterested or even turned off, keep your distance and look elsewhere. If you're getting mixed signals, talk to her and ask her how she feels about you. Let her know you're prepared to deal with the truth.

4. Girls go on dates to have a good time, not to be serious. Keep it casual. Plan the date carefully, but be flexible if she has other preferences. Try to go somewhere familiar so you'll know what to expect.

5. Movies are a good first date. It's dark, you don't have to talk a lot, and there'll be something to discuss afterward. It shows no imagination on your part, but it's easy.

6. Treat her with respect, and pay attention to what she has to say. Girls love guys who really listen. Spend most of your date listening to her.

7. End the date before she does. Tell her you had a great time and that you hope she did and that you'd like to see her again. This is a great way to let her know you're not the kind of guy who would ever put pressure on a girl.

8. If you enjoyed the date and feel that the two of you made a connection, send or give her a little gift at the right moment. Hint: girls love flowers.

9. Remember that on your first date, the object is to have fun and to be real with each other. If you both like each other, the rest will take care of itself.

What the Prom Will Cost the Guy

Back in the old days, guys paid for all prom expenses except the boutonnière (a flower you wear on the lapel of your jacket), which was the girl's contribution. But today's prom prices are sky-high, and most guys simply can't afford them, so it's become common for the girls to share the cost. Be honest with your date, and let her know where you stand early on. Give her the option of splitting some of the costs with you or tailoring prom night to your budget.

1. **Tickets:** $40–$50 per couple. If dinner is included, they're likely to cost anywhere from $90 to $150 for a pair.

2. **Dinner:** If it's not part of the prom package, chances are you'll spend another $50–$75 for dinner. Don't forget the 15% tip.

3. **Tuxedo:** $50–$150, depending on its quality and the extras you choose. The basic price generally includes everything — shoes, cuff links, shirt, tie, vest or cummerbund, the jacket, and the pants.

4. **Corsage:** $25–$50. It's supposed to match her dress.

5. **Photographs:** $35–$150. There's usually a photographer at the prom, and you can order whatever picture sets you want. (Be sure to bring a check or credit card with you so you don't have to carry cash, which may be stolen.)

6. **Limousine:** $400–$500. This is a biggie, so you should plan to split the cost with other couples.

What the Prom Will Cost the Girl

1. **The dress:** $75–$500, with an average of $250
2. **Shoes:** $50–$100
3. **Purse:** $25–$50
4. **Gloves:** $15–$25
5. **Hair ornaments:** $10–$50
6. **Miscellaneous accessories** (makeup, underwear, etc.): $100
7. **Hairdo:** $50–$60
8. **Manicure and pedicure:** $25–$100
9. **Boutonnière:** $5–$15

11 Tips for Renting a Limousine

Most limousine rentals are "mom and pop" businesses in which the owner does some of the driving. Even though there are, on average, only a dozen prom nights a year in any community, they are very important to the limousine operators. Demand polite, professional service, and show your respect for their property in return.

1. The best way to find a reliable company is to get a recommendation from someone who has already used it. When you book the limo, tell them who recommended you.

2. Do business with a company owner who treats you with respect. You should receive every bit of consideration and service. This includes being addressed appropriately, having the limousine stocked with sodas, having doors held open for you, and generally being treated like a VIP.

3. Get the company to put in writing the year, make, and model of the vehicle you will be renting. (Showing the young client a 2000 model but showing up on the big night in a 1992 stretch is a common trick of bad companies.)

4. Make sure the company has not been overbooked and will meet you on time or 15 minutes early in a clean vehicle. Confirm the arrangements a week before, a day before, and on the day of the event.

5. Teens tend to focus on the glitz and glamour of the vehicle, but the attitude, training, and professionalism of the chauffeur are just as important. If the person giving you information is rude or short with you on the phone, there is a strong possibility the chauffeur will act that way too.

6. Do not pay more than a 50% deposit. If possible, put the rental on a credit card. If the limousine is late or breaks down, you will be protected by your credit card provider.

7. When you book the limo, state the exact number of passengers on your trip, and do not attempt to overload the limousine. Remember that if you break any of their rules about drinking, smoking, and carrying on, you may find yourself back on your doorstep before the prom even begins. And you'll lose your deposit, too.

8. A cheap limousine may not be a safe limousine. Call your state public utility commission to find out if the company is licensed and has had any complaints filed against it.

9. If you are renting a vehicle for the entire evening, have the company acknowledge in writing that they will not try to squeeze in an airport trip while you're at the prom. Make sure the limousine is dedicated completely to you and your party and that you won't have to wait for the car at any point. It should be waiting for you.

10. Have your chauffeur pick up each passenger at home rather than meeting them all at one location. That way, everyone gets the same treatment and there's less chance that anyone will be late.

11. The limousine industry has a national trade association. Check out www.nla.org. for more guidance.

How to Give the Perfect Movie Kiss

1. If you have gum or anything else in your mouth, get rid of it.

2. Hold the person gently by the shoulders and look into their face. Try to look happy.

3. Stare into their eyes.

4. Open your lips slightly, inhale through your nose, and close your eyes slowly.

5. Move closer. Hold their face with your hands and kiss them on the lips. Keep your tongue inside your mouth. Gentle moaning and heavy breathing are good. The kiss should be long enough so that the person knows you are enjoying it but not so long that you can't breathe.

6. After the kiss, look into the person's eyes and smile.

3 Reasons That People Close Their Eyes When They Kiss

These are just possibilities.

1. Since kissing is sensual, rather than visual, closing your eyes allows you to concentrate on the kiss without any distractions.

2. You will get cross-eyed if you stare at each other from such a close distance. Your eyes can't focus on each other without straining.

3. Sometimes you want to imagine you're kissing someone else. Closing your eyes makes it easier.

7 Ways to Keep Your Breath Fresh

If there's kissing in your future—or you just don't want to offend anyone—here are some tips.

1. Don't smoke. Ever.

2. Avoid foods that typically cause bad breath: onions, garlic, and spicy foods, for instance.

3. When you brush your teeth, clean your tongue as well. There are little gadgets you can get at the drugstore that do the job.

4. Keep breath mints or gum with you at all times.

5. Avoid caffeine, especially in coffee. It dries out your mouth and makes bad breath even worse.

6. Drink 6–8 glasses of water a day.

7. Eat lots of citrus fruit, like oranges.

The Top 10 Signs That Someone Has a Crush on You

1. The person always seems to find an excuse to talk to you.

2. This person is always trying to get your attention, even if it's in obnoxious ways, like pulling your hair or making faces at you.

3. They really enjoy hearing stuff about you.

4. They try to ignore you when they are with friends, but they wind up staring at you anyway.

5. They stutter and stammer when you ask them a simple question.

6. They act differently around you than they normally do.

7. He always tries to impress you.

8. She defends you to other people.

9. The person turns red and acts embarrassed when you approach.

10. They tell you personal things about themselves and ask you to share your private thoughts as well.

5 Ways to Size Up a Prospective Love Interest

Your stomach does flip-flops when you see her; you can't take your eyes off him when he walks into the room. But do these people really have what it takes to rock your boat? Ask yourself these questions.

1. How did she treat her last boyfriend? Why did they break up?

2. What hopes and dreams does he have for the future, and how does he plan to achieve them?

3. What are her values? Does she live up to them?

4. Does he have a sense of humor?

5. Does she appreciate your special, unique qualities?

10 Ways to Let Someone Know You're "Interested"

Whether you'd just like to know more about the guy in your math class or you've caught the love bug and are dying to get that girl's attention, taking the first step can be terrifying. No one wants to get rejected—that's a normal fear. Fact is, if you do get rejected, you'll live. Go ahead. Make your move!

1. Smile. This is the best place to start. If you don't have the nerve to open your mouth, the smile at least lets her know that you're aware of her and that you're approachable.

2. Use body language. How you move and hold yourself has a lot to do with how people react to you. Stand tall and keep your head up. Walk with purpose. The trick is to appear confident even if you don't feel it.

3. Glance at the person often. When you're having a conversation, make eye contact. If you're talking with your friends and you see her across the street, look at her so she knows you've seen her. (But don't stare!)

4. Laugh. If she says something funny, laugh; let her know you're enjoying the conversation. Don't overdo it, though, and make sure that whatever you're laughing at was intended to be funny.

5. **Pay the person a compliment.** "Nice going on that test!" "Great game Friday night!" "I love your purple hair."

6. **Make yourself available.** Guys especially hate to talk to girls when they're surrounded by lots of friends. If you're in a class together, hang back from the crowd and see what happens when you're alone. Make it easy for the person to find you when you're on your own.

7. **Ask questions.** Once you get into a conversation, keep it moving along. Let her know you're interested in her and that you share other interests. Ask him about something he knows a lot about, so he'll have a chance to show off a little. Read the list of "12 Ways to Start a Conversation" on page 129.

8. **Make physical contact.** Touch his arm when he's talking to you or brush him "accidentally" when you pass him in the hall. Let him know you want to get closer.

9. **Get mutual friends on your team.** Maybe one of them can bring up your name in a conversation and say some nice things about you. Or try to arrange to get invited to events you know he'll be attending.

10. **Be memorable.** Don't be afraid to stand out from the crowd and do things a little differently. Let him know that you're unique.

6 Ways to Let Someone Know You're Definitely <u>Not</u> Interested

Here's how to tell someone that they need to move on. If you get these signs from someone you're interested in, back off. Maybe she'll appreciate the space and discover you on her own later.

1. Tell them! Don't avoid their e-mails or dodge them at school. Take them aside privately and let them know you think they're more interested in you than you are in them and you'd like some space. Tell them that you're flattered by their interest.

2. Don't string them along. Saying yes to something and then canceling at the last minute is cruel.

3. Try introducing them to someone you think would make a better match.

4. Let this person see you with the person you really care about.

5. Write the person a letter and say how you feel. Say that you appreciate their good qualities but that they should be with someone who appreciates them more than you do.

6. Let mutual friends know how you feel and hope the message gets around.

7 Steps to Ending a Relationship

1. If you're getting ready to dump somebody and you're afraid they may get violent, break the news in a public place.

2. Don't break up with someone in your house; you won't be able to get away when you want to end the conversation.

3. If you are going to break up in a public place, make sure you have arranged a ride home beforehand.

4. Don't make any promises or plans for the future.

5. Offer to return anything valuable they may have given you. Don't be mean about it. This is not the time to get into an argument over who really paid for the Train CD.

6. Give them a chance to say how they feel. Apologize for anything you've done that was hurtful.

7. Make the ending final.

15 Tips for Getting Dumped Without Losing Your Cool

It happens to everyone, and it's not the end of the world —it just feels that way. Whether you were expecting it or not, it can hurt. But you're going to get past it, and you're going to fall in love again. We guarantee it. Here are some things to do while you're waiting for your broken heart to heal.

1. Don't call and try to talk them out of dumping you. You will only be further humiliated.

2. Don't try to become their new best friend. You will only get hurt when they talk about dating other people.

3. Cry. Try not to be obsessive about this, and don't do it in public. Go someplace private and get it out of your system.

4. Don't keep all the stuff they gave you, like cards and notes. Either get rid of these things or put them someplace where you don't have to stare at them every day and be reminded of your sadness.

5. Do cool stuff for yourself. Rent a favorite movie, relax in a warm bubble bath, listen to your favorite music, dance. Try to unwind. Spend time by yourself and rediscover what good company you are. Read "100 Things to Do When There's Nothing to Do (All Alone and by Yourself)" on page 5.

6. Make a list of all your best qualities. Don't hold back—this is no time for modesty.

7. List the things you will do differently the next time you date. Did the person break up with you because you were too demanding? Maybe this is the time to think about making a change in how you deal with the opposite sex.

8. Talk to your pet. Tell him everything. If you don't have a pet, get one.

9. Get out of the house. Take yourself to a movie, the mall, or a party. Let your friends know you're still there and that you're available.

10. Exercise. This will definitely perk up your mood.

11. Be patient with yourself. You need to go through a healing process, and that's not something you can rush.

12. Avoid the frozen food section in the supermarket. A gallon of Rocky Road will not help, and you'll feel worse about yourself when it's gone.

13. Plan an event: a party, a concert outing, or just a small get-together with close friends. Have something on the calendar to look forward to.

14. Help someone who's hurting more than you are. If you can't find someone who's fits that category, you're not looking hard enough.

15. Don't give up on the opposite sex. "Don't ever run after a train, a bus, or a lover," we're told. "There'll be another one along shortly."

15 Ways to Tell If You're a Fool for Love

Romance can be fun, but when it starts interfering with your ability to maintain friendships, good grades, and family ties, it's time to get a life — your own. Here are some ways to tell if the relationship needs a time-out.

1. You sit by the phone and get nervous if anyone else uses it, even though you have Call Waiting. You won't leave the house without your cell phone.

2. You refused to see a movie with your friends, but you've now sat through it twice with her.

3. Anyone who has her attention instantly becomes your mortal enemy. You are jealous of his pet snake.

4. You call his house and then hang up when he answers just to hear his voice.

5. She loves green. You hate green. You wear green everything.

6. You refuse to make plans with anyone just in case she calls. Your sister's wedding suddenly seems like a big waste of time.

7. Even your diary is sick of hearing about him.

8. Your math grade has gone from an *A* to a *C-*. Guess who sits in front of you in math.

9. You pretend to like Eminem, Creed, and/or the Indigo Girls because you know she does.

10. You find yourself bungee jumping even though your idea of a good time is a book and a cup of cocoa.

11. You tell her you love her four cats and that you sneeze around them only because you're coming down with something. What allergy?

12. You sit through sports events that bore you silly.

13. You act totally absorbed when he talks about his 16-byte buffer connector but you don't know the difference between RAM and ROM.

14. You find yourself offering to help her mother carry groceries but can't remember the last time you helped your own.

15. You're upset because you can't find a Hallmark card for a six-and-a-half-day anniversary.

10 Signs That It's Real Love

A truly loving relationship means *both* people feel the same way.

1. You get butterflies in your stomach when you see each other.

2. You spend almost all of your time thinking about each other.

3. Being alone together makes you happy.

4. Stupid love songs don't seem so stupid.

5. Your relationship is a priority in both your lives.

6. You can't bear to watch each other flirt with anyone else.

7. You can't bear to see each other in pain.

8. The attachment you feel for each other is more than physical.

9. You can't imagine a future without each other.

10. You each get excited when you talk about the other.

5 Ways to Cope with a Broken Heart

Whether you are the dumper or the dumpee, first heart-breaks are awful because you've never had that experience before and you don't know how you're to get over the hurt. You will, although you may go through a few boxes of tissues before you do. That's okay. Here are some ways to cope.

1. Don't think about the breakup over and over again. Don't keep reliving the moment when he said, "Can't we just be friends?" There's no need to put yourself through that kind of misery. Focus on something else when you start thinking about your former flame.

2. When you are feeling sad, try picturing your former boy- or girlfriend in a laughable or ridiculous situation. This really works.

3. Don't dwell on how great the relationship was. Try to remember the things that led to the breakup.

4. If you feel like you've just gotten your heart torn out and fed to a pack of wild animals, it's time to pump up the volume on your self-esteem. If you find yourself thinking that you will never find someone as wonderful as the person that just dumped you, you've got to replace that yucky negative thought with a positive one. Make a list of all the great things about yourself and remember them whenever you start feeling sad. Hang out with people who love you and make you feel good about yourself.

5. Remember that you have just gained a new experience that will prepare you for the next time you break up. Think about what you will do differently next time.

20 Things You May Have Heard About Sex That Just Aren't True

Like most teens, you may have learned most of what you know about sex from friends. But a lot of this information may be false or misleading. If you have questions about sex, go to the library or speak with your parents, a teacher, or a physician. The following are some statements about sex that are just not true.

1. **Everybody's doing it.** No, they're not. And even if they were, so what? You should have sex only when you feel that you are ready.

2. **Masturbation is evil, dirty, and harmful.** No. It will not make you go blind, drive you insane, turn you into a perverted fiend, stunt your growth, give you a sexually transmitted disease (STD), make you sterile, or get you pregnant.

3. **You can't get birth control if you're under 18.** You can get birth control devices anywhere in the U.S. without your parents' permission.

4. **A girl can't get pregnant the first time she has sex.** A girl can get pregnant any time she has sex.

5. **You can tell if your partner has an STD.** Unless your partner is honest with you, it is often impossible to tell.

6. **Using birth control takes away the romance.** It's just the opposite. Using birth control can relieve fears about unwanted pregnancy.

7. **Birth control is the girl's responsibility.** Both partners should be prepared.

8. You're not a real man or woman if you are not having sex. Oh please!

9. There must be something wrong with you if you don't want to have sex. There *is* something wrong with a person who tries to coerce others into doing things they don't want to do.

10. You can't get an STD or HIV (the virus that causes AIDS) from oral sex.

11. Oral sex is a safe alternative to intercourse. Even though you can't get pregnant, you can still catch an STD or HIV.

12. If you love someone, you're going to want to have sex with that person. There are many ways of expressing love. If someone tells you, "You'd do it if you loved me," tell them, "If you loved me, you'd wait."

13. A girl can't get pregnant while she has her period. There's *always* a chance she can get pregnant.

14. Having intercourse while standing up or jumping up and down afterward will prevent pregnancy. This is just plain stupid. If something doesn't make sense to you, research it before you accept it.

15. Boys always initiate sexual activity. The girl's sex drive is just as strong as the boy's.

16. There's something wrong with a guy who hasn't had sex by the time he is 18. A guy shouldn't have sex until he's ready for it.

17. You can tell if a person is a homosexual just by looking at them. You can't tell anything about a person just by looking at them.

18. AIDS is a "gay" or homosexual disease. AIDS affects everyone.

19. Condoms don't work. Latex condoms can be effective if they're used properly, especially if you use a spermicide as well. Still, only 100% abstinence is 100% safe.

20. Having an orgasm while you're asleep (a "nocturnal" orgasm) means that there is something wrong with you. It's perfectly normal.

The 20 Most Commonly Asked Questions (and Answers) About AIDS

This list was compiled by students at Putnam County High School in Granville, Illinois.

1. Does everyone with HIV, the AIDS virus, have AIDS? No. AIDS is the end stage of HIV infection and may not appear for more than 10 years after infection.

2. Can I tell if a person has HIV by looking at him or her? No. A person can be infected with HIV and be capable of transmitting it to others for up to 10 years or longer before having any outward symptoms.

3. Can teenagers get HIV/AIDS? Yes. Teens, like anyone else, can get HIV. Many teens have HIV but have no symptoms, so they may not know they have the virus.

4. Can a person be infected with HIV by sharing needles and drug works? Yes. Sharing needles has become a major route of HIV transmission; the blood on the needle, not the drug, is the way HIV is spread.

5. Does the use of steroids have anything to do with HIV/AIDS? No. Steroids themselves can cause other problems, but not HIV or AIDS unless you are using a needle that has been contaminated by the HIV virus.

6. Is it true that people with HIV/AIDS have done bad things and deserve to be sick? No. AIDS is a disease caused by HIV, a virus that affects people for physiological reasons. Anyone—good or bad—can get it.

7. Can a person be infected with HIV and not even know it? Yes. There is often a long period between infection and first symptoms; it is thought that most of the people in the U.S. who have HIV are not aware of their condition.

8. Can you get HIV/AIDS by donating blood? No. Blood donation is completely safe. The needle used to draw the blood is sterile and is used only once, then discarded, so no infectious diseases can be transmitted in this way.

9. Can a blood test tell you if you have AIDS? There is no such test. The standard blood test is for antibodies to HIV, the virus that causes AIDS, and will tell if a person's blood contains HIV.

10. Can drinking alcohol lead to behaviors that can cause the spread of HIV? No. But drinking alcohol lowers the ability to make good decisions, and a person who is drunk may engage in risky behaviors that he or she would not try otherwise.

11. What is the only certain protection against HIV? Abstinence from sex and drugs.

12. Can you get HIV by kissing, petting, and sensual massage? No. These are the safer sexual behaviors that allow partners to give each other pleasure short of engaging in sexual intercourse or oral sex.

13. Do some STDs cause sores that make it easier to get HIV? Yes. Gonorrhea and herpes, especially, cause sores that can provide an easy entry for HIV, the virus that causes AIDS.

14. Is it true that sexually transmitted diseases are not dangerous, since they can be cured with medication? No. Symptoms of viral STDs, such as herpes and genital warts, can be controlled through medication *but these diseases cannot be cured.* Many bacterial STDs, such as chlamydia and gonorrhea, are not life-threatening, but they may cause extensive internal damage and discomfort if not diagnosed and treated.

15. Does using latex condoms during sex help prevent the transmission of HIV? Yes. But that doesn't mean they're 100% effective; they do break and leak. Still, if you're having sex, latex condoms are the best means of protection from sexually transmitted diseases.

16. Is there a vaccine to prevent HIV and AIDS? No. Current research focuses on a vaccine to prevent those with HIV from developing AIDS.

17. Can I get HIV if I have sex with only one other person? Yes. Because there is a big "if." Sex is safe only if neither partner is infected, and that's virtually impossible to know without a blood test.

18. Do birth control pills prevent HIV/AIDS? No. Birth control pills are extremely effective in preventing pregnancy, but they offer no protection against STDs.

19. If I know my sexual partner well, do I still need to use a condom? Yes. Even if you know your partner well, you cannot know about the health of his or her previous sexual partners.

20. Does sexual intercourse refer only to vaginal intercourse?
No. The term sexual intercourse refers to vaginal, anal, and oral intercourse.

4.
SCHOOL

No More Pencils, No More Books: How School Will Be Different in the Year 2025

In 2001, *Newsweek* asked leading teachers, inventors, and entrepreneurs for their vision of the classroom of the future and how learning will change. Here are some of their responses.

1. Students will be completely wireless! Instead of textbooks and notebooks, you'll have a tablet PC that will not only replace your texts and paper but also allow you to communicate—via videophone—with anyone. And because files can be shared, parents, teachers, and students can all follow a student's progress. Bill Gates, the chairman and chief software architect of Microsoft, calls this "connected learning," where people are "not as isolated from each other the way we are today."

2. There will still be classrooms, but they won't be nearly as structured as they are today, predicts John Doerr, a tech adviser who helped companies like Amazon and Netscape get where they are today. He says that instead of traditional tests, schools will find better ways to measure a person's ability. The purpose of education, he says, will be "to be set to learn for life on your own, to be ready to vote, to be a functioning citizen in the information economy."

3. Teachers will be coaches more than teachers per se. Linda Darling-Hammond, a professor of education at Stanford University, says they "will be in more of a coaching role, directing students to the resources they need to solve problems—a 'guide on the side' . . . rather than a 'sage on the stage.'?"

4. Your education will take place far beyond the classroom, to all the reaches of the world. "Technology and education will allow us to build bridges of understanding between people of different cultures around the world," says Maria Cantwell, a U.S. senator from Washington who looks forward to what she calls the global classroom. Brandon Lloyd, a 7th-grade teacher whose classroom is part of a pilot program that connects kids across the country with one another, explains that that will reduce prejudice in the world, since "students will be able to work with other kids, maybe in Syria and Israel, and exchange information." And since kids are able to approach things with less prejudice than adults (they've had less practice), they'll be able to grow—and encourage their children to grow—to be successful citizens of the world.

5. Your education will be more of an individual experience, and it will be designed for your abilities, needs, and goals. Says Danny Hills, a pioneer of supercomputing in the 1970s and now chairman of Applied Minds, an inventor's workshop in Glendale, Calif.: "Imagine you had a tutor who knew you well, knew that you liked concrete examples and seeing pictures, or being told a story. This tutor would know how to explain things in your terms, what would excite you, what would mean something to you." It will be like having your own personal search engine. "I can almost taste it!" says Hills.

6. Learning will become part of your social life, predicts investor Herb Allen. "The new social experience will be people gathering around intellectual topics to form social units, much as they did in Germany in the 1800s." Since you'll be able to locate people of similar interests on the Internet, and since learning will be a lot less structured than it is today, you might wind up becoming friends with three people in your state who live far away but who share your interests.

7. Learning will be oriented toward multimedia. Whereas previously almost everything took place on a blackboard and on paper, the assignments of the future will be multimedia presentations more often than simple essays. "You should see the movies that kids and teachers are making now," says Steve Jobs, the CEO of Apple. "I can show you a movie made by a 6th-grade teacher with her kids about learning the principles of geometry in a way that you will never forget." He firmly believes: "When students are creating, learning is taking place."

Take a Load Off (Your Backpack)

You can lighten your load and protect your health by following these guidelines.

1. Start out by buying a good backpack. All the seams should be reinforced, and there should be enough pockets to hold all your smaller items but not so many that you'll never remember where you put everything. You want something washable, so you don't have to throw it out because of lunch leaks, and you want something big enough to hold all your books. Cheap backpacks are usually just a little smaller than the better ones.

2. Don't sling your backpack over one shoulder from a single strap. Even if you change shoulders from time to time, it can cause spine curvature.

3. The straps should be padded and wide, and they should be pulled tight enough so that the backpack is close to your body. If not, the straps will pull your shoulders back, causing neck and back pain.

4. When you place books in your backpack, put the heavier items close to your back.

5. Get a backpack with a hip belt, which will take some of the weight off your back.

6. With all your books in it, your backpack should weigh no more than 5%–10% of your body weight. If it's any heavier, you will tend to walk leaning forward, which is bad for your posture.

The 5 Youngest High School Graduates

1. Brandenn Bremmer, Venango, Nebraska. In the summer of 2001, Bremmer graduated from the Independent Study program at the University of Nebraska, Lincoln, at the age of 10. His GPA was 3.7 and his IQ, 178. He is interested in studying music and science and hopes to get involved in cloning research when he's older.

2. Michael Kearney, Murfreesboro, Tennessee. In 1985, Kearney graduated from high school at the age of 5 years and 9 months and began studying for an associate of science degree at Santa Rosa Junior College, in California, at 6 years and 7 months. With an IQ above 200, he graduated from Santa Rosa and transferred to the University of South Alabama at 8. In 1990, he set the record for "Youngest Graduate" in the *Guinness Book of World Records* when he received his B.A. in anthropology at 10 years and 4 months. Finally, at 14, he earned his M.S. in chemistry from Middle Tennessee University. Kearney aspires to host his own TV game show for children.

3. Greg Smith, Keswick, Virginia. With a 4.57 cumulative GPA, Smith graduated in 1999 at the age of 10 from Orange Park High School in Florida. That same year, he began his studies at Randolph-Macon College in Ashland, Virginia. His ultimate goal is to have three Ph.D.'s by the age of 33 and become an aerospace engineer. He hopes to build space stations, become a biomedical researcher so he can cure diseases and reverse the aging process, and be president of the U.S. so he can bring peace to the world.

4. Tathagat Avatar Tulsi, Bihar, India. In 1996, at the age of 9 1/2 years, this whiz kid finished high school and received his B.S. in physics from Science College of Patna University at the age of 12. Tulsi's success earned him a name in the *Guinness Book of World Records* as "Youngest Graduate." His ambition is to conduct research in science and high temperature superconductors.

5. Sho Yano, Chicago, Illinois. With an IQ of around 200, Yano scored 1,500 out of 1,600 on his SATs at the age of 8 and graduated from high school through a home-schooling program. In the fall of 2000, at 9, the 4-foot genius began studying premed at Loyola University. His goal is to find a cure for AIDS and become a composer.

9 Nobel Prizewinners Who Hated School

1. **Winston Churchill, winner of the 1953 Nobel Prize in literature.** Churchill was schooled at home until he was 7, then sent to boarding school. He had looked forward to the companionship of other boys and to the adventure, but it didn't quite work out that way: "How I hated this school, and what a life of anxiety I lived there for more than two years. I made very little progress in my lessons, and none at all at games. I counted the days and the hours to the end of every term, when I should return home from this hateful servitude and range my soldiers in line of battle on the nursery floor." He once said that his only pleasure at the time was reading.

2. **Albert Einstein, co-winner of the 1921 Nobel Prize in physics.** One of the greatest thinkers of modern times, Einstein hated the structure of school and said that even a horse would turn down food if it was forced on him as education was. In fact, he was diagnosed as a slow learner early in his schooling. He has said: "It is, in fact, nothing short of a miracle that the modern methods of instruction have not yet entirely strangled the holy curiosity of inquiry; for this delicate little plant [student], aside from stimulation, stands mainly in need of freedom; without this it goes to wreck and ruin without fail."

3. **Richard Feynman, co-winner of the 1965 Nobel Prize in physics.** Feynman was a crucial member of the Manhattan Project, which developed the atomic bomb for the Allies during World War II, and a member of the special commission that investigated the explosion of the space shuttle *Challenger*. Mostly self-taught, he described the few short years he did attend public school as "an intellectual desert." Having learned algebra on his own, he once created a set of four equations and four unknowns to show off to his arithmetic teacher, who had to take it to the principal to find out whether it was correct.

4. **Arno Penzias, co-winner of the 1978 Nobel Prize in physics.** The vice president of research at AT&T Bell Laboratories, Penzias predicts that in the future, the best jobs will go to those with the best experience, not necessarily the highest grades. "I think we've tied acquiring knowledge too much to school," he has said.

5. **Bertrand Russell, winner of the 1950 Nobel Prize in literature.** This famous statesman promoted home schooling, saying that most education authorities cared nothing about children. He said that being schooled at home preserved the individuality of the student, explaining: "An orchestra requires men with different talents and, within limits, different tastes; if all men insisted upon playing the trombone, orchestral music would be impossible. Social co-operation, in like manner, requires differences of taste and aptitude, which are less likely to exist if all children are exposed to the same influences."

6. **Andrei Sakharov, winner of the 1975 Nobel Prize for world peace.** Soviet dissident Andrei Sakharov thought school was a "waste of time." He was schooled at home, where he gained an intellectual courage that helped him resist tyranny for most of his life.

7. **George Bernard Shaw, winner of the 1925 Nobel Prize in**

literature. Shaw said it best: "There is, on the whole, nothing on earth intended for innocent people so horrible as a school. To begin with, it is a prison. But it is in some respects more cruel than a prison. In a prison, for instance, you are not forced to read books written by the warders [guards] and beaten or otherwise tormented if you cannot remember their utterly un-memorable contents. In the prison you are not forced to sit lis-tening to the turnkeys discoursing without charm or interest on subjects that they don't understand and don't care about, and are therefore incapable of making you understand or care about. In a prison they may torture your body; but they do not torture your brains; and they protect you against violence and outrage from your fellow-prisoners. In a school you have none of these advantages. . . . You are forced to read a hideous im-posture called a school book, written by a man who cannot write: A book from which no human can learn anything: a book which, though you may decipher it, you cannot in any fruitful sense read, though the enforced attempt will make you loathe the sight of a book all the rest of your life."

8. **Rabindranath Tagore, winner of the 1913 Nobel Prize in literature.** Tagore was a superb writer, one of the founders of modern Bengali literature, and the first non-Western author to win the Nobel literature prize. He described school as being "like the shoes of a mandarin woman," saying it "pinched and bruised my nature on all sides and at every movement. I was fortunate enough in extricating myself before insensibil-ity set in."

9. **Sigrid Undset, winner of the 1928 Nobel Prize in litera-ture.** Undset hated school intensely and claimed it interfered with her freedom. She developed an elaborate technique of "zoning out" during classes.

The 5 Biggest Causes of Violence in Schools

1. Students bullying other students
2. Parents not being involved with their kids
3. Schools ignoring troubled teens
4. Guns and weapons being too easily accessible
5. Violence in the media

12 Ways to Prevent Violence at School

Recent statistics suggest that 25% of high school students fear school violence. Here are some pointers from the National Crime Prevention Council's Center for the Prevention of School Violence (www.ncpc.org).

1. Refuse to take a weapon to school, refuse to carry a weapon for someone else, and be sure to speak out about those who carry weapons.

2. Report any crime immediately to school authorities or police.

3. Report suspicious or upsetting behavior or talk by other students to either a teacher or counselor at school. You may save someone's life.

4. Learn how to deal with your own anger. Find out ways to settle an argument by talking it out, working it out, or walking away rather than fighting.

5. Help others settle disputes peaceably. Start or join a program designed to avoid violence, in which trained students help classmates find ways to settle arguments without fists or weapons.

6. Get permission to set up a teen court at school, in which kids serve as judge, prosecutor, jury, and defense attorneys. Courts can hear cases, make findings, and impose sentences, or they may lay down sentences in cases where teens plead guilty. Teens feel more involved and respected in this process than in an adult juvenile justice system.

7. Become a peer counselor, working with classmates who need support and help with problems.

8. Mentor a younger student. As a role model and friend, you can make it easier for a younger person to adjust to school and ask for help.

9. Start a school crime watch. A student patrol can help keep an eye on corridors, parking lots, and groups, and it offers a way for students to report concerns anonymously.

10. Ask each student activity group or club to adopt a theme against violence. The newspaper could run stories on how to prevent violence; the art club could illustrate the costs of violence. Sports teams could address ways to reduce violence that's not part of the game plan.

11. Welcome new students and help them feel at home in your school. Introduce them to other students. Get to know at least one student unfamiliar to you each week.

12. Start a peace pledge campaign, in which students promise to settle disagreements without violence, to reject weapons, and to work toward a safe campus for all. Try for 100% participation.

8 Things You Can Do at School to Help Save the Planet

1. If there's an ecology club, join it. If there isn't, start one with the goal of educating all the students about the effects of ecology on the planet and on our lifestyles and what they can do. The club can raise funds to support a larger effort in the community.

2. Encourage other students to participate in Earth Day, April 22. Visit www.earthday.com for more information.

3. Set up a paper recycling system for all the paper that students throw away in the course of a day. In general, try to use less paper. Use extra sheets as scrap paper.

4. We assume there's already a system to prevent waste in the cafeteria. Avoid food containers that are not made of paper.

5. When your assignment allows you to pick any subject for an essay, choose something on ecology.

6. Turn off the lights in rooms that are not being used.

7. Plant trees.

8. Talk to the principal about offering all students a course in tuning up a car.

U.S. Department of Education Guidelines on Religious Freedom in Public Schools

Whether prayer should be allowed in public school is a question that goes back to the first divisions between church and state, in the 15th century. These current rulings were issued by the Department of Education in 1995.

1. Students may read religious books, say prayers before and after meals and tests, and generally engage in such activities to the extent that they engage in secular activities that are equally nondisruptive.

2. Students may talk to other students about religious matters in informal settings, just as they may discuss any other topics.

3. Students can proselytize with other students, but they may not engage in religiously motivated harassment.

4. No student can be coerced into any religious activity.

5. Teachers and administrators cannot discourage or promote an activity because of its religious content. This applies to antireligious activity as well.

6. Schools may teach about religion and its role in society, and they can teach the Bible as literature. They cannot provide religious instruction.

7. Students may distribute religious literature under the same guidelines that allow them to distribute any other literature.

8. Students may be released to attend religious classes at another location. Teachers are not to encourage or discourage such activities.

9. Schools may teach lessons in common civic values but must be neutral with respect to religion.

The Bill of Rights for Gay Students

Federal law requires all schools to have a harassment policy, although it should not specify race, gender, or sexual orientation. The law also requires schools to permit student groups to meet and form alliances. For more information, contact the P.E.R.S.O.N. Project at www.youth.org/loco/PERSON Project/.

1. The right to attend school free of verbal and physical harassment and be assured that education, not survival, is the priority.

2. The right to attend school where respect and dignity for all is a standard set by the boards of education and enforced by every teacher and principal.

3. The right to have access to accurate information about gay people, free of negative judgment and delivered by trained adults who not only inform but affirm them.

4. The right to positive role models, both in person and in the curriculum.

5. The right to be included in all the support programs that exist to help teenagers deal with the difficulties of adolescence.

6. The right to legislators who guarantee and fight for their constitutional freedom rather than ones who reinforce hate and prejudice.

7. The right to a legacy free from hatred and unchallenged discrimination.

8. The right to consider themselves capable of being strong, happy, healthy, and successful.

9. The right to question in an environment that does not presume heterosexuality and that honors their level of development.

10. The right to public disclosure and privacy on their own terms in a school environment that honors professional confidentiality.

How American Students Stack Up

The Program for International Student Assessment (PISA) was developed to assess the reading, mathematics, and science literacy of 15-year-olds in participating countries. Students from 32 of the world's most developed countries were tested on how well they could apply their knowledge gained in and out of school.

1. Fourteen countries ranked higher than the U.S. in overall literacy, with Finland, Canada, and New Zealand at the top. The combined scores included the ability to interpret and reflect on texts and retrieve information.

2. U.S. students ranked 18th in math; Japan, Korea, and New Zealand ranked highest.

3. The U.S. placed 14th in science, with Korea, Japan, and Finland at the top.

4. The U.S. had among the highest percentages of students scoring in the top 10% in overall reading skill, behind only Canada, Finland, and New Zealand. But the U.S. also had more students at the lowest level than several countries.

5. Girls outperformed boys in reading literacy in every country.

6. There was no difference by gender in math or science in the U.S.

7. The relationship between family wealth and performance in the U.S. was the same as that in other highly industrial nations, with higher performances tending to reflect higher socioeconomic status.

15 Signs That You'll Make a Great Teacher Someday

1. You take attendance at family dinners.

2. You correct birthday cards and send them back to the people who sent them to you.

3. You refer to the weekend as a time-out.

4. You prefer chalk to chocolate.

5. Your friends call you "Mrs. Tingle" and you take it as a compliment.

6. You tend to say things like "I'm not repeating myself; I'm just reviewing the material."

7. Your journal entries contain footnotes.

8. You think *Snow Day* is the worst movie ever made.

9. You get up at 7:00 A.M., even on weekends.

10. Your favorite time of year is finals.

11. You have more than two science experiments going on in your room at any given time.

12. You'd rather teach yourself physics than go to the mall.

13. You ask your parents for extra credit in exchange for doing chores.

14. When you were little, you were disappointed to learn that Donald Duck's nephews didn't invent the Dewey decimal system.

15. You have nightmares about home schooling.

How High School Students Describe Their Last Report Card

This list (and the eight that follow) is based on studies conducted by the Horatio Alger Association of Distinguished Americans, which celebrates the lives of Americans who have overcome adversity. They publish *The State of Our Nation's Youth Report,* which collects the results of surveys that help people show more sensitivity to the concerns of young people. The survey was conducted by phone and included 1,014 students aged 14–18 across the country.

Mostly A's	20%
A's and B's	33%
Mostly B's	8%
Mix of B's and C's	26%
Mostly C's	7%
Mostly below C's	6%

Hours per Week Most High School Students Spend on Homework

0–5 hours	58%
6–10 hours	26%
11–15 hours	9%
16–20 hours	3%
More than 20 hours	3%

Girls' Favorite School Subjects

1. Art/music/drama
2. English
3. Physical education
4. Languages
5. History
6. Science

Boys' Favorite School Subjects

1. Physical education
2. History
3. Art/music/drama
4. Science
5. Math
6. Computers

Teens' Average Participation in Extracurricular Activities

No activities	15%
One activity	36%
Two activities	19%
Three or more activities	30%

How Students Define Success in Life

Having close family relationships	84%
Having a close group of friends	60%
Making a contribution to society	49%
Having an active spiritual life	44%
Making a lot of money	35%
Being famous or respected in your field	27%
Being attractive or popular	8%

The 12 Most Popular Extracurricular Activities

1. Athletic teams and clubs
2. Band/orchestra
3. Drama/theater
4. Honor societies
5. Service/volunteer groups
6. School publications
7. Career-oriented clubs

8. Cheerleading/dance teams
9. Language clubs
10. Student government
11. Debate team
12. Science clubs

What Most Teens Plan to Do After High School

Continue my education	74%
Get a job	34%
Travel	18%
Join the armed forces	10%
Join a volunteer organization	8%
Get married	7%
Other	2%
Not sure	2%

The Ages of Compulsory School Attendance in Each State (and the District of Columbia)

State	Ages	State	Ages	State	Ages
Alabama	7–16	Kentucky	6–16	North Dakota	7–16
Alaska	7–16	Louisiana	7–17	Ohio	6–18
Arizona	6–16	Maine	7–17	Oklahoma	5–18
Arkansas	5–17	Maryland	5–16	Oregon	7–18
California	6–18	Massachusetts	6–16	Pennsylvania	8–17
Colorado	7–16	Michigan	6–16	Rhode Island	6–16
Connecticut	7–16	Minnesota	7–16	South Carolina	5–17
Delaware	5–16	Mississippi	6–17	South Dakota	6–16
D.C.	5–18	Missouri	7–16	Tennessee	7–17
Florida	6–16	Montana	7–16	Texas	6–17
Georgia	7–16	Nebraska	7–16	Utah	6–18
Hawaii	6–18	Nevada	7–17	Vermont	7–16
Idaho	7–16	New Hampshire	6–16	Virginia	5–18
Illinois	7–16	New Jersey	6–16	Washington	8–18
Indiana	7–18	New Mexico	5–18	West Virginia	6–16
Iowa	6–16	New York	6–16	Wisconsin	6–18
Kansas	7–16	North Carolina	7–16	Wyoming	7–16

High School Rank in Graduation Rates in Each State (and the District of Columbia)

Georgia	51	57%	Delaware	25	75%
Tennessee	50	59%	Wyoming	24	76%
Mississippi	49	60%	Kansas	23	76%
District of Columbia	48	60%	Virginia	22	76%
Arizona	47	60%	Utah	21	77%
Alabama	46	62%	Missouri	20	77%
New Mexico	45	63%	Rhode Island	19	77%
Florida	44	63%	Maine	18	77%
Nevada	43	63%	Michigan	17	77%
North Carolina	42	66%	South Dakota	16	78%
Louisiana	41	66%	Ohio	15	78%
Oregon	40	67%	West Virginia	14	78%
Texas	39	68%	Maryland	13	79%
Alaska	38	70%	Montana	12	80%
Colorado	37	70%	Massachusetts	11	80%
Kentucky	36	71%	New Jersey	10	80%
Arkansas	35	71%	Connecticut	9	81%
Hawaii	34	72%	Illinois	8	82%
South Carolina	33	72%	Minnesota	7	84%
Washington	32	72%	Vermont	6	85%
California	31	73%	Pennsylvania	5	85%
New York	30	74%	Nebraska	4	85%
Indiana	29	74%	North Dakota	3	87%
New Hampshire	28	74%	Wisconsin	2	87%
Oklahoma	27	75%	Iowa	1	93%
Idaho	26	75%			

4 Signs That You're Not Getting into Yale

1. Your probation officer refuses to write you a recommendation.

2. It's March, and you're not quite sure who your teachers are this semester.

3. When you tried to make an appointment at the college guidance office, they thought you were joking.

4. Everyone in your family went to Harvard.

4 Ways to Kiss Up to Your Teacher

If you've been screwing up in class, being disruptive, and ignoring small details—like your homework—the best way to kiss up is to get your act together. Here are some other ways to get ahead.

1. Make sure your teacher knows who you are. If you're new to the school, take time after class to introduce yourself and let your teacher know something about your background.

2. Look lively. If you're not really interested in the material, try to find a way to motivate yourself. Pay attention in class.

3. Stay a few pages ahead in your textbook. Even if you just review it to get an idea of what's to come, you'll have an easier time impressing teachers with your class participation. They *love* this.

4. Let them know you're trying. If you're having trouble with a subject, ask the teacher for some extra time before and after class for help. Or find out if you can do a project for extra credit.

5 Things Your Teachers Don't Want You to Know

1. They're not always mad when they act mad. They do that to get your attention. (It works!)

2. They're as nervous as you are on the first day of school. (We only get one chance to make a first impression!)

3. They, too, are concerned about important things like what they're having for lunch, whether they can get to the bathroom, and how many more days there are until Friday.

4. They count the days until Thanksgiving, winter break, and summer.

5. They sometimes know more than they act like they know. That's why they always ask questions you suspect they know the answers to. They're trying to get you to learn on your own.

13 Phrases to Listen for When the Teacher Is Lecturing

When you hear these words, there's a good chance that the next point made will appear on an exam. Also, look at the teacher's eyes; if he looks down at his notes, he's checking an important point he's about to make.

1. "So in conclusion . . ."
2. "Remember that . . ."
3. "The basic reason . . ."
4. "Essentially . . ."
5. "A perfect example . . ."
6. "Therefore . . ."
7. "Notice that . . ."
8. "Last but not least . . ."
9. "And most important . . ."
10. "A major development . . ."
11. "The basic concept here . . ."
12. "From this we have learned . . ."
13. "Finally . . ."

10 Tips for Taking Great Notes

Your notes can be your salvation. Guard them carefully. Be sure your name is in each of your notebooks and files.

1. **Read the assignment before class.** The material will be much more familiar, and you'll already know what the important points are. (You'll also impress the teacher!)

2. **Don't overwrite.** If you try to write down every word the teacher says, you'll never get past "Good morning, class." Make up abbreviations for conjunctions and often-used terms ("and" = "A"; "international" = "int"; "revolution" = "rv").

3. **Date your notes.** It will be easier to locate them later for test reviews.

4. **Write notes only on one side of the page.**

5. **Try not to always have to look down at the page when you're writing.**

6. **If the teacher is talking too fast, ask her to slow down.**

7. **After class, go over your notes as soon as you can and clean them up.** Cross out anything that turned out to be unimportant.

8. **Share your notes with others.** Everyone takes notes differently; there's a good chance that someone else wrote down something you missed.

9. **Spend a few minutes at the end of the school day (or in study hall) organizing your notes.**

10. **If you can take a tape recorder to school, don't take notes.** Just really listen to what's being said and organize the information when you get home.

8 Ways to Improve Your Memory

1. **Use your imagination.** Research tells us that you memorize more easily when you use both halves of your brain—the left side, which controls things like logic, words, lists, and numbers; and the right side, which controls rhythm, imagination, color, and spatial awareness. Using your imagination by creating visual connections can help you learn more easily. For instance, if you want to remember to get home on time, think of a huge clock face staring at you. Or link items together to create a story in order to remember a shopping list: A green (lettuce) cow (milk) ate a sandwich (bread and bologna) on the moon (cheese).

2. **Create acronyms for memorizing lists.** For instance, to remember the names of the Great Lakes, think of HOMES: *H*uron, *O*ntario, *M*ichigan, *E*rie, and *S*uperior. *N*ever *E*at *S*our *W*atermelon will help you remember the four directions: north, east, south, west. ROY G. BIV can help you remember the colors of the rainbow: red, orange, yellow, green, blue, indigo, and violet. Try to make up your own, similar mnemonic devices.

3. **To remember long numbers,** divide them into a series of smaller numbers and try to create associations for that number. For instance, 186,663,410 becomes 18 (the age at which you'll be "legal"), 666 (the devil's number), 34 (perhaps the number of your house?), 10 (your curfew).

4. **To remember dates,** associate them with dates you al-

now. For instance, April 6 might be four days after your
November 25 is Christmas Day except a month ear-
year 1519 can be remembered as the ages of two peo-
you know. (Of course, this will only work for a year!)

5. **Talk it out.** It's easier to learn material that you've heard.
Try discussing the subject out loud. Or read it into a tape
recorder and listen to it as you fall asleep at night. The very
best way of learning something is to teach it to someone. If no
one's around, try the dog, your teddy bear, or the mirror.

6. **Make up rhymes.** "Columbus sailed the ocean blue in
1492." To treat shock: "If the face is red, raise the head; if the
face is pale, raise the tail."

7. **Type all your notes into the computer.** Just typing them
will cause you to think about them, and you'll remember the
material longer.

8. **Put everything on Post-it notes** and stick them every-
where until you've learned the material.

6 Steps to Writing a Great Essay

1. **Choose a subject.** One of the most common mistakes
students make is that they pick a subject that's too general.
Think about the length of your essay and the resources you
have available. Choose a realistic topic.

2. **Gather your resources.** Make sure you have access to the
books you need and the addresses of Web sites that might be
useful. If you need to conduct interviews for your essay, get
them done and transcribed.

3. **Gather your notes.** You now want to go through all of
your resources and mark the material you want to include in
your essay. If you're not sure whether you'll need something,
mark it anyway, so you can find it just in case. When you're
done, clear everything else out of your work area.

4. **Outline the essay.** The more detailed your outline, the
easier it will be to write the final essay. Once you have done this
part, the rest practically "writes itself." Your essay — any good
essay — should follow this structure:

- The introduction, in which you state your thesis
- The main points (three is a good number to cover)

- A section elaborating on each of your main points
- The secondary points (two, perhaps)
- A section elaborating on each of your secondary points
- The conclusion

5. **Write the essay, sticking to your outline.** If you're in the middle of a paragraph and suddenly get another idea, don't just add it. Consult the outline to make sure you insert the point where it logically belongs. Prove your points and give examples. Use direct quotes when you can; don't paraphrase them if they make a point well enough on their own. Don't use stiff and formal language if that's not your style. If you're not using a computer, write in pencil on every other line (so you'll have room to edit). If you want to make a point that you can't quite figure out, leave a space for it and come back to it later.

6. **Edit the paper.** Be realistic. If it's only supposed to be 500 words long and you've gone on for ten pages, you haven't done the assignment. Edit it down; try to imagine what your teacher will think is important, and eliminate everything else. Even if you've stayed within the assigned length, chances are there are words in each sentence that can be eliminated. Be succinct. At this point you also want to check any facts you're not sure of— numbers and chart information and sources. When your final essay is ready, check the spelling and punctuation *twice*. Before you consider your essay finished, ask yourself the following questions:

- Have I covered all the points in my outline?
- Did I prove my point?
- Is my introduction interesting?
- Do all my sentences follow in a logical order?
- Does the first sentence of each paragraph give an idea of what the paragraph is about?

14 Ways to Describe Yourself

Whether you're writing a college essay or applying for a job, you'll often be asked to "tell us a little something about yourself." The thing is, you don't have to respond by describing every detail of your life since the day you were born. They're not interested in everything that happened to you; they're interested in how you react to the world around you. Here are several things you can write or talk about that, if written with sincerity, will reflect the real you.

1. Describe how you felt on the most important day of your life.

2. Write about how your favorite book affected you.

3. Talk about the person you admire most and tell which qualities of theirs you are trying to develop yourself.

4. Talk about what you look for in a friend.

5. Describe yourself as your friends would describe you.

6. Describe the thing in the world you are most passionate about and explain why it exhilarates you.

7. Concentrate on your greatest accomplishment and talk about what you did to achieve that goal.

8. Explain how you have coped with the worst thing that ever happened to you.

9. Talk about where you'd like to be in ten years.

10. Define the word *success*.

11. Write about the most exciting place you've ever visited and why you would want to live or work there someday.

12. Tell about the day you first figured out that you wanted to do whatever it is you're applying for, even if you were 4 at the time.

13. Talk about the relationship between you and your siblings.

14. Write about yourself in the form of a list: "6 Reasons I'd Make a Great Cadet"; "7 of My Favorite People and What I Learned from Each One." Write explanatory paragraphs for each of your entries.

The 12 Biggest Complaints About Homework (And What You Can Do About Them)

1. **"I just can't focus on my homework. I have trouble concentrating."** High school students study an average of three hours a day, more if there's a test. That's a long stretch of time, and no one expects you to tie yourself to the chair and get it all done in one clip. In fact, you'll learn more if you take frequent *short* breaks—say, ten minutes for each half hour of studying.

2. **"Homework stresses me out."** Make a list of everything you have to do and take a good look at it. Circle the stuff that has to get done by the next day. Then, next to each item left on your list, write the day of the week you can get it done. If you stick to your plan, you'll get through it all just fine. To relieve stress while you're doing your homework, take breaks and do something physical or nutty—stand on your head!

3. **"I've got to cram for tomorrow's exam and I don't think I can get it done."** You're right, you can't. If you've been procrastinating (look it up!), now's the time to pay the piper. Which doesn't mean the world is ending. For tomorrow's test, try to learn part of the material as well as you can. Try dividing the work in half and concentrating on the half you already know best. And let this be a lesson!

4. **"I'm not motivated."** Chances are, you have no goals yet and therefore can't see where your education fits into your future. It's time to get some goals! Talk to people who have interesting jobs to find out if any of them are right for you. Talk to the career counselor at school and surf the Web just to see what opportunities are out there. For getting your homework done, though, you'll need some short-term goals that have nothing to do with schoolwork. For instance, promise yourself some new CDs if you can get through this week's math mountain.

5. **"There's this one subject that I'm completely confused about because my grandmother was sick so I had to go to Vermont with my mother, so I missed some days of school and couldn't make up the work right away because my father's car was stolen so I couldn't get a ride to school and the bus people are on strike. It wasn't my fault!"** The first thing you need to do is start taking responsibility for this mess. When college advisers look at your test scores, they're not going to want to hear about Granny and that testy transmission. Talk to your teacher and 'fess up about just how behind you are. Ask for help in making a plan to catch up. Think about getting the homework e-mailed to you or dropped off by a friend the next time you miss school.

6. **"I can't get organized."** Organized isn't something you get to be in a day; it takes an investment of your time, and once you have a system set up, you need to maintain it. Start by getting rid of the clutter—the note your best friend passed you in study hall about who was out of school today; the lunch forms that never got filled out—all the junk. Then organize the rest of it. Each subject should have its own notebook or section of your binder. Classroom handouts should be neatly inserted in your binder (buy a hole punch). You should have files at home for stuff you need to keep but that you don't need to be carrying around (most important, old tests). Get a notebook just for making lists—of what needs to be done by tomorrow, the next day, the next week, and so on. Consult your organizational system regularly, and you'll know exactly where you belong at any time. Think of it as a map to your future.

7. **"I work. I don't have time for homework."** Yes, you do. Make a list of your priorities. Your education should be way up there above saving up for the dirt bike you've been dreaming about since you were 10. Get a time-planner or a desk agenda and start making appointments for yourself—an appointment to do homework, an appointment to work, an appointment for chores, etc. If there's simply not enough time for everything, then it's probably time to streamline your life in some way. You're going to have to cut back somewhere, but eliminating homework is not an option.

8. **"I was doing fine in this subject and then something happened, and now I'm lost."** You probably missed something along the way. Learning is like building blocks. You start with a foundation and grow from there. If you've been skipping assignments, it's no wonder you're lost. Go back to a place in your text before you got "lost." Review something you already know well and move ahead from there. You should also think about getting a tutor, especially if finals are approaching and there's not a lot of time.

9. **"My house is like a zoo. I can't study there."** Then find someplace else to study. Go to the library or offer to monitor study hall for extra credit after school. As for your noisy sibs, try negotiating with them—two hours of quiet each night in exchange for two hours with your X-Box on the weekend. If all else fails, try earplugs.

10. "I like doing homework, but I get easily distracted." You need a routine. You should be doing your homework every day at the same time and in the same place. Before you begin, gather everything you'll need—books, pencils, references, even snacks if you get hungry. Forget the phone. When you start doing your homework, tackle the hard stuff first. Stick to your routine. Take fewer study breaks and keep them short. Don't play video games on your break. Do something that will help you concentrate—like some stretching exercises or resting with your eyes closed.

11. "I'm good at this subject, but I'm such a slow reader that it takes me forever." Most people can double their reading speed *and improve their comprehension* by adopting a few simple habits. For one thing, you can try to avoid "saying" the words in your head when you read. Since your brain thinks faster than your mouth can move, you'll be able to cover a lot more ground. Also, make it a habit to read everything twice—once quickly, just to get an idea of the subject, and then a second time, more carefully and thoroughly. But the best way of all to improve reading speed is to practice, practice, practice. The more you do it, the faster you'll get. It doesn't matter if you're reading textbooks, comics, or cereal boxes, just as long as you spend some time reading *every day*.

12. "I hate homework." Just do it.

21 Tips for Getting Good Grades on Tests

Tests to get into schools, tests to get jobs, tests to take other tests! Do they ever end? No.

1. When studying for a test, read the material straight through, then go back and read it again. This time, underline important points. Circle words that you're unfamiliar with. When you do your final review, pay special attention to these terms.

2. Never wait until the last minute to study for a test; you'll panic. The best time to study is two days before. Then, the night before, review the material and get a good night's sleep.

3. Divide the test material in half and team up with a friend.

dependently, but get together a few days before the test
urns teaching each other the material you've covered.
study with friends as long as you're really studying.

4. Talk to the teacher a few days before the test. Say you want to make sure you're focusing on the right material and explain your understanding of what will be covered.

5. Keep old tests and use them to study for the new ones. Most teachers ask certain kinds of questions, and you'll be ahead of the game—and a lot less nervous—if you know what to expect. (Here's where older siblings come in handy; if they've taken the course, they can be a great help.) When looking through your own tests, pay special attention to the questions you got wrong. Try to determine the reason for most of the wrong answers. Did you forget to study the material, or did you misunderstand the question? Did you run out of time? Take measures to correct your main problems.

6. A good way to learn something well is to hear it. Read your textbook out loud or try teaching it to someone else.

7. The night before the test, as you fall asleep, picture the important material in your mind. This is when your brain is most open to learning. You'll be surprised how much you can memorize at this time.

8. Your brain needs proper food before a test. Eat a good breakfast if the test is in the morning. If it's in the afternoon, avoid carbohydrates for lunch. See the list of "11 Foods to Eat Before a Test," page 175.

9. Bring everything you think you'll need to the test—pens and pencils, a ruler and calculator if they're appropriate, reference books if they're allowed, and a wristwatch, so you can keep track of the time.

10. Wear comfortable clothes. You'll have an easier time concentrating if you don't feel restricted in any way.

11. Before you go to the classroom to take the test, find a quiet spot and review the important material again. Last call!

12. Get to the classroom early so you're ready when the test begins. Don't sit near friends who might distract you.

13. When you read the test instructions, do so slowly and thoroughly. Make sure you have all the pages you're supposed to have. If you don't understand something, ask for help right away. Make sure you know whether there will be a penalty for guessing.

14. Take your time on the test, and use all the time allotted. Consult your watch often.

15. To deal with nervousness, take deep breaths and try to picture yourself leaving the classroom when the test is over. Think of how relieved you'll feel.

16. Answer the easy questions first. This will help you build your confidence. If you can't answer a question, put an X in the margin and go on to the next one. You'll come back to it at the end.

17. In true-false questions, remember that if part of the statement is false, the *whole* statement is false.

18. In matching columns of phrases with each other, cross them out as you connect them. Then deal with the leftovers by process of elimination.

19. With multiple-choice questions, try to recall the answer before you read the choices. Then, as you read the choices, immediately cross out the answers you're sure are wrong.

20. For essay questions, make a short outline of your answer before you write the essay. State your main point in the first sentence; get right to the point.

21. If you've memorized lots of details for the test, write down the ones you think you may forget as soon as the test starts.

11 Foods to Eat Before a Test

These foods won't make you smarter, but studies show they can help keep you alert by fighting the effects of carbohydrates (candy, bread, sugar), which tend to make you more calm or sleepy.

1. Fish
2. Turkey breast
3. Skim milk
4. Low-fat yogurt
5. Lean beef
6. Nuts, especially peanuts
7. Broccoli
8. Apples
9. Pears
10. Peaches
11. Grapes

10 Exercises for Your Brain

Your brain, like all the other parts of you, needs exercise to function well. Here are some alternatives to zoning out.

1. Picture your house. Draw a mental map of all the rooms. Now try to rearrange the rooms so that your house is completely different.

2. Think about how many windows there are in your house. How many doors? How many chairs? Closets?

3. Recite tongue-twisters.

4. Read a magazine article and try to work three facts you have learned into your conversation that day.

5. Think up a new ending for your favorite book or movie.

6. Write down a word that has more than 15 letters and see how many smaller words you can make from it.

7. Memorize a poem.

8. Make a copy of a crossword puzzle. Work on one copy of it and time yourself. When you're done, try to fill in the second copy in half the time.

9. Read your computer instruction manual and teach yourself to do something new without the computer in front of you.

10. List five statements that support something you really believe in, like freedom of speech. Now come up with five arguments against the thing you believe in.

11 Things You Oughta Know About Cheating

1. Cheating makes you a liar.

2. The one who gets hurt most by cheating is you.

3. When you cheat in school, you are denying yourself knowledge and the satisfaction of having gotten a good grade on your own.

4. Just because others are cheating doesn't mean it is okay for you to do so.

5. If you feel the need to cheat in school, it shows that you are weak in that subject. Getting help is a much better way of getting ahead.

6. Cheating on a boyfriend or girlfriend is very uncool. If you don't want to be in an exclusive relationship, you should get out of it.

7. You are not doing anybody a favor by covering up for a cheater.

8. Reasons for cheating are purely selfish. Nobody ever cheats for the sake of another person.

9. Each time you cheat, it becomes easier to cheat again.

10. 'Fessing up for cheating will not only help clear your conscience but will be the first step in regaining your self-respect and the respect of others.

11. When cheaters cheat, everyone is cheated. Especially if it's an exam that will be graded on a curve. The cheater will affect his classmates' grades.

14 Tips if You're Nervous About Public Speaking

If the thought of getting up in front of the classroom sets your palms sweating and your heart pounding, you're not alone. Public speaking is one of the top fears of most adults. Now is a good time to conquer your phobia once and for all. Here are some tips.

1. Organize your thoughts into a simple outline: an introduction, the body of your speech, your final thoughts. Prepare a card for each part of the speech and list the points you will make. You will speak from these notes. Number your cards so if you drop them, you can put them back in order easily.

2. One of the biggest mistakes people make in a speech is trying to cover too much information. When you plan your speech, count on making only three or four main points in the body.

3. Practice—but don't overdo it. Deliver your talk in front of the mirror a few times, then just concentrate on learning your notes. If you practice too much, you'll sound overrehearsed and insincere.

4. Don't be afraid to use humor, which draws in your audience. Another way to do that is to start out with a (rhetorical) question, such as "What do you think it was like to be the first man on the moon?" Your real purpose here is to give them a reason to listen.

5. When you're talking, try to scan the room so that you've made eye contact with most of the people (or at least a few in each section in a large auditorium). If you're too scared to look at all of them or if this distracts you, find a friendly face somewhere in the center of the room and focus on that person. As you get more comfortable, start glancing at the people sitting around that person. If you *really* can't bring yourself to look at anyone, look at the spaces just above their heads; you'll appear to be looking at the person behind them.

6. If you make a mistake, don't make a big deal about it; you may wind up calling attention to an error no one else has noticed. If it's a big, obvious mistake, like your brain goes dead and you suddenly forget your last name, just take a few deep breaths, smile at the audience, say "Excuse me," take a deep breath, and resume your talk. They'll relax if you appear to be back in control.

7. When you're talking, think of someone you know who is confident and would do this perfectly. Pretend you are that person.

8. Use normal language; be yourself. Don't use words if you're not completely sure of their pronunciation and meaning. Your audience will forgive you if you're nervous, but not if you come looking like you're trying to be someone you're not.

9. Talk just a little slower than you think you need to. Everyone tends to rush. Speak loudly and clearly. Your voice has to be loud enough to be heard by the person sitting farthest away.

10. If your friends try to make you laugh while you're speaking, smile at them briefly and don't look at them again.

11. Smile. A lot.

12. Don't sway when you speak.

13. Don't put your hands in your pockets. Use them to gesture, but only if these movements feel natural. If you tend to fidget, keep your hands at your sides and pinch your index fingers and thumbs tightly to remind yourself to keep still.

14. Remember that your audience wants you to succeed.

11 Tips for Tutors

These tips can make the difference between a good tutor and a great tutor.

1. Spend some time with your student and find out what makes him tick—what his expectations are, what really interests him, and what fears he might have.

2. Find out what skills your student already has before you begin teaching new ones.

3. If you can, talk to your student's teacher to find out how you can be most helpful.

4. Review the course material. Get a copy of your student's textbook if you can.

5. Keep track of the progress your student is making. Get exam results and go over the questions your student missed.

6. Don't just give answers or solve problems while the student watches. Ask her leading questions that will help her solve the problems alone.

7. Your teaching sessions should never be interrupted. No phone calls. No food. A bathroom break is okay.

8. Be patient and pleasant. This will help give your student the confidence she needs.

9. Never raise your voice to a student.

10. Always be enthusiastic and encourage your student to succeed. When they do well, cheer them on. Your basic pep talk.

11. Always exhibit ethical and professional behavior. This is, after all, a job.

11 Tips for Looking Good in Your School Picture

1. Wear something that makes you feel like *you*.

2. Wear a solid color but not white or black. Also, avoid shiny fabrics and buttons. Deep colors like navy or red, pastels, and denim usually photograph well.

3. Avoid hair ornaments or a lot of jewelry. Barrettes should be small and unobtrusive.

4. Wear whatever makeup you wear normally. (If you don't wear any, check out the list of "7 Makeup Tips for Girls Who Don't Wear Makeup," page 38.) If your face is shiny in places, a thin application of face powder will give you a softer look. (Guys, too!)

5. This is the worst time possible to try out that blue mohawk you've been contemplating. Wear your hair the way you normally do.

6. If you get a zit, try covering it up with some light foundation that matches your skin tone. Too much will make it look like you tried—unsuccessfully—to cover up a zit.

7. Stand (or sit up) straight.

8. Don't fidget.

9. Practice your smile, especially if you wear braces.

10. Don't blink during the flash. (Good luck.)

11. Relax.

5 Common Scholarship Scam Come-ons

Legitimate scholarship programs don't go looking for you. If a company approaches you claiming that it can help you get scholarships and uses any of the following phrases, avoid it at all costs. At some point, when you're asked for your credit card number, you'll *know* you're being taken.

1. "This scholarship is guaranteed or your money back."

2. "You can't get this information anywhere else."

3. "We do all the work."

4. "You have been selected by a national foundation."

5. "You're a finalist!"

6 Ways to Get Money for College

1. Grants and scholarships. This is money that doesn't have to be repaid. There are tons of scholarships available that are awarded not only for scholarly merit but also to various minorities and families with special hardships. Find them at www.fastweb.com or www.fastaid.com.

2. Subsidized federal Stafford loan. The government lends money to needy students. There's no interest here; the government pays it for you.

3. Unsubsidized federal loans. These are available to all students, but interest (7.5%) accrues, and you have to start paying it back within 6 months after you graduate from college.

4. Perkins loan. This is a subsidized loan that you get directly from the college, with an interest rate of only 5%.

5. Plus loan. The government lends you enough money to make up the difference between the financial aid you've received and the actual college costs.

6. Work-study programs. The college gives you a job and takes your paycheck in exchange for tuition.

15 Fun Things You Shouldn't Do on the First Day of Class

If you want to still have friends on the second day, don't do any of these:

1. Introduce yourself to the class as "the master of disaster."

2. Ask all your questions in rap form.

3. Wear a scarf and gloves to class, and every few minutes ask the teacher to turn up the heat.

4. Stand up while holding up your textbook and say, "COOL!"

5. Sit in the front and wink at your teacher whenever you make eye contact.

6. In the middle of a lecture, ask your teacher if he can explain where babies come from.

7. Present your teacher with a list of your demands.

8. Take photos of your teacher during class. Be sure to use flash bulbs.

9. When your teacher turns on his laser pointer, scream, "USE THE FORCE!"

10. Address the teacher as "your worship."

11. Spend the lecture blowing kisses to an imaginary audience.

12. Stand up to ask a question. Curtsey before sitting down.

13. Shout "NO WAY!" after every sentence of the lecture.

14. Interrupt every few minutes to ask the teacher, "Can you spell that?"

15. Every 10 minutes or so ask the teacher, "Will that be on the test?"

5.
THAT'S
ENTERTAINMENT

The 7 Worst TV Moms

Those grumpy, bossy, annoying mothers are great as comedians, but could you possibly live with them? After checking out these moms, you might never complain about yours again.

1. Claudia, *Grounded for Life*. Ever since Claudia got pregnant after high school, she and her husband have been "grounded for life." As the mother of your typical dysfunctional TV family, she really has no concern for her brood at all. She's a reckless woman who's broken into her daughter Lily's private e-mail, robbed a dry cleaner's, and argued with a nun. And to top it all off, she's known as the neighborhood "hot mom." TV may have some great maternal role models, but Claudia sure isn't one of them.

2. Endora, *Bewitched*. You've heard of husbands thinking their mothers-in-law are witches. Well, Darrin's mother-in-law, Endora, is the real thing. Stubborn and stern, Endora is always furious that her witch daughter, Samantha, married a mortal, and she calls him names like Durwood or Dum Dum. She casts spells on him when she's mad and obsesses about every aspect of Samantha and Darrin's life. She continually pops up in their house unexpectedly.

3. Estelle Costanza, *Seinfeld*. As George Costanza's mother, Estelle is a loud, grouchy mom who loves her son but makes his life miserable. She always frets about George's life and complains that she's never been able to brag about him. She fights with her husband incessantly and is always unhappy.

4. Gale Leery, *Dawson's Creek*. Gale is certainly not a respectable mother. As a married woman and TV anchor, she had an affair with her co-anchor behind her husband's back. And worse, her son Dawson saw the cheating couple kissing. Not exactly the right way to teach your family good values.

5. Lois, *Malcolm in the Middle*. As the mother of four reckless boys, Lois is known for her short temper and cruel punishments. For instance, when she found her anniversary dress burned and thrown in the toilet, she forced her sons Reese and Malcolm to stand as close together as possible in a corner while her youngest son, Dewey, had a gas problem. Then they had to spin around several times with baseball bats to their foreheads and crawl under the couch, which was infested with rotting food, bugs, and piles of dirt. Suddenly, being grounded sounds like paradise.

6. Peg Bundy, *Married with Children*. Peg Bundy refuses to cook for her family, clean the house, or do laundry. She won't get a job and spends most of her time sitting at home eating bonbons and watching the Home Shopping Network. Dressed in her high-heeled shoes and slutty outfits, she wobbles around the house whining and complaining. Peggy Bundy is a lousy mother with only one good quality: she sure knows her stuff when it comes to shopping!

7. Roseanne Conner, *Roseanne*. Overweight and crotchety, Roseanne defined a new generation of dysfunctional moms. She groaned and whined her way through motherhood and constantly greeted her two daughters with either a complaint or an insult. Roseanne actually loved her family deeply; she just had a weird way of showing it.

The 11 Best TV Moms

These are the moms you don't have to come home to—they come home to you. Just turn on your TV, and they're there with smiling faces, clean homes, and meat and potatoes ready on the dinner table. These are the mothers we all grew up with and sometimes dreamed about. They know how to settle arguments, raise kids properly, and always say the right thing. Well, what do you expect? They had scriptwriters to help them out. Where are those scriptwriters when *we* need them?

1. Amy Gray, *Judging Amy*. Amy Gray's character in *Judging Amy* represents the struggles of today's single career mothers. After a divorce, Amy left New York City with her daughter for a judgeship in her Connecticut hometown. After moving in with her own mother, she experienced the constant everyday battles a mom must face. As Amy plays her many roles of mother, daughter, and professional, she tackles difficult day-to-day problems such as finding alternative care for a sick child and dealing with the guilt of working outside the home. A far cry from June Cleaver.

2. Carol Brady, *The Brady Bunch*. Raising six kids isn't easy, but Carol managed to do it with such Brady ease. From cute little Cindy to whiny Jan to hormone-racing Greg, Carol loved all her kids and raised them with good, wholesome family values. She was always there to settle arguments between the kids, exchange a few laughs with housekeeper Alice, and wait with a pretty dress and a warm smile for loving hubby Mike to come home at the end of the day.

3. June Cleaver, *Leave It to Beaver*. Although June Cleaver wasn't the most exciting TV mom, she had that vintage beauty about her that made you just want to stay at home with your TV dinner and curl up in your fuzzy duster. As a 1950s homemaker, she set the standard of what a mother should be for many other TV moms—and real moms, too. She always looked nice, had pork chops or meatloaf on the table, and made sure that Beaver was properly behaved. June Cleaver was neither a career mom nor a strong, tough, independent role model, but she kept the family together, the house clean, and everyone happy.

4. Laura Petrie, *The Dick Van Dyke Show*. Good ol' Laura Petrie, the dutiful wife of Rob Petrie, always kept the family together. She was the one who encouraged Rob to stand up at his job. She was also the one who helped her son Ritchie grow into a good little boy. And she always looked spiffy. But Laura wasn't all bunny rabbits and candy canes. She opened the door to a female fashion revolution with her beatnik-black stirrup stretch pants, a trend that became a fad among the housewives of America. Smart, wholesome, and sexy, Laura was a supermom of the '60s.

5. Lily Samler, *Once and Again*. In one episode, Lily's teen daughter Grace says to her mother one night, "You're a good sister, Mom. I just think you should know that before you go to sleep." *Once and Again* is a show about two families brought together through a second marriage. After her divorce, Lily falls into a hot and steamy relationship with Rick Sammler, who also gets a divorce and becomes her new handsome hubby. But after Lily's daughter walks in on an intimate moment between the couple, Lily tries hard to maintain her role as mother while preserving a loving relationship with her kids. Lily's character shows what it's like to be a 40-year-old woman, still holding some of the same emotions and desires of her youth while remaining a strong and devoted mother.

6. Lorelei Gilmore, *Gilmore Girls.* Lorelei Gilmore isn't perfect, even though she looks it. She was a teenager when she had her daughter, Rory, and chose to raise her on her own. This difficult decision caused a dramatic need for independence and resulted in a falling-out between her and her wealthy parents. Because of her youth, good looks, and close relationship with her teen daughter, people think they're sisters. They're nearly best friends, though, which is close enough. And despite Lorelei's escapades, she still tries to keep her home a loving and friendly environment for Rory and give her a "proper" upbringing.

7. Lucy Ricardo, *I Love Lucy.* Yeah, Lucy, played by Lucille Ball, stayed home, cooked, cleaned the house, and took care of Little Ricky all at once, but there was more to her 1950s demeanor. Loud, funny, and always trying to steal the spotlight from her husband, Ricky, she was one of the first TV moms to yearn for more than housewifery. Whether she was juggling chocolates on a conveyor belt, starring in a "Vitavetavegimin" commercial, or stomping grapes, she kept us laughing while she became America's most ironic role model.

8. Marge Simpson, *The Simpsons.* When your husband swallows a hallucinogenic chili pepper, your son glues a bird beak on his face with Krazy Glue, and your daughter paints green oatmeal all over her father and brother, you need a mom in control. Marge Simpson is definitely the perfect mom for the not-so-perfect family. Mother of three (or four, including hubby Homer), she stays calm and rational while establishing good family values. Although she may not have perfect hair and a topnotch career, she loves her family despite their shortcomings and keeps the house spotless. Marge Simpson represents the best of the stay-at-home moms.

9. Murphy Brown, *Murphy Brown.* In 1992, when America's favorite TV career woman decided to have her baby out of wedlock, Murphy became one of the most famous sitcom single mothers in history. The ratings soared, especially after our vice president at the time, Dan Quayle, said, "It doesn't help matters when prime-time TV has Murphy Brown, a character who supposedly epitomizes today's intelligent, highly paid professional woman, mocking the importance of fathers by bearing a child alone and calling it just another lifestyle choice." Despite the controversy, Murphy ended up raising a bright young boy (possibly even brighter than Dan Quayle).

10. Roseanne Conner, *Roseanne*. Here's living proof that everyone has a good side and a bad side. Roseanne made our list of "The Worst TV Moms" (page 184), but she belongs here as well. As brusque and sarcastic as she was, Roseanne always tried to tell her kids the truth about everything. She was no hypocrite—if she didn't like someone, she let them know. She also knew the value of a sense of humor and let everyone in the family know that love and a family bond are more important than the money problems the family was always facing. She taught her kids to care about others and demonstrated it by letting Darlene's boyfriend David move in with them when he had no home of his own.

11. Shirley Partridge, *The Partridge Family*. Shirley Partridge, a widowed mother of five, skilled guitar player, and member of the family pop band, could keep the family's fame-driven career intact and still have time to make them lunch. As Mom on the *Partridge Family*, the popular '70s sitcom, Shirley established her supermom role while other TV mothers were still submissive. Confident and talented, Shirley had what it takes to be a supermom superstar.

Matt Groening's Top 10 Episodes of The Simpsons

10. "There's No Disgrace Like Home," Season 1. In this episode, the family tries shock therapy with Dr. Marvin Monroe. My favorite quote is Homer's saying, "When will I learn? The answers to life's problems aren't at the bottom of a bottle. They're on TV!"

9. "Krusty Gets Busted," Season 1. Sideshow Bob commits his first crime when he frames Krusty for a robbery at the Kwik-E-Mart. I love Krusty's terrible slogan for his literacy campaign: "Give a hoot! Read a book!"

8. "Natural Born Kissers," Season 9. Homer and Marge rekindle their passion by getting intimate in public or in dangerous situations. My favorite shot in this episode occurs in the bed-and-breakfast: the maid walks in on Homer and Marge, causing Homer to cover his nipples with teacups.

7. "Treehouse of Horror VII," Season 8. Bart discovers Hugo, his evil twin, Lisa creates a higher form of life, and Kang and Kodos morph into Bob Dole and Bill Clinton. My favorite quote is Marge's opinion of Clinton after Kodos says, "I am Clin-Ton. As overlord, all will kneel trembling before me and obey my brutal commands. End communication." Marge responds, "Hmm, that's Slick Willie for you, always with the smooth talk."

6. "Homer's Enemy," Season 8. A new employee, Frank Grimes, becomes bitter when he sees how successful a boob like Homer can be. This is a favorite episode among most fans as well. Frank is a dose of reality in the world of Springfield, which makes his observations hysterical.

5. "In Marge We Trust," Season 8. Marge offers her sympathetic ear when Reverend Lovejoy gives up on his parish. Also, Homer discovers that Mr. Sparkle, a character on a Japanese soapbox, bears his own likeness. I love the completely politically incorrect way the writers depict Japanese businessmen. It's a parody on the stereotypes Americans believe to be true.

4. "A Streetcar Named Marge," Season 4. Marge takes the part of Blanche Dubois in Springfield's musical version of *A Streetcar Named Desire*. My favorite moment is Apu's singing as the newspaper boy.

3. "Much Apu About Nothing," Season 7. Homer jumps on the anti-immigration bandwagon before realizing Apu will be deported. The episode pokes fun at our own insecurities as a country.

2. "Life on the Fast Lane," Season 1. Marge flirts with her bowling instructor, Jacques, when Homer gives her a bowling ball for her birthday. My favorite moment is the *Officer and a*

Gentleman parody, when Homer says he's going to take Marge to the back seat of his car and he won't be back "for ten whole minutes."

1. **"Bart the Daredevil," Season 2.** After seeing Captain Lance Murdoch perform (barely) death-defying feats at the Springfield Speedway, Bart becomes a daredevil himself. My favorite moment in this episode is when Homer realizes he's not going to make it across the gorge.

40 Things That Bart Simpson Has Written on the Blackboard at the Beginning of <u>The Simpsons</u>

1. They are laughing at me, not with me.
2. I will not fake my way through life.
3. I will not call my teacher "Hot Cakes."
4. I will not encourage others to fly.
5. I will not Xerox my butt.
6. I will not instigate a revolution.
7. I will not draw naked ladies in class.
8. I did not see Elvis.
9. I will not trade pants with others.
10. I will not drive the principal's car.
11. I will not sell school property.
12. Spitwads are not free speech.
13. A burp is not an answer.
14. I will not belch the National Anthem.
15. I will not grease the monkey bars.
16. I will not hide behind the Fifth Amendment.
17. Hamsters cannot fly.
18. I am not a dentist.
19. Underwear should be worn on the inside.
20. I will not expose the ignorance of the faculty.
21. I will not conduct my own fire drills.
22. Goldfish don't bounce.
23. I will not eat things for money.
24. I will not yell "She's Dead" during roll call.
25. I will not barf unless I'm sick.

26. I will not carve gods.
27. I will not aim for the head.
28. I will not snap bras.
29. This punishment is not boring and pointless.
30. My name is not Dr. Death.
31. The principal's toupee is not a Frisbee.
32. Mud is not one of the four food groups.
33. I will not sell miracle cures.
34. I do not have diplomatic immunity.
35. I am not authorized to fire substitute teachers.
36. The Pledge of Allegiance does not end with "Hail Satan."
37. Garlic gum is not funny.
38. I will not do anything bad ever again.
39. "Bart Bucks" are not legal tender.
40. I will finish what I star

25 Answers to TV Trivia Questions

1. Leland Palmer.
   (Who killed Laura Palmer on *Twin Peaks?*)
2. *My So-Called Life.*
   (On what show did Clare Danes get her start?)
3. Mark, Randy, and Bradley.
   (What are the names of the three sons on *Home Improvement?*)
4. Malibu Sands Beach Club.
   (What was the name of the beach club where the gang hung out on *Saved by the Bell?*)
5. $7,000.
   (On *Friends,* what did Phoebe promise to give Chandler to stop smoking?)
6. Minnesota.
   (On *Beverly Hills 90210,* where did the Walshes live before they moved to Beverly Hills?)
7. The Gate.
   (What was the name of the magazine on *Suddenly Susan?*)
8. Cochran.
   (What was Uncle Jesse's last name on *Full House* before it became Katsopolis?)

9. Hoëk and Cadoogan.
(What are Ren and Stimpy's last names?)

10. *Cheers.*
(From what show did *Frasier* spin off?)

11. Geoffrey.
(What was the name of the butler on *Fresh Prince of Bel-Air?*)

12. Optimus Prime.
(Who was the leader of the good Transformers?)

13. Christmas.
(On *Three's Company*, what was "Chrissy" short for?)

14. Flash.
(What was Roscoe's dog's name on *The Dukes of Hazzard?*)

15. Nanoo nanoo.
(What was Mork's signature greeting on *Mork and Mindy?*)

16. Gleek.
(What was the monkey's name on *The SuperFriends?*)

17. Vicki.
(What was the name of the robot girl on *Small Wonder?*)

18. Milk and Pepsi.
(What were Laverne and Shirley's favorite drinks?)

19. "Hey you guys!"
(How did *The Electric Company* start each episode?)

20. Raquel and Trevor Achmanic.
(Who lived next door to ALF?)

21. Apollo and Zeus.
(What were the names of the dogs on *Magnum P.I.?*)

22. Kirk and Candace Cameron.
(Name the siblings who starred in *Growing Pains* and *Full House*, respectively.)

23. Martha Quinn, J. J. Jackson, Mark Goodman, Alan Hunter, Nina Blackwood.
(Who were the first five DJs on MTV?)

24. Chuck Cunningham.
(What was the name of the older brother you rarely saw on *Happy Days?*)

25. Wily Kit and Wily Kat.
(Name the twins on *The Thundercats*.)

The Real Names of the X-Men

Cyclops	Scott Summers
Wolverine	Logan
Storm	Oro Munroe
Jubilee	Jubilation Lee
Gambit	Remy LeBeau
Beast	Dr. Hank McCoy
Professor X	Professor Charles Xavier
Nightcrawler	Kurt Loder

Mistakes in 12 of Your Favorite Flicks

Although millions of dollars were spent on each of the following films, mistakes abound (as they do in just about all films). When you watch a movie, use your *whole* brain to find them. These are just a few examples.

1. *Almost Famous* (2000). It's 1969, and William is looking through a stack of record albums his sister has given him. The collection includes Joni Mitchell's *Blue,* which wasn't released until 1971. Similarly, the airplane that Penny Lane flew on when she returned home has small vertical stabilizers on the wingtips—which weren't invented until the early '90s. And when the band is heading toward New York City and crossing a bridge, you can see the famous Citicorps Center, which was built in 1978.

2. *Back to the Future* (1985). The many time inconsistencies here are especially ironic given the nature of the film. Someone clearly was not paying attention to detail. The episode of *The Honeymooners* that Lorraine's parents are watching in 1950 didn't air until 1955; in 1955 Marty plays a Gibson ES-355 guitar, a model that didn't exist until 1959; Marty McFly hears the song "Mr. Sandman" three years before it was released.

3. *Charlie's Angels* (2000). When Cameron Diaz is driving the race car, she hits a red car, which then flips over and hits a blue car. The blue car has no driver. (All the crash dummies must have been on vacation.) When the girls pull into the drive-through to get something to eat, they look at a picture of a thin guy. But when the camera angle changes, the picture has changed.

4. *A Christmas Story* (1983). When the father's "award" arrives, the family gets up to see what it is, leaving dinner on the table. But when you see the table again, all the food and dinnerware have disappeared. When the box is being wheeled into the house, it has a rope around it, but when we see it in the house, the rope is gone. Also, in this scene, when the father is unwrapping the prize, he gets a lot of the packing material on his back. But when he stands up, his back is clean.

5. *Dirty Dancing* (1987). When Johnny gets locked out of his car in the rain, he reaches down to grab a post out of the ground to use to break the window. But it isn't raining where the post is—three feet away. In the scene where Johnny and Baby are driving back from the Sheldrake Hotel, they're speeding along comfortably—quite a trick with the car in Park. Also in this scene, the scenery behind Johnny's head seems to be going backward.

6. *Edward Scissorhands* (1990). When Edward gets locked in the room at Jim's house and the security alarm goes off, the system is deactivated and the door unlocks. But the door opens inward, and Edward could not have unlocked it with his scissorhands. So how did it open? And watch the scene where Edward is cutting Joyce's hair on the lawn. There are clouds in the background. But when we see closer shots of Edward's face, the sky is completely blue. The clouds change dramatically from shot to shot in this scene.

7. *Forrest Gump* (1994). Forrest reads *US Today Magazine* in 1970, but it didn't begin publication until 1982. While Gump is fishing, he picks up a Mello Yello can, but they weren't made at the time; and near the end of the movie, when Forrest visits Jenny, it's supposed to be July 4, 1976. But we see a shot of the Statue of Liberty with a gold torch, and it wasn't painted gold until 10 years later.

8. *Ghostbusters* (1984). In the scene where Gozar is telling the Ghostbusters to choose the form of their destructor, Peter mentions J. Edgar Hoover and says that they need to clear their minds. If he was thinking of J. Edgar Hoover at the time, shouldn't he have showed up instead of the marshmallow guy? And when the eggs are popping out onto the counter in Dana's apartment, if you look closely you can see the levers in the egg carton flipping each one out. When Ray and Winston are driving across the Brooklyn Bridge in the Ectomobile, Ray quotes a verse of Scripture and claims it's from Revelation 7:12. It's actually from Revelation 6:12.

9. *Home Alone 2: Lost in New York* (1992). When Kevin first enters the hotel, he asks where the lobby is and is told go straight ahead and turn left. But in the next shot we see him turning right. And look for the scene when Kevin is throwing bricks at Marv and Harry. If you watch the moment of the first throw in slow motion, you can see that Marv has blood on his forehead before the brick hits him. Finally, when Kevin is running away from the bandits, he drops a string of pearls on an icy corner. But when the bandits slip on them, there are far more pearls than Kevin dropped.

10. *Raiders of the Lost Ark* (1981). When Indy is being dragged underneath the truck, you can see a trench that they must have dug in the ground so he wouldn't scrape his back. When Indy is packing for his trip, Marcus warns him of the great power of the ark, but Indy dismisses him, saying he doesn't believe in all that hocus-pocus. But this movie takes place after *Temple of Doom*. Wasn't he paying attention? And although the movie takes place in the 1930s, there's a map showing Iran and Iraq, which were called Persia at the time.

11. *Romy and Michele's High School Reunion* (1997). When Kristy Masters is onstage talking about everyone's accomplishments, we see a shot of Heather with a stain on the front of her dress. It shouldn't be there, because it's not until the next scene—when Kristy announces that one of the jocks is now with the Dallas Cowboys—that Heather dribbles her beer to show how "impressed" she is. When Ramon's XJS Jaguar is parked outside the reunion, the rearview mirror is missing in a few of the shots. And isn't it weird that when Michele has her dream, she knows exactly what everyone looks like?

12 *Willy Wonka and the Chocolate Factory* (1971). After Augustus Gloop gets sucked away and he and his mother get left behind, the group boards a boat that has only enough seats for the remaining characters. The same thing happens when they get into the sudsy vehicle—now there are even fewer seats. Did Willy Wonka know what was going to happen? Also, when

Charlie is watching TV and hears about the golden tickets for the first time, he turns around to talk to Grandpa Joe. But when he does, the TV is off. And how can they afford a TV but not a loaf of bread?

The 22 Scariest Movies of All Time

1. *Alien* (1979; directed by Ridley Scott). An alien is born on a spaceship and proceeds to pick off the crew one by one. Great suspense from beginning to end, with gut-wrenching violence, slime, and shocking surprises.

2. *The Birds* (1963; directed by Alfred Hitchcock). Local birds wage an all-out war on the people of a small village.

3. *The Blair Witch Project* (1999; directed by Eduardo Sanchez and Daniel Myrick). In the opening titles, we are told that in 1994 three young student filmmakers go into the woods of Burkittsville, Maryland, in search of a legendary witch: "A year later, their footage was found." The film's style and even its production quality lead us to believe that it's a real documentary. One by one, each student is picked off by some ghostly entity. Scary snot scenes.

4. *The Cabinet of Dr. Caligari* (1919; directed by Robert Wiene). One of the most influential films of all time. Dr. Caligari is a magician and hypnotist. His staff includes his henchman Cesare, who unknowingly carries out all of Caligari's evil doings.

5. *Carrie* (1976; directed by Brian de Palma). Based on Stephen King's first novel, this is the story of a shy teenage girl, Carrie White, whose telekinetic powers lead her to exact revenge on her mean classmates and her mom, a religious fanatic.

6. *Diabolique* (1955; directed by Henri-Georges Clouzot). The wife of the headmaster of a school for boys tires of his abusive ways and teams up with his mistress to drown him and make it appear as a suicide.

7. *The Exorcist* (1973; directed by William Friedkin). This film about an innocent young girl who is possessed by an evil demon did more for pea soup than any Campbell's commercial. A true classic.

8. *Halloween* (1978; directed by John Carpenter). Six-year-old Michael Myers stabs his sister, Judith, to death on Halloween. Fifteen years later, he escapes from the institution he had been sent to and returns to his hometown, where he sets his sights on three teenage babysitters and a string of sequels.

9. *The Haunting* (1963; directed by Robert Wise). During a research project to prove the existence of ghosts, Hill House, a large mansion with a long history of violent death and insanity, comes alive. The mysterious and clairvoyant Theodora and the insecure Eleanor (whose psychic abilities seem to open her up to whatever spirits inhabit the old mansion) begin to realize that they have gotten more than they bargained for when the ghostly presence in the house manifests itself in horrific and deadly ways. Based on Shirley Jackson's well-loved book *The Haunting of Hill House*.

10. *Misery* (1990; directed by Rob Reiner). This is a strange tale about a crazed fan who saves her favorite author, then locks him up in her house and tortures him into writing his next novel to her specifications.

11. *The Night of the Living Dead* (1968; directed by George A. Romero). The entire story takes place over the course of one night. It follows the plight of a group of seven people who take refuge in a farmhouse as the horrifying phenomenon of the living dead begins. Named by some as the best fright film ever.

12. *A Nightmare on Elm Street* (1984; directed by Wes Craven). This movie revived the teen horror genre and led to six sequels about Freddy, the burn victim–child killer.

13. *Nosferatu* (1922; directed by F. W. Murnau). This silent film is the very first adaptation of Bram Stoker's *Dracula*. It most closely follows the plot of the book and is possibly the best vampire movie ever made. This vampire is the ugliest one in film history.

14. *Poltergeist* (1982; directed by Tobe Hooper). A family is terrorized by ghostlike entities. The spirits make contact with the family's youngest child, Carol Ann, and abduct her into the spirit realm via their television.

15. *Psycho* (1960; directed by Alfred Hitchcock). The scariest of them all, at least when it was released. A women arrives at the now-infamous Bates Motel, run by Norman Bates, who is obsessed and controlled by his mother. The woman is brutally murdered in the now-classic "shower scene," which kept many kids—and adults—opting for the bathtub for years to follow.

16. *Repulsion* (1965; directed by Roman Polanski). There really aren't many horror films that can compare with this story of an asocial and depressed Belgian girl named Carol who lives in London with her sister. When her sister leaves on vacation with her boyfriend, the dark forces tormenting Carol take over completely, and we see her go totally insane.

17. *Rosemary's Baby* (1968; directed by Roman Polanski). Rosemary is a pregnant young housewife in New York whose actor husband has literally made a deal with the devil. Her pregnancy seems normal until she starts suspecting that the neighbors in her apartment building hold some evil influence over her husband and that her unborn baby is at stake.

18. *Seven* (1995; directed by David Fincher). This mystery-thriller is about a pair of homicide detectives who must solve a puzzling series of murders based on the seven deadly sins. They begin an investigation that draws them deeper into the twisted world of a killer.

19. *The Shining* (1980; directed by Stanley Kubrick). Jack Torrance takes on the job of caretaker of a large Colorado hotel while it is closed during the winter months. Jack's wife and young son, a creepy-looking kid with a psychic gift (called Shining), begin suspecting that Jack is going crazy. They're right.

20. *The Silence of the Lambs* (1991; directed by Jonathan Demme). FBI trainee Clarisse Starling is recruited to attempt to get through to a brilliant psychotic criminal, "Hannibal the Cannibal" Lecter, in the hope that he can help her catch a deranged serial killer.

21. *The Sixth Sense* (1999; directed by M. Night Shyamalan). An 8-year-old sees dead people and is frightened by his paranormal powers. The only person he can speak with is a psychologist, who helps him try to uncover the truth about his supernatural abilities. With scary ghost scenes and a surprise ending, this film is a must.

22. *Suspiria* (1978; directed by Dario Argento). An American ballet student travels to Germany to continue her studies and stumbles across a coven of witches who run the school. Throatrippings, gory stabbings, maggot attacks, hangings, and glass mangling make this one of the goriest films ever. The razor-wire scene is truly intense.

9 Great Coming-of-Age Films

A coming-of-age story is one in which the main character experiences a critical turning point or event that results in a loss of childhood innocence. The movie usually spans only a short period of time, like an evening, weekend, or summer.

The fact that a film is rated R doesn't make it bad for you— it just means that it's probably appropriate for you to discuss its content with an adult who can provide clarification in places. If you can't get into these films on your own, invite your parents along and ask them to sit as far away as humanly possible (just kidding!).

1. *Almost Famous* (R, 2001). This story is told almost entirely through the eyes of 15-year-old William Miller, whose love of rock music completely changes his life when he travels with Stillwater, a '70s rock band. William is a novice journalist who wants to write a great story. His personal involvement with the band and its groupies, though, threatens his ability to tell the truth. Based on the life of writer-director Cameron Crowe.

2. *American Graffiti* (PG, 1973). This is the story of four characters, recent and soon-to-be high school graduates, during one momentous late summer night in 1962. While cruising the streets on a Friday night, the four weave in and out of each other's lives as they make major decisions and confront various traumas. This film started a trend of other popular teen-oriented films and was the first movie to use rock 'n' roll music all through its soundtrack.

3. *Billy Elliot* (R, 2000). An inspiring story of a young boy from a working-class family who finds a passion that will forever change his life. An 11-year-old miner's son, Billy is sent for boxing lessons but stumbles upon a ballet class, which he secretly joins. Billy's talent takes flight, but when his father discovers his son's ambition, Billy must fight for his dreams and his destiny.

4. *Boyz 'N the Hood* (R, 1991). Tre is a good kid growing up amid gangs in the 'hood in East Los Angeles. He becomes sick of gunfire and seeing the lives of his friends ruined by gang violence. With the guidance of his father, Tre observes an unjust world while growing to be a young man of character.

5. *The Breakfast Club* (R, 1985). Five very different high school students are trapped in school detention on a Saturday. They start out hating one anther but in the course of the day discover they share various bonds. In the end, they unite against their evil and corrupt detention principal.

6. *The Karate Kid* (PG, 1984). The story is about a bullied teenager named Daniel overcoming his tormentors and becoming a man under the guidance of the wise, compassionate karate master Mr. Miyagi. The relationship between the boy and his Okinawan handyman teacher is one of the most charming teacher-student relationships on film. Daniel's relationship with his mom is also one of the most realistic portrayals in a mainstream movie.

7. *Rebel Without a Cause* (not rated, 1955). This film portrays rebellious, restless, misunderstood, middle-class American youth. It's the story of three troubled teenagers who struggle with their self-esteem and inability to communicate with their parents. It was the last film for the charismatic cult star James Dean, who died in a tragic car accident the year the film was released.

8. *Stand by Me* (R, 1986). This film, based on a Stephen King novella called *The Body*, is about four friends who travel for two days to find a dead body, discovering themselves along the way.

9. *Welcome to the Dollhouse* (R, 1996). This is the story of Dawn Wiener, an awkward 7th-grader who is taunted by her peers because of her appearance. Even her teachers seem to take great joy in tormenting her. Dawn's older brother is "the king of the geeks," and her parents offer her no support whatsoever. Dawn never triumphs, but she does survive, and we get the feeling that she'll somehow manage the many hurdles that she will no doubt face throughout her life.

16 Great High School Movies

1. *Blackboard Jungle* (not rated, 1955). A teacher in a New York slum school fights to win the respect of his pupils. The teacher faces physical abuse, mental cruelty, and self-doubt, but in the end he somehow manages to get through to these alienated teens. The opening credits are backed by Bill Haley's "Rock Around The Clock," making this the first use of rock music in a feature film.

2. *The Brady Bunch Movie* (PG-13, 1995). Based on the TV show, the movie gives us the big house full of Bradys, living in their '70s innocence in the '90s. Grunge and CDs may be the norm in the '90s, but the Bradys still live in the eight-track world of the '70s. Look for neat cameos from some original Bradys and most of the Monkees.

3. *Buffy the Vampire Slayer* (PG-13, 1992). Buffy is a typical mall teen, concerned with shopping and cheerleading, until a mysterious man proclaims that her destiny is to slay the vampires who have suddenly infested Los Angeles. Buffy takes up the challenge, fighting off the vamps and their seductive leader.

4. *Clueless* (PG-13, 1995). Alicia Silverstone stars as the Beverly Hills mall rat Cher. She is popular, wealthy, and extremely superficial, manipulating her way through life. She lies and sweet-talks her teachers into raising her grades. To Cher, shopping, matchmaking, and makeovers are the keys to a happy life. Can these values lead to happiness? For Cher, anything is possible.

5. *Dead Poets Society* (PG, 1998). An English teacher in a very conservative prep school inspires his students by reading poetry to them. He challenges them to write their own poetry and to seize life every day as if it were their last.

6. *Ferris Bueller's Day Off* (PG-13, 1986). Ferris wants to get away with just one more sick day before he graduates from high school. He sweet-talks his best friend into borrowing his dad's precious Ferrari and sneaks his girlfriend out of class so they can all spend one glorious day of freedom. Their escapades lead to fun, adventure, and almost getting caught. This is one of the funniest high school movies ever.

7. *Hoosiers* (PG, 1986). A new basketball coach comes to town and leads the high school team to a series of victories. He helps make the team—and each person on it—better than they thought possible. A truly inspiring and well-acted film.

8. *Lucas* (PG-13, 1986). This wonderfully sensitive film stars Corey Haim as Lucas, a nerdy 14-year-old kid who skipped two grades and now has a difficult time fitting in with his older classmates. He makes friends and falls in love with Maggie, who is in love with Lucas's jock friend. Lucas is so jealous that he doesn't realize that there is another girl who likes him.

9. *Mr. Holland's Opus* (PG, 1995). Glenn Holland is a musician and composer consumed with a love for music; his life's ambition is to write one memorable piece of music. But instead he finds himself sharing his love of music with his students, and his passion leaves an indelible mark on their lives. He realizes that things don't always turn out the way we planned and that his legacy will be greater than he ever dreamed.

10. *My Bodyguard* (PG, 1980). An undersize high school student fends off attacking bullies by hiring a king-size, withdrawn bully as his bodyguard. Their "business" relationship, however, develops into a true friendship. An adolescent coming-of-age film with more intelligence and sensitivity than most.

11. *Peggy Sue Got Married* (PG-13, 1986). This comedy is about an unhappily married woman who falls unconscious at her 25th high school reunion and awakes as an 18-year-old back in high school in 1960, so she gets the chance to do it all over again.

12. *Rock 'n' Roll High School* (PG, 1979). Featuring the music of the Ramones, this high-energy cult classic is about a high school out to thwart the principal at every turn. Songs include "Teenage Lobotomy," "Blitzkrieg Bop," "I Wanna Be Sedated," and the classic title track "Rock 'n' Roll High School" among others.

13. *Sixteen Candles* (PG, 1984). This hilarious comedy of errors features Molly Ringwald as an awkward teen who's been dreaming of her 16th birthday. But the excitement of her sister's wedding causes everyone to forget it, and her birthday becomes her worst nightmare.

14. *Stand and Deliver* (PG, 1988). This is the true story of Jaime Escalante, an engineer from Bolivia who leaves the business world to become a teacher. His students are the youth of L.A.'s barrio, and he uses unorthodox methods to inspire them to learn.

15. *Teaching Mrs. Tingle* (PG-13, 1999). A sadistic English teacher unjustly accuses one of her students of cheating. Leigh Ann and her friends go to Mrs. Tingle's house to plead their case and beg for mercy, but the heartless witch refuses to listen to them. During a struggle, Mrs. Tingle is knocked out, and the teens come up with a plan to exact revenge.

16. *To Sir, With Love* (not rated, 1967). A black high school teacher has a difficult time connecting with his white British students. It's only after he tosses their schoolbooks aside and teaches them how to survive in the real world that his connection with them is complete. The title song, "To Sir, With Love," by Lulu (who appears in the film), was a huge hit.

10 Stupid Things to Ask a Videoshop Assistant

1. "What kind of movies do you have?"

2. "Just how long is 'The Never Ending Story'?"

3. "I kept the original tape. Is it OK if I just return a copy?"

4. "Can you help me? I'm looking for something I haven't seen?"

5. "Do you have a machine to erase subtitles?"

6. "Can I watch this here?"

7. "Do you have a version of *Titanic* with a happy ending?"

8. "Can you help me to stop my VCR from blinking twelve o'clock all the time?"

9. "Do you have anything funny?"

10. "Do you have (insert title currently playing at the movie theater)?"

5 Former Members of the Mickey Mouse Club

In 1989, Disney decided to bring back its popular children's show with an *All-New Mickey Mouse Club* in a format similar to that of the original series from the 1950s. The variety show featured an MTV-like atmosphere of energetic singers and dancers. All of the following wore ears.

1. Christina Aguilera
2. J. C. Chasez, of 'N Sync
3. Justin Timberlake, of 'N Sync
4. *Felicity*'s Keri Russell
5. Britney Spears

The Best Manga for Teens

Manga, Japanese comic books, are a huge industry in Japan, with thousands of titles available for all ages and tastes; many of them have been translated into English. Gilles Poitras, the author of *The Anime Companion: What's Japanese in Japanese Animation,* a guide to many cultural details found in anime and manga, has selected some of the best manga for teens. If you are a manga or anime fan and want to know more about this fascinating art form, visit Gilles's Web site, www. koyagi.com.

1. *Astro Boy,* by Tezuka Osamu (Dark Horse Comics), series. Tezuka's classic story of a robot boy. While this manga was written for children, it is surprisingly sophisticated and deals with issues of discrimination, war, and dignity.

2. *Domu,* by Otomo Katsuhiro (Dark Horse Comics), 1 vol. The first manga to receive the top prize for science fiction in Japan, this is an extremely beautiful work by one of the best manga artists, who is also the author of *Akira* and *Roujin Z. Domu* involves a psychic battle between two inhabitants of a large apartment complex, one who has secretly brought misery to the other inhabitants for years and the other out to stop these crimes.

3. *Fushigi Yugi,* by Watase Yu (Viz Communications). Miaka is struggling to get into an exclusive high school (in Japan you have to take entrance exams for high school). An incident happens when she is in a special collection at the National Library of Japan, and she finds herself in another world, a world very much like ancient China. She is recognized as the priestess of Suzaku, and to get home she must bring together seven he-

roes. The gathering proves to be a daunting task with many emotional consequences. One of the heroes is gay and very sympathetically portrayed.

4. *Hina,* by Akamatsu Ken (Tokyopop Press), series. When he was a child, Keitaro and a girl promised they would get into the highly prestigious Tokyo University and meet again. Keitaro keeps failing the entrance exams and refuses to give up, to the point that he moves to his grandmother's inn after an argument with his parents. But he has not been there in years, and he quickly, and embarrassingly, discovers that not only has his grandmother gone on a long trip but the inn is now a hostel for young women. His aunt, who has her own business, tells him—over the objections of many of the women—that he can be the caretaker.

5. *Nausicaä of the Valley of the Wind,* by Miyazaki (HayaoViz Communications). The only manga series from the internationally famous director Miyazaki. The story began in the 1980s but sat unfinished for a decade until fan pressure convinced Miyazaki to complete the tale. This is the story of Nausicaä, a young princess who finds herself and her small kingdom caught up in a war between larger empires.

6. *Neon Genesis Evangelion,* by Sadamoto Yoshiyuki (Viz Communications), series. This manga is based on the highly acclaimed TV series from Gainax, aimed at an older audience. It is a science fiction extravaganza that is more about human feelings and trust than dealing with some very alien attackers.

7. *Peach Girl, v. 1,* by Uena Miwa (Tokyopop Press). Momo is a high school girl with a problem: she tans very easily, and in Japan tans are a style popular among girls who have a reputation for loose morals. She also once heard that Toji, the boy she has a crush on, does not like tanned girls. By avoiding the sun as much as she can and applying lots of sunblock, she has managed to lighten her skin, but she is on the swimming team, which means she still gets a certain amount of exposure to sunlight. Another set of problems turns up. Kiley, the school playboy, has his eye on her, and Sae, who hangs out a lot with Momo, has her eye on Toji and is willing to play very dirty to get him.

8. *Ranma,* by Takahashi Rumiko (Viz Communications). The third and most successful anime series adaptation of a

Takahashi Rumiko manga series. Ranma is a young martial artist who has had an unfortunate accident. Akane is Ranma's fiancé, the result of an arrangement between their fathers. Much of the story is about how these two strong-willed children deal with the situation they find themselves in.

9. *Short Program,* by Adachi Mitsuru (Viz Communications), 1 vol. Adachi is a master storyteller, and this collection of short tales is an excellent example of his work. These are wondrous glimpses into important moments in the lives of the characters as well as into human interactions in Japanese society.

10. *Spirit of Wonder,* by Tsuruta Kenji (Viz Communications). Tsuruta is known for producing very few manga, but people don't mind, as the quality of his work is so high. This volume is a series of tales about a young Chinese woman who has inherited her family restaurant in a British coastal town. Her lodgers provide income but also trouble for the young "Miss China," which means entertainment for us. There is also a Spirit of Wonder anime available.

12 Magazines That Publish Teen Writing

1. *BlueJean* is devoted to publishing what young women are thinking, saying, and doing. Accepts submissions of writing, artwork, photography, comics, crafts, and original music from girls ages 13–24.

    c/o Blue Jean Media
    1115 E. Main St.
    P.O. Box 60
    Rochester, NY 14609
    716-288-6980
    www.bluejeanonline.com

2. *The Concord Review* is a quarterly journal of essays written by history students. Started in 1987, it publishes essays (average, 5,000 words) on a wide variety of topics by secondary school students.

    P.O. Box 661
    Concord, MA 01742
    800-331-5007 or 978-443-0022)
    www.tcr.org

3. *Creative Kids* publishes stories, poetry, plays, and photography by kids for kids, 5–18. Get this magazine to find out what really talented kids are up to.

P.O. Box 8813

Waco, TX 76714

800-998-2208

www.prufrock.com/mag

4. *Creative Writing for Teens* offers teens a chance to build their online portfolio by submitting their work in a number of categories. Contributing authors are provided with an author's page, which will include a bibliography of their published work and an autobiography.

www.about.com

5. *Impact Magazine for Readers and Writers* tries to provide a place on the Web for creative writing by students. It accepts submissions (short essays, book reviews, and poetry) but emphasizes *short*. The magazine also provides a place where students can share book reviews that encourage creative and critical thought.

c/o Viterbo Student Union

827 Winnebago St., #447

La Crosse, WI 54601

608-796-3454

www.jungleweb.net

6. *Merlyn's Pen* is a large annual magazine for writers ages 12–18. It gives feedback on all work that is submitted.

P.O. Box 910

E. Greenwich, RI 02818

800-247-2027

www.merlynspen.com

7. *Potato Hill Poetry* is a bimonthly magazine for teachers and students in K–12. Poems, exercises, artwork, essays.

81 Speen St.

Natick, MA 01760

508-652-9908

www.potatohill.com

8. *Skipping Stones* publishes writing and art by kids 7–18. In addition to stories, poems, and illustrations, it also offers jokes, recipes, magic tricks, science experiments, and movie and book reviews.

P.O. Box 3939
Eugene, OR 97403
541-342-4956
www.treelink.com/skipping

9. *TeenInk* is a national magazine, a Web site, and a book series written by teens for teens. It contains a wide variety of student work: nonfiction, fiction, poems, community service reports, interviews, college essays, college reviews, and book, concert, movie, music, video, and video game reviews. It also publishes artwork, photographs, and cartoons.

P.O. Box 30
Newton, MA 02461
617-964-6800
www.teenink.com

10. *Teen Poets Society* provides a forum for teens to discuss their creative writing and an informal setting for feedback on their work. It brings together teens with similar interests (writing, in this case).

c/o Haverhill Public Library
99 Main St.
Haverhill, MA 01830
978-373-1586
www.teencybercenter.org

11. *Teen Voices* publishes the opinions of any young women, regardless of their writing ability.

c/o Bay Area Teen Voices
3543 18th St., #18
San Francisco, CA 94110
415-255-7162
www.teenvoices.com

12. *YO! Youth Outlook* is an award-winning monthly publication by and for young people who have stories to share. Features solid reporting pieces and first-person essays, comic strips, and poetry pages.

c/o Pacific News Service
660 Market St., Suite 210
San Francisco, CA 94104
415-438-4755
www.youthoutlook.org

12 Rock 'n' Roll Action Figures

1. The Beatles
2. The BeeGees
3. Alice Cooper
4. Eminem
5. Jerry Garcia
6. Janis Joplin
7. Kid Rock
8. KISS
9. Metallica
10. Jim Morrison (the Doors)
11. Ozzy Osbourne
12. Angus Young (AC/DC)

12 Helpful Hints for Trading Card Collectors

1. Store your cards in a notebook with plastic pages, or place them in a plastic sleeve or shield and keep them in a storage box. Storage supplies are available at trading card and comics stores.
2. Keep cards away from food and liquids.
3. Don't store cards in places that are very hot or damp.
4. Never hold cards together with rubber bands. You'll damage their edges, which will reduce their value.
5. Sort cards by manufacturer, year (set), and number, not by team or players.
6. Establish a friendly relationship with the owner of your card shop. Let him know what you're looking for so that he can set it aside for you. Give him a list, and check back often.
7. Go online to find others who collect the same cards you do and see if you can trade.
8. Go to trade shows, where many dealers sell cards. You'll be able to compare prices and get an idea of what your cards are worth.
9. Scout garage sales for additions to your collection.
10. Buying cards individually is usually more expensive than buying sets.
11. The best cards to collect are those with mistakes on them.
12. Always buy, sell, and trade *fairly*.

How to Store Comic Books Safely

Most paper has acid in it, and this is what makes paper age: it turns brown and crumples easily. We can't stop the aging process, but we can slow it down. Take care of your comics if you plan to sell them someday.

1. Protect each comic book in its own acid-free plastic or Mylar bag. Comic book dealers carry them. Mylar bags should be changed every two or three years.

2. The comic books, in their bags, should be stored vertically (standing up), not lying on top of another. They should be stacked in special acid-free boxes.

3. Store the boxes in a cool (40°–50°), dark place with a relative humidity of 50°. Avoid heat, ultraviolet light, and dampness.

4. Keep your collection away from polluted air and dust.

22 Collectible Lunchboxes

Collecting—anything—can easily become an obsession. Stephen Sansweet's Star Wars items number over 300,000; his collection has grown to such huge proportions that he has to keep it in a separate building. At least lunchboxes don't take up a lot of space.

1. Barbie and Midge, 1963 — $215
2. Battlestar Galactica, 1978 — $105
3. Beatles, 1966 — $400
4. Beeny & Cecil, 1963 — $150
5. Boston Bruins, 1973 — $525
6. Bullwinkle, 1962 — $800
7. Bullwinkle, 1963 — $200
8. Dark Crystal, 1982 — $54
9. Dragon's Lair, 1983 — $149
10. ET Extra Terrestrial, 1982 — $47
11. Fall Guy, 1981 — $75
12. Gene Autry, 1954 — $425
13. Green Hornet, 1967 — $360
14. Howdy Doody, 1954 — $450

15. Jetson's dome-shaped box, 1963 —	$1,500
16. Little Friends, 1982	$500
17. Lost in Space, 1978–79	$145
18. Mickey Mouse, 1935	$1,000
19. Monkees, 1967	$212
20. Mork and Mindy, 1979 —	$42
21. Ronald McDonald, 1982	$50
22. Strawberry Shortcake, 1981 —	$60

7 Ways to Tell if Your Beanie Baby Is a Fake

The Beanie Baby craze reached such a frenzy at one point that probably everyone has at least one kicking around in the back of the closet somewhere. Unfortunately, there are plenty of counterfeit Babies out there, and if you're a serious collector, that's especially bad news. Magazines and Web sites devoted to Beanie Babies often list the fakes, and if you buy only from reputable vendors, you can protect yourself that way as well. Here are some things to look for.

1. Fake Beanie Babies have faces with far less detail than real ones.

2. The eyes should be shiny. Fake Beanie Babies have dull eyes that are often spaced irregularly.

3. The fabric should have a soft, velvety feel. Fakes use fabrics that tend to be more nubby.

4. Fakes have sloppy stitches; they're inconsistently sized and sewn.

5. The neck ribbon should be shiny on both sides, and it should not be sewn on.

6. On authentic Beanie Babies, the tag (called a "swing tag") has gold foil surrounding the heart. On fakes, the gold is just gold ink, not shiny foil. Overall, the tags on the fakes are thinner, and the printing isn't as neat.

7. Look at the colors. If you're holding "Pinky" and it's red, something's wrong.

6 Benefits of Playing Video Games

1. They're a great introduction to new technologies.
2. You get to practice following directions.
3. Many games provide practice in problem-solving and logic.
4. They help improve fine motor and spatial skills.
5. It's a good activity to share with people of all ages.
6. They're more entertaining than television, plus you get to participate.

The Trouble with Video Games

1. An overdependence on video games, always played alone, could foster social isolation.
2. Most video games are sexist, portraying women as weak, helpless, or sexually provocative.
3. Game environments are often based on plots of violence, aggression, and gender bias.
4. The games rarely require independent thought or creativity.
5. Overzealous players can confuse reality and fantasy.
6. They cost a fortune!

Computer and Video Game Ratings

A lot of the flak about video games comes from people (parents count as people) who worry that pixellated violence might escalate into the real thing. In the never-ending quest to make sure kids are protected from terrible things (like words and pictures), the government put pressure on software developers to come up with a video game rating system.

Actually, they came up with two. The Entertainment Software Rating Board—which includes some of the big cheeses from Nintendo, Sega, Sony, and other humongous cartridge and CD-ROM game guys—dreamed up a system that's a lot like movie ratings. Games are labeled according to the age of the appropriate audience. Depending on the game, the label can also include a description of the content, such as "realistic blood and gore" or "use of tobacco and alcohol" or—horrors! —"contains gambling."

Entertainment Software Rating Board System

Rating	Stands for	Meaning
EC	Early Childhood	Suitable for ages 3 and up, with no material that parents would find inappropriate. Some games may require reading or other skills.
KA	Kids to Adults	Suitable for ages 6 and up. Appealing to people of many ages and tastes. May include minimal violence, some comic mischief, or crude language.
T	Teen	Suitable for ages 13 and up. May include violent content, profanity, and mild sexual themes.
M	Mature	Suitable for ages 17 and up. May include more intense violence or profanity, and more mature sexual themes, than products in the Teen category.
AO	Adults Only	Suitable only for adults. May include graphic depictions of sex and violence. Not intended to be sold or rented to people under 18.

Meanwhile, the makers of computer-based games created the Recreational Software Advisory Council. This group uses a scale of 1–4 to rate the amount of violence, nudity and sex, and profanity. Game makers fill out a questionnaire; the answers are analyzed by a computer, which then spits out the rating. In this system, age doesn't count.

RSAC Consumer Software Content Guide

Rank	Violence	Nudity	Sex	Language
ALL [Suitable for all audiences]	Harmless conflict; some damage to non-living things	No nudity or revealing attire	Romance; no sex	Inoffensive slang; no profanity
LEVEL 1	Damage or destruction of non-human living beings	Revealing attire	Passionate kissing	Mild expletives and profanity
LEVEL 2	Damage or destruction of living beings including humans; some blood	Bare buttocks; brief display of female breasts	Clothed sexual touching	Moderate expletives; non-sexual anatomical references
LEVEL 3	Destruction of living beings including humans; blood and gore	Non-sexual frontal nudity	Non-explicit sexual activity	Strong language; obscene gestures
LEVEL 4 [Extreme Content]	Wanton or gratuitous violence; torture; rape	Provocative frontal nudity	Explicitly sexual activity; sex crimes	"Four-letter" words; crude or explicit sexual references

10 Signs That You're an Internet Junkie

1. You type "com" after every period.

2. You tell your teacher that you need to go to the bathroom to download.

3. You name your pets Yahoo, eBay, and Amazon.

4. You fail all your high school subjects on purpose and repeat the year just for the free Internet access.

5. You tell the bus driver you live at http://234.grand.ave /house/colonial.html.

6. When you get up in the middle of the night to go to the bathroom, you stop to check your e-mail.

7. Your pet has its own Web site.

8. When you check your mail and it says, "No new messages," you go into a fit of depression.

9. You tilt your head sideways when you smile.

10. Logging off seems so final.

6 Reasons That Your Etch-a-Sketch Is More Efficient Than Your Computer

1. To turn on your computer, you have to hit a switch and wait for it to boot up. With an Etch-a-Sketch, you just pick it up and shake it.

2. To undo an action on your computer, you have to click on "Undo." With an Etch-a-Sketch, you just pick it up and shake it.

3. To create a new document on your computer, you have to open a new document window. With an Etch-a-Sketch, you just pick it up and shake it.

4. To revise a document on your computer, you have to open the document and edit it. With an Etch-a-Sketch, you just pick it up and shake it.

5. To turn off your computer, you have to close down the program and log off. With an Etch-a-Sketch, you just pick it up and shake it.

6. No more wasted time reading e-mails and surfing the Internet!

Note: To save a document on your Etch-a-Sketch, *don't* shake it.

10 Things We "Learn" from Video Games

1. There is no problem that cannot be overcome by violence.

2. Piloting any vehicle is simple and requires no training.

3. If you see food lying on the ground, eat it.

4. If someone dies, they disappear.
5. Money is frequently found lying on the street.
6. Ninjas are common and fight in public frequently.
7. Whenever huge, fat, evil men are about to die, they begin flashing red or yellow.
8. All martial arts women wear revealing clothes and have great bodies.
9. All martial arts men have rippling muscles and angry expressions.
10. *Carpe diem!* You live only three times!

The 100 Most Frequently Challenged Books of 1990–2001

Book burning sounds like something that went out with the 20th century—not true. All across the U.S., parent, school, and church groups burned copies of the Harry Potter books to show their disapproval of their occult themes. Censorship is a bigger problem than you might realize. Judy Blume has said, "It's not just the books under fire now that worry me. It is the books that will never be written. The books that will never be read. And all due to the fear of censorship . . . young readers will be the real losers." The American Library Association reports that these were the most frequently challenged books of the last decade. Read them.

1. *The Adventures of Huckleberry Finn,* by Mark Twain
2. *The Adventures of Tom Sawyer,* by Mark Twain
3. *Alice* (series), by Phyllis Reynolds Naylor
4. *Always Running,* by Luis Rodriguez
5. *American Psycho,* by Bret Easton Ellis
6. *The Anarchist Cookbook,* by William Powell
7. *Anastasia Krupnik* (series), by Lois Lowry
8. *Annie on my Mind,* by Nancy Garden
9. *Are You There, God? It's Me, Margaret,* by Judy Blume
10. *Arizona Kid,* by Ron Koertge
11. *Asking About Sex and Growing Up,* by Joanna Cole
12. *Athletic Shorts,* by Chris Crutcher
13. *Beloved,* by Toni Morrison

14. *Bless Me, Ultima,* by Rudolfo A. Anaya
15. *Blubber,* by Judy Blume
16. *The Bluest Eye,* by Toni Morrison
17. *The Boy Who Lost His Face,* by Louis Sachar
18. *Boys and Sex,* by Wardell Pomeroy
19. *Brave New World,* by Aldous Huxley
20. *Bridge to Terabithia,* by Katherine Paterson
21. *Bumps in the Night,* by Harry Allard
22. *Carrie,* by Stephen King
23. *The Catcher in the Rye,* by J. D. Salinger
24. *The Chocolate War,* by Robert Cormier
25. *The Color Purple,* by Alice Walker
26. *Crazy Lady,* by Jane Conly
27. *Cross Your Fingers, Spit in Your Hat,* by Alvin Schwartz
28. *Cujo,* by Stephen King
29. *Curses, Hexes and Spells,* by Daniel Cohen
30. *Daddy's Roommate,* by Michael Willhoite
31. *A Day No Pigs Would Die,* by Robert Newton Peck
32. *The Dead Zone,* by Stephen King
33. *Deenie,* by Judy Blume
34. *The Drowning of Stephen Jones,* by Bette Greene
35. *Earth's Children* (series), by Jean M. Auel
36. *The Face on the Milk Carton,* by Caroline Cooney
37. *Fade,* by Robert Cormier
38. *Fallen Angels,* by Walter Dean Myers
39. *Family Secrets,* by Norma Klein
40. *Final Exit,* by Derek Humphry
41. *Flowers for Algernon,* by Daniel Keyes
42. *Forever,* by Judy Blume
43. *Girls and Sex,* by Wardell Pomeroy
44. *The Giver,* by Lois Lowry
45. *Go Ask Alice,* by Anonymous
46. *The Goats,* by Brock Cole
47. *Goosebumps* (series), by R. L. Stine
48. *The Great Gilly Hopkins,* by Katherine Paterson
49. *Guess What?* by Mem Fox
50. *Halloween ABC,* by Eve Merriam
51. *The Handmaid's Tale,* by Margaret Atwood
52. *Harry Potter* (series), by J. K. Rowling

53. *The Headless Cupid*, by Zilpha Keatley Snyder
54. *Heather Has Two Mommies*, by Leslea Newman
55. *The House of Spirits*, by Isabel Allende
56. *How to Eat Fried Worms*, by Thomas Rockwell
57. *I Know Why the Caged Bird Sings*, by Maya Angelou
58. *In the Night Kitchen*, by Maurice Sendak
59. *It's Perfectly Normal*, by Robie Harris
60. *Jack*, by A. M. Homes
61. *James and the Giant Peach*, by Roald Dahl
62. *Julie of the Wolves*, by Jean Craighead George
63. *Jump Ship to Freedom*, by James Lincoln Collier and Christopher Collier
64. *Kaffir Boy*, by Mark Mathabane
65. *Killing Griffin*, by Lois Duncan
66. *A Light in the Attic*, by Shel Silverstein
67. *Little Black Sambo*, by Helen Bannerman
68. *Lord of the Flies*, by William Golding
69. *Mommy Laid an Egg*, by Babette Cole
70. *My Brother Sam Is Dead*, by James Lincoln Collier and Christopher Collier
71. *Native Son*, by Richard Wright
72. *The New Joy of Gay Sex*, by Charles Silverstein
73. *Of Mice and Men*, by John Steinbeck
74. *On My Honor*, by Marion Dane Bauer
75. *Ordinary People*, by Judith Guest
76. *Pillars of the Earth*, by Ken Follett
77. *The Outsiders*, by S. E. Hinton
78. *The Pigman*, by Paul Zindel
79. *Private Parts*, by Howard Stern
80. *Running Loose*, by Chris Crutcher
81. *Scary Stories* (series), by Alvin Schwartz
82. *Sex Education*, by Jenny Davis
83. *Sex*, by Madonna
84. *Slaughterhouse-Five*, by Kurt Vonnegut
85. *Sleeping Beauty Trilogy*, by A. N. Roquelaure (Anne Rice)
86. *Song of Solomon*, by Toni Morrison
87. *The Stupids* (series), by Harry Allard
88. *Summer of My German Soldier*, by Bette Greene
89. *The Terrorist*, by Caroline Cooney

90. *Tiger Eyes*, by Judy Blume

91. *To Kill a Mockingbird*, by Harper Lee

92. *View from the Cherry Tree*, by Willo Davis Roberts

93. *We All Fall Down*, by Robert Cormier

94. *What's Happening to My Body? Book for Boys: A Growing-Up Guide for Parents & Sons*, by Lynda Madaras

95. *What's Happening to my Body? Book for Girls: A Growing-Up Guide for Parents & Daughters*, by Lynda Madaras

96. *Where Did I Come From?* by Peter Mayle

97. *Where's Waldo?* by Martin Hanford

98. *The Witches*, by Roald Dahl

99. *Women on Top: How Real Life Has Changed Women's Fantasies*, by Nancy Friday

100. *A Wrinkle in Time*, by Madeleine L'Engle

30 Adult Novels That Teens Enjoy

The Mid-Continent Public Library in Independence, Missouri, recommends these books to teens whose reading skills allow them to understand adult language. The subject matter is appropriate for all ages, and they were selected to serve as bridges from children's to adult literature.

1. Emily Brontë, *Wuthering Heights*. Through Heathcliff's obsessive passion for Cathy, readers are introduced to a theme that has attracted artists for centuries. A work of towering genius, read by young teens for its wild and eccentric romanticism.

2. Rita Mae Brown, *Bingo*. Not only words but cannonballs fly when the Hunsenmeir sisters, both in their 80s, compete for the affections of the new man in town.

3. Sheila Burnford, *Bel Ria*. Follows the wanderings of a little performing dog in France, England, and at sea during World War II. Vivid descriptions of wartime.

4. Orson Scott Card, *Ender's Game*. In this award-winning novel, aliens have attacked the planet Earth twice and have nearly destroyed the human race. To prepare for another attack and ensure our planet's victory, world leaders direct the breeding of military whiz kids by teaching them war games. Ender

Wiggin proves himself the most brilliant of all the young trainees by winning all the games. But will his abilities be enough to save the planet?

5. Marion Chesney, *Lady Fortescue Steps Out*. In a society where no one must know you are poor, Lady Fortescue gets found out. Book 1 of the 6-volume Poor Relations series.

6. Tracy Chevalier, *Girl with a Pearl Earring*. This historical novel, told through the eyes of 16-year-old Griet, is set in the Netherlands during the 17th century. Griet's life changes when she becomes employed by the legendary artist Vermeer. She poses for him and is drawn into a sequence of events that change her life.

7. W. J. Corbett, *Pentecost and the Chosen One*. After inheriting the leadership of the mice on Lickey Top, a young mouse, beset by doubts and feelings of inadequacy, ignores the problems of the community until a momentous trip to the city teaches him about courage, duty, friendship, and his own qualities as a leader.

8. Patricia Cornwell, *Cruel and Unusual*. Kay Scarpetta, the chief medical examiner of Virginia, is unnerved when, following the execution of a serial killer, she finds new victims murdered with the same MO.

9. Margaret Craven, *I Heard the Owl Call My Name*. As he lives and works among the Indian people in several remote Canadian villages, a dying young Anglican missionary becomes sensitive to the strains and the richness of their lives. Spiritual without being preachy.

10. Lindsey Davis, *Silver P-I-G-S*. A Roman detective travels to Roman Britain to discover who is smuggling silver and how.

11. Daphne du Maurier, *Rebecca*. In the awkward role of bride to the dashing and enigmatic Maxim de Winter, timid Rebecca finds his manor house, Manderly, haunted by the spirit of his first wife and pervaded by a sense of impending doom.

12. Dave Eggers, *A Heartbreaking Work of Staggering Genius*. After the death of his parents, Eggers, 22 years old, is appointed the "parent" of his youngest brother, Toph. Raising his brother is a challenging experience, and the author's often cynical insights and observations present the reader with the story of how he dealt with his life and with all of his fears and experiences.

13. Ernest J. Gaines, *Autobiography of Miss Jane Pittman*. Through the character of his compelling 110-year-old heroine, Gaines interprets and personalizes the black experience in America—from slavery to the present.

14. Sue Grafton, *A Is for Alibi*. California P.I. Kinsey Millhone is hot on the trail of an 8-year-old murder.

15. Judith Guest, *Ordinary People*. Shattered by the accidental drowning of one son and the attempted suicide of another, a family gropes for reconciliation.

16. Robert Heinlein, *Friday*. A created person "whose mother was a test tube and whose father was a knife" travels the known worlds in search of "home."

17. Frank Herbert, *Dune*. Exotically detailed science fiction about a member of a genetically superior family who realize their destiny on the barren planet of Dune.

18. Tom Holt, *Who's Afraid of Beowulf*? Epic fantasy develops as an ancient Norse king returns to life to fight his arch enemy the sorcerer-king, now a computer enthusiast.

19. Shirley Jackson, *We Have Always Lived in the Castle*. A genuinely chilling psychological horror story by the gifted author of the equally scary *Haunting of Hill House*.

20 Harper Lee, *To Kill a Mockingbird*. An engaging and unsentimental portrait of southern small-town life in the 1930s. It is narrated by 8-year-old Scout, whose world changes when her lawyer father attempts to prove the innocence of a black man accused of raping a white woman.

21. Gregory Maguire, *Confessions of an Ugly Stepsister*. The author lets us in on the real story behind that timeless fairy tale "Cinderella." What motivated the wicked stepmother into being so cruel? What were the stepsisters really like? Why would a prince marry a commoner like Cinderella? And what became of Cinderella's family?

22. Connie Porter, *Imani All Mine*. This tragic story is told through the eyes of a 15-year-old girl, Tasha, who struggles to raise her own daughter, Imani, in a neighborhood filled with poverty, drugs, and violence. Using the language of the street, Tasha reveals that she was a rape victim, but she handles herself with pride and keeps on going even while her world seems to be falling apart.

23. Chaim Potok, *The Chosen*. The search for personal identity within the framework of a strong religious tradition is explored in this story about Jewish fathers and sons.

24. Reynolds Price, *A Long and Happy Life*. Wanting only "a long and happy life" with a boy who does not love her, Rosa Mastian is the memorable heroine of this often-overlooked novel.

25. Phillip Pullman, *Ruby in the Smoke*. Sally's investigation of her father's death leads her into a world of stolen rubies and opium.

26. Judith Merkle Riley, *A Vision of Light*. A gripping tale of 14th-century England told through Margaret Ashbury, a divinely inspired midwife.

27. John Steinbeck, *Of Mice and Men*. Tremendously strong, feeble-minded Lennie is protected by his friend George but ultimately falls victim to his own primitive innocence. Dealing simply with basic emotions, the story arouses pity and an awareness of the limits of innocence.

28. Mary Stewart, *Crystal Cave* (also *Hollow Hills; Last Enchantment*). Adventurous, fast-paced recreations of the Arthurian legends centering on Merlin, from his birth in Wales to his infatuation with Nimue.

29. Amy Tan, *Joy Luck Club*. Jing-mei (June) never understood her mother until she was coerced into taking her place at the weekly mahjong and gossip session.

30. T. H. White, *The Once and Future King*. A tongue-in-cheek portrayal of chivalry enlivens this masterful modern version of the life of King Arthur. Through fantasy, humor, and White's compassionate vision, legendary heroes become human, and the tragic grandeur of the Arthurian epic is given meaning.

12 Books That Compile Teen Voices

1. *Dear Diary I'm Pregnant: Teenagers Talk About Their Pregnancy*, Annrenee Englander, compiler, 1997

2. *Girls in America: Their Stories, Their Words*, Carol Cassidy, 2000

3. *Hear These Voices: Youth at the Edge of the Millennium*, Anthony Allison, 1999

4. *No More Strangers Now: Young Voices from a New South Africa,* Timothy McKee, interviewer, 1998

5. *Ophelia Speaks: Adolescent Girls Write About Their Search for Self,* Sara Shandler, 1999

6. *Picture the Girl: Young Women Speak Their Minds,* Audrey Shehyn, 2000

7. *Real Boys' Voices,* William Pollack, 2000

8. *Remix: Conversations with Immigrant Teens,* Marina Budhos, 1999

9. *The Secret Life of Teens: Young People Speak Out About Their Lives,* Gayatri and Michelle Patnaik, 2000

10. *Seen and Heard: Teenagers Talk About Their Lives,* Mary Motley Kalergis, 1998

11. *What Are You? Voices of Mixed-race Young People,* Pearl Guyo Gaskins, editor, 1999

12. *Why Do They Hate Me? Young Lives Caught in War and Conflict,* Laurel Holliday, 1999

11 Classic Teen Authors

1. Katharine Hull, 15, and Pamela Whitlock, 16, went to school together in England. One day, while taking shelter from a rainstorm, they decided to collaborate on a book by children, about children, and for children. Their novel, *The Far-Distant Oxus,* was published a year later, in 1937, and was hailed by critics as an instant classic in both Europe and the U.S.

2. Anne Frank's diary was published in English in 1952 as *The Diary of a Young Girl.* Written when Anne was a teenager, it describes her family's life in hiding during World War II because they were Jewish. After two years of confinement in the attic of a warehouse in Amsterdam, Holland, the family was discovered by the Nazis and taken to a concentration camp. Only Anne's father survived. When the diary was found, he saw to its publication in 1947. It has been translated into more than 50 languages.

3. S. E. (Susan Eloise) Hinton started her writing career in high school, beginning the first draft of *The Outsiders* at the age of 15; it took her a year and a half to complete it. A book about youth gangs and their confrontations, it was published in

1967, when she was 17. It has sold more than a million copies.

4. Gordon Korman wrote his first book, *This Can't Be Happening at MacDonald Hall,* as a 7th-grade English project. By the time he graduated from high school, he had written and published five more books, including *Go Jump in the Pool* and *Beware the Fish.* All are available in paperback editions.

5. At the age of 18, Edgar Allan Poe had his first book published, *Tamerlane and Other Poems* (1827). Best known today for his tales of horror, he also wrote poetry and critical essays and worked as a magazine editor.

6. Ernest Hemingway wrote poems and stories as a high school student in Oak Park, Illinois, and his first published story, "The Judgment of Manitou," appeared in his school literary magazine when he was 16.

7. Sylvia Plath published a short story, "And Summer Will Not Come Again," in *Seventeen* magazine soon after her high school graduation. She was not yet 18.

8. Langston Hughes wrote his first poem for his 8th-grade graduation. As a student at Cleveland Central High School, he published poems in the school magazine and edited the yearbook. In January 1921, not yet 19, Hughes published two poems, "Fairies" and "Winter Sweetness," in *The Brownie's Book,* a magazine for African-American children.

9. Louisa May Alcott was a prolific teen writer, just like her character Jo in *Little Women* (1868). Alcott was first published at age 18, in 1851, when *Peterson's Magazine* printed her poem "Sunlight." She published many works for children and adults and edited a children's magazine.

10. F. Scott Fitzgerald's first publication came at 13, in 1909, when his story "The Mystery of the Raymond Mortgage" appeared in the school magazine at St. Paul Academy in St. Paul, Minnesota.

11. James Joyce was an 18-year-old student at University College in Dublin when his critical review of Ibsen's *When We Dead Awaken* in the journal *Fortnightly Review* was published.

17 More Teens Who Wrote Books That Got Published

1. Gil C. Alicea (16 years old), *The Air Down Here: True Tales from a South Bronx Boyhood*, 1995

2. Amelia Atwater-Rhodes (14), *In the Forests of the Night*, 1999; *Demon in My View*, 2000

3. Irwin Cait (13), *Conquering the Beast Within: How I Fought Depression and Won*, 1998

4. Maureen Daly (17), *Seventeenth Summer*, 1942

5. Jamie DeWitt (12), *Jamie's Turn*, 1984

6. Miles Franklin (16), *My Brilliant Career*, 1901

7. Kimberly Fuller (16), *Home*, 1998

8. Zach Hample (18), *How to Snag Major League Baseballs*, 1999

9. Latoya Hunter (12), *The Diary of Latoya Hunter: My First Year in Junior High*, 1992

10. Benjamin Lebert (16), *Crazy*, 2000

11. Dave Lindsay (15), *Dave's Quick 'n' Easy Web Pages*, 1999

12. Megan McNeill Libby (16), *Postcards from France*, 1998

13. Mark Pfetzer (17), *Within Reach: My Everest Story*, 1998

14. Dav Pilkey (19), *World War Won*, 1987

15. Alexandra (Ally) Sheedy (12), *She Was Nice to Mice*, 1975

16. Mary Shelley (19), *Frankenstein*, 1816

17. Katie Tarbox (15), *Katie.com: My Story*, 2000

9 Great Novels About Siblings

1. Jane Austen's *Sense and Sensibility, Pride and Prejudice,* and *Persuasion,* novels in which relationships between smart, silly, or warmhearted sisters feature prominently, have been well loved as both books and films.

2. *The Brothers Karamazov,* by Fyodor Dostoevsky. An epic masterpiece about a troubled family in czarist Russia that deals with four brothers, their love-hate relationship with their father, and the bonds between them.

3. *The Catcher in the Rye,* by J. D. Salinger. Seventeen-year-old Holden Caulfield, the narrator of this novel, is a rebellious schoolboy who doesn't trust the values of the adult world. He relates events that occurred during three December days the previous year. Holden probes and investigates his own sense of emptiness and isolation while the people around him ignore his pain and suffering.

4. *East of Eden,* by John Steinbeck. Set in the rich farmlands of California's Salinas Valley, the story follows the intertwined destinies of two families—the Trasks and the Hamiltons—whose generations helplessly reenact the fall of Adam and Eve and the poisonous rivalry of Cain and Abel.

5. *Franny and Zooey,* by J. D. Salinger. Franny and Zooey, sister and brother, have a long theological and personal discussion in which we learn about the bonds they shared as children and their relationship to their other siblings.

6. *Plainsong,* by Kent Haruf. In the small town of Holt, Tom Guthrie, a high school teacher, fights to keep his life together and to raise his two boys after their depressed mother moves to her sister's house. The boys, not yet adolescents, struggle to make sense of adult behavior and their mother's apparent abandonment. A pregnant teenage girl, kicked out by her mother and rejected by the father of her child, helps them all learn the true meaning of family.

7. *The Poisonwood Bible,* by Barbara Kingsolver, is a historical novel that takes place during the Congo's struggle for independence and follows the fortunes of the Price sisters: four young girls taken there by their missionary father Nathan and his long-suffering wife Orleanna. The novel is narrated by the four children as they grow and reveal changing attitudes toward Africa, their father, and one another.

8. *The Sound and the Fury,* by William Faulkner. Published in 1929, this book introduced his "heart's darling," the beautiful and tragic Caddy Compson, whose story Faulkner told through separate monologues by her three brothers—the idiot Benjy, the neurotic, suicidal Quentin, and the monstrous Jason.

9. *To Kill a Mockingbird,* by Harper Lee. Set in 1930s Alabama, the story is narrated by young Scout Finch. Her father, Athens Finch, is a lawyer who defends a black man accused of attacking a white girl. A moving portrayal of the tragedy that is racism.

8 Excellent Novels About Baseball

1. *The Bingo Long Traveling All-Stars and Motor Kings,* by William Brashler. Between baseball seasons in the 1930s, the poorly paid black players would travel from the South to the North, offering to play the best talent each town along the way had to offer. The All-Stars would have to balance their talent against the tolerance level of each community—no town put up gracefully with black players defeating local white heroes. In some communities it could even result in violence.

2. *The Celebrant: A Novel,* by Eric Rolfe Greenberg. Considered by many to be one of the best baseball novels ever, it chronicles the development of an immigrant Jewish family in the 1930s. Great characters.

3. *Joy in Mudville,* by Gordon McAlpine. This fantasy tracks a home run hit by Babe Ruth as the ball travels across the country, pursued by a man who believes it to be proof that Martians have come to visit Earth.

4. *The Last Days of Summer,* by Steve Kluger. A moving coming-of-age tale of future sportswriter Joey Margolis and his improbable relationship with the Giants rookie sensation Charlie Banks. The place is Brooklyn, the time is the early '40s, and young baseball fanatic Joey needs a hero.

5. *The Natural,* by Bernard Malamud. This morality tale features one of the most memorable characters in all of literature: Roy Hobbs, a talented athlete whose promising career is derailed by a youthful indiscretion.

6. *Screwballs,* by Jay Cronley. Possibly the funniest baseball novel ever written. The hero is a team manager who loves baseball and uses every stratagem known to man and God to motivate his team. With force and awkwardness, he arm-wrestles them into a World Series championship.

7. *Shoeless Joe,* by W. P. Kinsella. A moving fantasy about baseball, fathers and sons, and mythology.

8. *The Year the Yankees Lost the Pennant,* by Douglas Wallop. A hopeless fan of the hapless Washington Senators ("first in war, first in peace, and last in the American League") sells his soul to the devil for a chance to be a baseball player good enough to help his team beat the unstoppable New York Yankees.

5 Excellent Novels About Basketball

1. *The Cockroach Basketball League,* by Charles Rosen. Rosen depicts a coach struggling to make his CBA team play like a team rather than a bunch of would-be stars trying to build up their individual stats so they can be called up to play *real* basketball in the NBA. He takes his team to the CBA championship in spite of everything.

2. *Ghost,* by Peter Barsocchini. A pro basketball player is trying to deal with the death of his father while wondering about just what kind of man he was. A charming subplot centers on a basketball hustler in need of a good friend and rescuer.

3. *Massy's Game,* by Jack Olsen. On the court, 8'2" Massy can do no wrong. But no one roots for this Goliath. He is cursed and spat upon by irate fans, elbowed, punched, kneed in the jewels by competing players, and universally despised. One of the most original sports novels, this fast-moving story makes a strong and provocative comment on our entire society.

4. *Slo Mo!,* by Rick Reilly. Here's a laugh-out-loud story of likable, amazingly naive, 17-year-old Mo Finsternick, plucked out of high school to play for the NBA because he's 7'8" and has an unfailing 3-point shot. Raised in a cave cult with virtually no exposure to the modern world, he is duped by agents and jealous teammates.

5. *Winning the City,* by Theodore Weesner. This novel is about a 15-year-old basketball player who is cut from the roster because he plays the same position as the son of a rich man who is willing to finance the team. Consumed by the unfairness of it, the boy is determined to find another team to play on and to win the city championship against his school despite great odds.

4 Excellent Novels About Football

1. *The Man Who Ruined Football,* by Elston Brook. A middle-aged man holds the key to a winning football season—he can kick a football through the goalposts every single time, no matter what the distance. This makes his team unbeatable and upsets the football gamblers something awful. And when gamblers get mad, they often try to get even.

2. *The Pigskin Rabbi*, by Willard Manus. A young rabbi who has lost his religious conviction has returned to his first love, football, playing with a Dutch team. Signed by the New York Giants, he instantly becomes a star, especially when they hire his old Yiddish-speaking sandlot buddy. A great toss-and-catch combination, they communicate in Yiddish, which confuses their opponents. Their teammates learn not only Yiddish from them but also a spontaneous, joyous way to play the game.

3. *Titans*, by Tim Green. Quarterback Hunter Logan, at the top but aging and looking for financial security, does a little sports gambling. When the nephew of a Mafia don finds out about it, he threatens Logan, demanding that he fix games or place his family at risk.

4. *Toss*, by Boomer Esiason and Lowell Cauffie. Esiason, a longtime NFL quarterback, gives a gripping portrayal of an NFL team that's been engineered for failure in order to lower its value and force a sale. The team's manager drafts troublemakers to instigate antagonism among the players. But the $6 million rookie quarterback Derek Brody wins his teammates over and convinces them that winning is possible.

7 Excellent Novels About Girls in Sports

1. *Balls*, by Gorman Bechar. This book is about Louise "Balls" Gehrig, the first woman to play Major League baseball. Filled with comedy, romance, suspense, and, of course, baseball.

2. *Can't Miss*, by Michael Bowen. Insights into plausible interactions between a female rookie ballplayer and the other players, managers, and sportswriters make this a memorable read.

3. *Courting Pandemonium*, by Frederick Barton. A talented young basketball player struggles with feminist issues when she must choose between the scholarship she's worked hard for and her identity as a team player. Filled with great basketball action and coaching strategy.

4. *Dead to Rights*, by Anna Maxes. Regina Lichtman, who works for an organization that resembles the NCAA, sets out to investigate a women's soccer coach, Pierce Nolan, whose remarkable successes seem to be due to foul play. Anyone who has interfered in the coach's plans has suffered an unfortunate accident. Reggie also discovers that the coach has some very powerful allies whose goals are more evil than just success on the soccer field.

5. *Iced!*, by Judith Alquire. Alison Gutherie, 40, coaches the Toronto Teddies in the new women's professional ice hockey league. Through her, we follow the team's fortunes to the season's end and get to know the players and their diverse reasons for playing hockey. Gutherie endures a rickety team bus, poor lodgings, a hotheaded goaltender who gets her team into penalty trouble, an owner who embarrasses the league with frilly uniforms, and her own infatuation with a much younger team member.

6. *A League of Their Own*, by Sarah Gilbert. A novel based on the movie that stands on its own merits as a good story about two sisters who compete in the women's professional baseball league of the 1940s.

7. *A Whole Other Ballgame: Women's Literature on Women's Sports*, Joli Sandoz, ed. An anthology of sports stories and poems by Adrienne Rich, Fannie Hurst, Marge Piercy, Betty Bao Lord, Maxine Kumin, Tess Gallagher, and Laurie Colwin. They all explore and explain the passionate experiences of women in sport and the possibilities that sports and competition hold out to the human spirit.

5 Steps to Great Sportsmanship

What does it take to be a winner, to achieve the kind of excellence we see repeatedly from professional athletes such as Tiger Woods, Wayne Gretzky, Martina Navratilova, and Michael Jordan? In June 2001, *Newsweek* magazine asked a dozen true dominators what it takes to be the best of the best. They all agreed on the following five points.

1. Genius is 99% perspiration. You need to get in there and work and then work harder and then work even harder. Practice, practice, practice! That can get boring, but Joe Montana of the San Francisco '49ers warns against skimping on hard work: "A lot of guys say, 'Yeah, I watched two hours of game film last night.' But they're not really studying what's going on. They may as well have been watching television." Practice pays off, claims tennis great Martina Navratilova: "Every great shot you hit, you've already hit a bunch of times in practice."

2. Let the other guy get nervous. The true greats share an uncanny ability to always keep their cool. This is important, not only because you'll do better if you're calm and can concentrate on the task at hand, but also because it tends to scare the competition. "Believe it or not," said Wayne Gretzky, "the bigger the game, the calmer I seem to get." Says Yankee outfielder Reggie Jackson, "I'm comfortable *because* other people are nervous." You can rattle your opponents with a cool head.

3. Don't just dominate, intimidate. Tiger Woods shows up on the golf course in a blood-red sweater. Dale Earnhardt wore dark sunglasses and drove an intimidating black and white race car that looked like a 200 mph pirate ship. Bob Gibson, the ferocious pitcher for the St. Louis Cardinals, won't even *talk* to players on the opposing team before a game. He explains: "When people get to know you, they get more comfortable with you. And then they get more comfortable against you."

4. Have a sense of history. Know what feats have been performed already and what it will take to beat them. Don't settle for a few short moments of glory. Real winners want to dominate over the long term and be remembered. Pedro Martinez of the Boston Red Sox constantly compares himself to the players he respects the most, so he always has a sense of where he's going. "I want to go to the places they've been and test myself," he explains.

5. Never ever be satisfied. Tiger Woods is a great example of a sportsman who always tries to reach the next rung on the ladder, no matter how high he has already climbed. Every victory seems to make him work harder. A loss should only make the next win more important, and a win should not be too satisfying for too long. Says sports commentator Bob Costas about Michael Jordan, whose obsession with victory made him virtually unstoppable, "He's got to know it's unlikely that he can do anything to increase his standing. . . . He's doing it because he just can't bear not to."

10 Characteristics of a Good Team Player

The ability to cooperate, communicate, respect, and get along with others is a valuable trait, whether you're in the boardroom or operating room, rock band or chorus line. And there's no better place to learn these skills than on the playing field.

1. A team player would rather see his team win than be the star of a losing team.

2. A team player is a collaborator who provides a sense of purpose and gets the team to create a set of goals.

3. A team player appreciates the efforts of teammates if they work as hard as they can.

4. A team player doesn't mind taking suggestions from others.

5. A team player never feels selfish.

6. A team player doesn't look down at anyone who is different.

7. A team player is willing to help a lesser player improve her game.

8. A team player focuses on the task at hand and doesn't need to be in control.

9. A team player is willing to listen to criticism.

10. A team player trusts other people.

10 Things You Can Do to Prevent Sports Injuries

1. Every student participating in athletics should first receive a physical exam, including a general exam and an orthopedic exam. The general exam should include checks on height, weight, blood pressure, pulse, respiration, eye, ear, nose, chest, and abdomen. The orthopedic exam should focus on joint flexibility, joint range of motion, and an examination of past bone and joint injuries.

2. Athletes should work with trainers and coaches year-round to maintain their condition with appropriate exercises and nutrition. They should engage in conditioning programs for at least six weeks before the start of daily practice.

3. Limit workouts and practices to no more than two hours.

4. The night before an event, athletes should drink electrolyte fluids to reduce the risk of dehydration.

5. Athletes should be entitled to unrestricted amounts of fluids during a game to prevent dehydration and other forms of heat-related illness.

6. All athletes should use equipment that fits properly. It should be checked before and after each use to make sure it's in proper working condition and replaced or repaired immediately if there are any problems.

7. The appropriate protective equipment should be worn in all practices as well as during competition.

8. Shoes should provide the necessary support for each individual sport.

9. Mouth guards should be used in all collision sports, including ice hockey, football, and rugby. They're also recommended for all contact sports, including basketball, baseball, lacrosse, and soccer. Not only do they help prevent dental injuries, they can also absorb shocks from blows to the jaw or head and reduce their severity.

10. Players should stretch properly before and after workouts of any kind. They should also have at least a fifteen-minute warm-up period before any game or practice, and an appropriate cool-down period afterward is recommended. Athletes should also warm up for five minutes during any prolonged breaks in the game (including half-time, between periods, etc.).

10 Tips for Catching Balls at Major League Baseball Games

Baseball fan Zach Hample's lifetime goal was to catch 100 Major League baseballs. He caught 128 balls in 1992 alone, and by the end of 1996 he had accumulated over 1,000 balls. Here are some of the secrets he reveals in his wonderful book, *How to Shag Major League Baseballs.*

1. Go to batting practice. It will be a lot harder to catch a ball during a game. You should try to be the first person to enter to get the best spot, which is usually in the first row on the right field line. Ask someone at the box office which gates open the earliest and be the first one in.

2. If you're in a good spot and in a section by yourself, you might be able to ask a player to throw you a ball. If you know the player's name, you improve your chances.

3. If you make a habit of asking players to throw you a ball, don't wear the same clothes to every game or they'll begin to recognize you.

4. Bring a glove. You can try bringing a fishnet, but it may be taken away from you. Some people even bring umbrellas to scoop up balls.

5. If you tie a piece of string to your glove, you may be able to retrieve balls that are sitting on the field just out of reach. Just swing your glove out and drag the ball back to you.

6. Focus on the batter during the game and at batting practice so you don't miss an opportunity.

7. The best areas during batting practice are near one of the foul poles, beyond the outfield fence but in fair territory, or any area in foul territory where the netting of the batting cage won't interfere with the balls' trajectory. Or any area where you can be alone and avoid competition.

8. If you are familiar with the players' batting styles, you can move around the stadium during batting practice and improve your odds. For instance, if a player is a lefty, he will pull the ball to the right.

9. Avoid sitting in the bleachers; it's the worst place to catch balls.

10. When coaches hit fungos during fielding practice, there will be a lot of balls in play and hit into the stands. Be ready.

20 Really Extreme Sports

Extreme sports can often lead to extreme injuries. Guys get injured more often than girls; inline skaters get injured the most. The most common occurrences are broken bones, strains, sprains, serious bruising, and facial cuts. But studies show that nearly 75% of all people who get injured during extreme sports incurred their injuries because they wore NO protective gear! We don't advise you try any of these sports, but if you choose to, be prepared. Learn everything you can about the sport, follow the rules, take *all* safety measures, and make sure your parents know what you are doing.

1. **Big wave tow-in surfing.** Generally done in Maui, Hawaii, tow-in surfing has come into its own as a bona fide subsport of surfing. It involves surfing in waves exceeding the height of a four-story building. Riders try and catch the tallest wave for as long as they can.

2. **Bob skeletoning.** A rider travels head-first on a metal toboggan at speeds in excess of 80 mph down a bobsled run.

3. **Bungee jumping.** This sport is now practiced worldwide, and millions of people have enjoyed this ultimate adrenaline rush.

4. **Canyonning** is an odd sport that combines the disciplines of rock climbing, caving, and swimming.

5. **Ice climbing** is a worldwide sport, popular in the world's greatest mountain ranges.

6. **Mountain biking and overland motorbiking.** For bike enthusiasts, the ultimate challenge is to test your skills against the harshest and least forgiving terrain.

7. **Hang gliding** gives you an unparalleled sense of freedom. You use the movements of the air across your body and the wind's force to stay aloft.

8. **Windsurfing** offers the speed of skiing, the freedom of sailing, and the sheer exhilaration of surfing—and you can have your equipment off the car roof, rigged and ready, in under 5 minutes.

9. **Extreme skiing** is the descent by ski of any exposed face or couloir (a steep mountainside gorge) of 40°.

10. **Speed skiing.** Flying on a cushion of air, speed skiing has been called the fastest unpowered sport on earth.

11. **Snowboarding** has been around for longer than most people imagine. It began in the 1970s, with Californian surfers taking the style and feel of surfing to the mountains.

12. **Surfing** is great for anyone with strong swimming skills.

13. **Cross country (XC).** Mountain bikers on light bikes race around long, off-road circuits of natural tracks. The emphasis is on endurance, fitness, and technical riding skills.

14. **Cyclocross.** A winter event for road racers who don't mind getting muddy. It's similar to XC, but the bikes are not as suitable for the conditions.

15. **Downhill racing.** Riders race against the clock or another rider down steep descents at very high speed. This is the most dangerous biking sport.

16. **BMX dirt biking** involves outdoor jumps. Great if you're lucky enough to live near a woodland or hilly area.

17. **Motocross, or MX,** is off-road motorbike racing, incorporating jumps and turns on specially prepared bikes.

18. **Skydiving** was once reserved for daredevil stuntmen, but it is becoming more and more accessible.

19. **Free fall** is the more skilled and more dangerous part of skydiving. For enthusiasts, the dangers are outweighed by the buzz you get from falling toward Earth at speeds of more than 100 mph.

20. **Tethered riverboarding** is the art of surfing a permanent swell or pocket in the rapids of a river while connected to a bungee cord–like device.

20 of the Best Party Dance Songs of the 1990s

1. "Baby Got Back," Sir Mix-A-Lot, 1991
2. ". . . Baby One More Time," Britney Spears, 1999
3. "Be My Lover," La Bouche, 1996
4. "Believe," Cher, 1999
5. "Escapade," Janet Jackson, 1990
6. "Everybody Dance Now," C & C Music Factory, 1991
7. "Good Vibrations," Marky Mark & the Funky Bunch, 1991
8. "Groove Is in the Heart," Deee-Lite, 1991
9. "Ice Ice Baby," Vanilla Ice, 1991
10. "I'm Too Sexy," Right Said Fred, 1992
11. "Jump," Kriss Kross, 1992
12. "1, 2, 3, 4 (Sumpin' New)," Coolio, 1996
13. "Roam," The B-52s, 1990
14. "Rumpshaker," Wreckx-N-Effect, 1993
15. "This Is How We Do It," Montell Jordan, 1995
16. "U Can't Touch This," M. C. Hammer, 1990

17. "Vogue," Madonna, 1990
18. "Waiting for Tonight," Jennifer Lopez, 1999
19. "Wannabe," Spice Girls, 1997
20. "Whoomp! There It Is," Tag Team, 1993

The Dementia Top 20

Tony Goldmark, our favorite new musical comedy genius, lists his picks for "most demented" music. Catch his Internet radio show, "The Looney Bin," at http://www.dqydj.com /tony/looneybin.htm and hope he plays some of the classics from his two records, *Songs Guaranteed to Annoy Your Parents* and *Masterpiece Weirder*, which includes his famous "Kill the Backstreet Boys."

1. "Banana Boat (Day-O)," Stan Freberg (*Stan Freberg's Greatest Hits* or *The Very Best of Stan Freberg*). In perhaps the best of radio satirist Stan Freberg's copious list of recordings, a bongo player tries to ask Harry Belafonte to "sing softer, man. Like I don't dig loud noises."

2. "Dancin' Fool," Frank Zappa (*Shiek Yerbouti; Strictly Commercial;* or *Dr. Demento's 20th Anniversary Collection*). Dozens upon dozens of antidisco records were released in the late '70s, but this one, by the late avant-garde musical rebel-genius Frank Zappa, is probably the best.

3. "Doctor Worm," They Might Be Giants (*Severe Tire Damage*). One could teach an entire class on They Might Be Giants' lyrics and what they might mean; very few TMBG songs go out of their way to make sense. But that just adds to the dementia!

4. "Fish License/Eric the Half-A-Bee," Monty Python (*Monty Python's Previous Record* or *Monty Python: The Final Rip-Off*). True to Python's muse, these two tracks form a story about a man attempting to get a license to own a fish named Eric, then breaking into song about a half-a-bee. Silly, silly, I say.

5. "Hello Mudduh, Hello Fadduh! (A Letter from Camp)," Allan Sherman (*My Son the Greatest* or *Dr. Demento's 20th Anniversary Collection*). You just can't beat the classics. There was a time in this country when literally every 12-year-old kid was singing this song, so it has left an indelible mark on our society that remains even today.

6. "Hooray for Captain Spaulding," Groucho Marx (*Heeere's Groucho!*). Another classic, albeit from an even older generation. This musical number, originally in the Marx Brothers' film *Animal Crackers*, is as zany and madcap as anyone could possibly get.

7. "I Love You, Baby," Space Ghost (*Space Ghost's Musical Bar-be-que*). It was this song that introduced a good many unsuspecting, "normal" people to the comedy mastermind known to the universe as Brak. Their lives were never the same again.

8. "Irish Ballad," Tom Lehrer (*Revisited or Songs and More Songs by Tom Lehrer*). Tom Lehrer is perhaps the greatest American comedy music writer of the 20th century, and this folk song about a psychotic Irish girl is one of his greatest.

9. "Kevin and God," Radio Free Vestibule (*Sketches, Songs and Shoes*). RFV is a comedy trio from Quebec best known for a bit called "Bulbous Bouffant." But I think this sketch, about a guy who talks to God and forgets to tell people, is even funnier.

10. "Man on the Flying Trapeze," Spike Jones & His City Slickers Doodles Weaver (*The Best of Spike Jones* or *Musical Deprecation Revue: The Spike Jones Anthology*). Spike Jones was definitely the greatest musical comedy genius of the 1940s. In this track he teams up with Doodles Weaver, one of his many City Slickers, for a version of this song that defies description.

11. "Mounted Animal Nature Trail," the Arrogant Worms (*C'est Cheese* or *Live Bait*). Another Canadian troupe, the Arrogant Worms uniquely combines first-rate folk music with everything from social satire to silly kid stuff (often both in the same song).

12. "Nookie/Break Stuff," Richard Cheese (*Lounge Against the Machine*), www.ideatown.com/richardcheese. One of the many alter egos of musical comedian Mark Jonathan Davis, Richard Cheese (who performs alternative music in a Las Vegas lounge style) is the most successful and arguably the funniest.

13. "Old Philosopher," Eddie Lawrence (*Dr. Demento's 25th Anniversary Collection*). The spiel of an old man who tells people to "never give up," even when they are bankrupt and about to drown in mud, is both weirdly ridiculous and somewhat inspiring.

14. "Psychic Voicemail Hotline," Tom Smith (*Plugged*). The funniest song (IMO, at least) by Tom Smith, one of the world's most famous performers of filk (funny folk songs about sci-fi), is the tale of a psychic phone line that knows just a bit too much.

15. "Royal Canadian Kilted Yaksmen Anthem," Ren & Stimpy (*You Eediot!*). Okay, if you were a kid in the early '90s in a household that had cable TV, you probably knew this song by heart at some point. If you listen to it again today, I bet you'll find it has lost none of its humor over time.

16. "They're Coming to Take Me Away, Ha-Haaa!" Napoleon XIV (*The Second Coming* or *Dr. Demento's 20th Anniversary Collection* or *The Very Best of Dr. Demento*). The snare drums. The clapping. The gradually increasing speed of the lead vocal. The hypnotic tale of an insane man on his way to the funny farm, where life is beautiful all the time. You know it, you love it.

17. "Ti Kwan Leep/Boot to the Head," the Frantics (*Dr. Demento's 20th Anniversary Collection* or *The Very Best of Dr. Demento*). The Frantics, one of Canada's funniest comedy troupes of all time, is best known for this tale of a guy who goes to a martial arts lesson and gets more than he bargained for.

18. "Voodoo," Adam Sandler (*What's Your Name?*). Adam Sandler is often funnier on his albums than in his movies, especially in the case of this underappreciated classic, dedicated to "all the bad people of the world."

19. "What Do You Want Me to Do About It?" Henry Phillips (*On the Shoulders of Freaks* or *Number 2*). In this song, every verse begins with a list of problems in the world today and ends with "But what do you want me to do about it?" A lesser singer-songwriter might completely botch this idea, but Henry makes it work.

20. "What's Up, Spock?" the Great Luke Ski (*Fanboys 'n da Hood* or *Carpe Dementia*). A very good friend of mine, not to mention a major dementia talent, Luke Ski will make you proud to be a geek. "What's Up, Spock?," which crams the entire 30-plus-year history of *Star Trek* into a 5-minute rap, is probably his greatest bit ever.

The 17 Greatest Weird Al Songs of All Time

"Weird Al" Yankovic has combined music, comedy, and performance to become the greatest comedy music performer of his time. "Eat It," his spoof of Michael Jackson's "Beat It," hit the charts in 1984, and most people thought he was a funny one-hit wonder. He's more popular today than he's ever been before.

Tony Goldmark lists here the 17 funniest Weird Al songs ever created. DRUM ROLL!

1. "Achy Breaky Song," *Alapalooza; Permanent Record: Al in the Box; Greatest Hits Vol. 2.* In one of his most biting yet deserved satires ever, he targets the man who made America vomit, Billy Ray Cyrus. In this number, he lists the artists he would rather hear (Vanilla Ice, Yoko Ono, and Slim Whitman are on the list).

2. "Albuquerque," *Running with Scissors.* In this 11-minute track, Al punctuates a whimsical story of his move to Albuquerque with plenty of out-of-left-field lines and events only he could have possibly thought of. Hey, you've got weasels on your face.

3. "The Alternative Polka," *Bad Hair Day.* Al has released over half a dozen "polka medleys"—medleys of current songs performed polka style—but this is arguably the best. The polka version of NIN's "Closer" will change your life.

4. "Amish Paradise," *Bad Hair Day.* This might be Al's greatest parody ever in terms of both impact and humor. Nobody but Al could have conceptualized "Gangsta Amish," much less perform it, without making it sound like really bad white rap.

5. "The Biggest Ball of Twine in Minnesota," *UHF: Original Motion Picture Soundtrack and Other Stuff.* Another major fan favorite, this ode to roadside attractions has prompted Al fans the world over to flock to Darwin, Minnesota, where Al is more or less a folk hero for immortalizing the town's greatest landmark in song.

6. "The Check's in the Mail," *"Weird Al" Yankovic.* Though it's an underappreciated original, this delightfully perky ode to Hollywood agents sounds like it was plucked from a Broadway musical with the same title. Hmmm, now there's an idea . . .

7. "Dare to Be Stupid," *Dare to Be Stupid; Greatest Hits; Permanent Record: Al in the Box*. Another memento from the 1980s, this Devo-inspired ditty continually delights fans in concert nonetheless. Just think, if everyone would just dare to be stupid, what a stupid world this would be.

8. "Everything You Know Is Wrong," *Bad Hair Day*. A brilliant ode to They Might Be Giants and a reminder of why he's never called "Normal Al" Yankovic. "I was walking to the kitchen for some Golden Grahams when I accidentally stepped into an alternate dimension . . ."

9. "Generic Blues," *UHF: Original Motion Picture Soundtrack and Other Stuff; Permanent Record: Al in the Box*. A raucous blues number of the highest order, this song takes every great cliché about blues music and turns it on its head. "I woke up this morning, then I went right back to bed."

10. "I Lost on Jeopardy!" *"Weird Al" Yankovic in 3-D; Greatest Hits; Permanent Record: Al in the Box; The TV Album*. An ode to the world's most endearing game show, this cut is cooked to perfection by the addition of Don Pardo ("You don't get to come back tomorrow! You don't even get a lousy copy of our home game!"), the most popular game show announcer of all time.

11. "It's All About the Pentiums," *Running with Scissors*. "Always at my PC, double-clicking on my mizouse." A Puff Daddy parody, this rap song uses hip-hop braggadocio to talk about computer technology. Bonus points for the awesome Drew Carey cameo in the video as Mase.

12. "Livin' in the Fridge," *Alapalooza; Permanent Record: Al in the Box*. Ironic, isn't it, that of all the food songs Al has released, the funniest is about leftovers? In this delightful Aerosmith parody, Al uses Steven Tyler's paranoid vocals in referring to old food that has developed consciousness.

13. "Midnight Star," *"Weird Al" Yankovic in 3-D; Permanent Record: Al in the Box*. An incredible spoof of the fine literacy of the supermarket tabloids, this song is also notable for the fact that it later became the title of a Houston fanzine all about Al. I want to know, I want to know.

14. "Pretty Fly (for a Rabbi)," *Running with Scissors*. You don't have to be Jewish to get this song, but it does help. Using a large array of Hebrew and Yiddish phrases and Judaic references, this song is at the top of my list of "Songs That Should Have Been Made into Videos."

15. "Ricky," "Weird Al" Yankovic; *Greatest Hits; Permanent Record: Al in the Box; The TV Album.* A fabulous spoof of the 1950s TV bonanza that was *I Love Lucy,* this track features the multitalented Tress MacNeille (master of cartoon voices for shows like *The Simpsons, Futurama,* and *Animaniacs*) as the redhead herself.

16. "Smells Like Nirvana," *Off the Deep End; Permanent Record: Al in the Box; Greatest Hits, Vol. 2.* The timing of this song couldn't have been better. When it was released, everyone was up to their knees in Nirvana despite their utterly unintelligible lyrics, and Al's song and video were just what the doctor ordered. Bargle Nawdle Zouss.

17. "Yoda," *Dare to Be Stupid; Permanent Record: Al in the Box; Greatest Hits, Vol. 2.* You know it, you love it. The song about the little green man from Dagoba continues to delight fans twenty years after its creation. If you have never been part of an entire crowd of people at an Al concert singing "Yoda, Yo Yo Yo Yo Yoda," then you, my friend, have not lived.

12 Tips for Buying a Stereo

Buying a stereo system can be frustrating. There are so many choices, and salespeople are often not as helpful as you would hope. Follow these tips, and you'll have an easier time choosing the one that's just right for you.

1. Figure out how much money you can spend. This will help narrow your options. But to determine the difference between a bargain and cheap junk, you'll have to do some research. Magazines such as *Consumer Reports* often publish issues on stereo equipment that name which brands are high quality and which cost way more than they are worth.

2. Large discounters generally charge less than small specialty stores, but the service you'll get at a large store may not be as good as the help you get at a local store.

3. Speakers are the most important part of any system and should be your first consideration. The only way to determine how good speakers are is by listening to them. [The] sound you hear at the store will be different th[an] hear at home, you'll still get a good idea of what t[...]

4. If you have a small room, you won't need l[...] They may look great, but the sound will [...] whelm the neighbors and you'll never use the[...] capacity.

5. Buy a good set of headphones so you can crank up the sound to ear-splitting volume if going deaf is on your "to do" list.

6. If you are planning on going away to college someday, get a portable system.

7. Most one-piece stereo systems come with a two- to- five-CD changer. Go for the larger capacity if you are generally lazy.

8. Comparison shop. You may be able to save enough in one store to pay for your headphones.

9. Many stores offer sales at various times of the year. You may be able to get a better stereo if you're willing to wait.

10. Before you leave the store, make sure that the stereo you are buying is not damaged and has not been returned to the store by a former owner. Keep your receipt. When you unpack the stereo, fill out the warranty card and send it to the manufacturer.

11. Pushy salespeople may try to sell you a certain model because the store needs to get rid of it. Don't let them influence you. Buy the stereo that you want, not what they want you to buy.

12. Ask an older person to accompany you to the store. Stereo salespeople are programmed to take advantage of young people. Put your pride aside.

12 Steps to Starting Your Own Band

Being in a band can be a great experience. Even if you never aspire to stardom, music is a great way to express yourself, get involved with other people, and wear clothes that are against the law in some states. You'll find more information about each of these steps—and tons of great advice from the pros—at www.starpolish.com, which covers every aspect of musicianship.

Learn to play an instrument. When you listen to music, you tend to notice the guitar line or the rhythm? Pick an instrument that reflects your musical interest—something that you want to play because *you just gotta play it.* You can learn on your own, but you'll get there faster if you take lessons. Whatever you choose, make sure it fits into your life. If your parents have a thing about peace and quiet, maybe drums are the wrong choice for you.

2. Get three friends to learn an instrument. Of course, these should be different instruments from the one you play. If you're all learning your instruments at the same time, there's less chance that one of you will "pull a star trip." (Don't miss *Almost Famous,* whatever you do.) On the other hand, if you join a band in which everyone has more experience than you, you'll have better mentors. You can find kindred spirits by posting notices at school, in your community, and at music stores. Your notice should let people know what kind of music you're into, the level of your experience and interest, and your goals.

3. Find a rehearsal space. If someone in your band has a basement and deaf parents, great. Otherwise, try to rehearse at school or in a space that you might have to pay for. Look for a place that isn't too humid (bad for drums) and that has good security.

4. Get some songs. If you all write songs together, everyone in the band will feel more involved in performing them, plus your band will be more likely to develop its own sound. A good way to learn about songwriting is to listen to your favorite songs and analyze their structure. Think about what makes you love them, and try to include those elements in your tunes. Or choose a dozen or so songs from the millions of great songs already out there and practice them.

5. Practice, practice, practice! Practice different versions of the songs you've chosen, and don't be afraid to try out new things. You'll have to spend tons of time practicing, so make sure everyone in the band gets along and that you're all having fun.

6. Cut a demo. You don't have to go to some big recording studio; you can do it in your living room. If the songs are good enough, the people you send the demo to will likely ignore the sound quality. Get a four-track recorder (a device that allows you to record four different instruments at the same time); it costs around $500. Your demo should have no more than three songs on it.

7. Land a gig. Once you have about a dozen songs perfected, you're ready for your first gig. Start out small—at a community event, a school program, or at someone's birthday party. To get a gig, you will have to get club owners to listen to your demo. Be organized. Include a note describing your band, and then, about a week after you've sent in the tape, follow up with a phone call. If a club owner does hire you, chances are you won't be paid. First gigs are usually paid for by the cover charge collected at the door, and you're expected to get your friends to show up. Advertise: put up signs at school and around the neighborhood, especially in music stores. If your school has a radio station, make sure the DJ mentions your show.

8. Play your first show. Possible first-gig problems: the drummer breaks his sticks, the sound system sucks, the van that was going to transport you breaks down, only 13 people show up, the singer forgets the lyrics, your grandmother shows up, and you freeze. These will make great war stories someday. Learn from them and discuss them with your bandmates. Think about how much fun it will be to talk about these adventures in your first *Rolling Stone* interview!

9. Shop your demo to labels. After months of rehearsing and experience, you might want to start sending your demo to some independent record labels. Call the company and ask for the names of the A&R (artist and repertoire) people. They're the ones who sign bands. If they like you, you'll probably hear back within a few weeks and they'll want to come to your next show. If they're interested in signing you, it's time to . . .

10. Get a manager. This person will get a percentage of your money, and it will be her job to find and negotiate gigs, argue about money, and generally advise you about choices. A good, honest, experienced manager is just about the best thing that can happen to you.

11. Start your own label. It will cost a bundle and you'll work harder than you ever imagined (doing your own publicity, production, and record sales), but having your own label means you can do exactly what you want. If you love the creative process of putting your songs together and total control is important to you, this may be the best route for you. It's a serious commitment, but the rewards can be great.

12. Send us free tickets to your first arena gig!

The All-Time Top 10 Karaoke Songs

1. "My Way," Frank Sinatra
2. "Crazy," Patsy Cline
3. "Love Shack," the B-52s
4. "I Will Survive," Gloria Gaynor
5. "YMCA," the Village People
6. "Summer Nights," John Travolta and Olivia Newton-John
7. "I Got You Babe," Sonny and Cher
8. "New York, New York," Frank Sinatra
9. "The Rose," Bette Midler
10. "Endless Love," Diana Ross and Lionel Ritchie

25 Pop Stars Who Were Teenagers When They Hit the Charts

1. Aaliyah. At the age of 15, the New York singer's 1994 debut album, *Age Ain't Nothing but a Number,* went platinum and spawned a pair of gold singles: "Back & Forth" and "At Your Best (You Are Love)."

2. The Backstreet Boys sold more than 55 million records worldwide in less than three years. And both U.S. albums— *Backstreet Boys* and *Millenium*—have received the Diamond Award from the RIAA for sales of more than 10 million each.

3. The Beastie Boys. High schoolers Adam Yauch and Mike Diamond founded the Beastie Boys, which had the first rap-rock hit appealing to the non-hip-hop-listening (read: white) masses, and it had the first rap album, *Fight for Your Right (to Party),* to go to #1 on the Billboard album charts.

4. Boyz II Men. They began their recording career with the debut album *Cooleyhighharmony,* in May 1991. The first single,

"Motownphilly," vaulted up to #3 on the Billboard singles chart by July. The second single, a remake of "It's So Hard to Say Goodbye to Yesterday," hit #2.

5. **Brandy**. At the age of 14, Brandy got her first record contract with Atlantic Records. Her self-titled debut LP appeared in 1994, launching a series of hits, among them "I Wanna Be Down," "Baby," and "Brokenhearted."

6. **Jerry Butler**'s career began at the age of 18 when he and Curtis Mayfield formed a rhythm and blues group, the Impressions, in Chicago in 1958. The same year, Butler wrote a song, "For Your Precious Love," which launched Butler and the Impressions.

7. **Chubby Checker** first gained fame as a teen when his recording "The Twist" exploded onto the music scene in 1960. Known as "King of the Twist," Chubby is a record-breaker who has sold over 250 million records to date. He is the only person on the planet who has had the same single record go #1 twice in different years.

8. **Eddie Cochran**. At the age of 18, Eddie was cast in the 1956 rock 'n' roll film *The Girl Can't Help It*. His performance of "Twenty Flight Rock" was electrifying. As well as making him a teenage idol, it brought him a recording contract with Liberty Records.

9. **Cher** was only 18 when she met Sonny Bono, who became her producer and husband. The internationally known duo released "Dream Baby," which became a hit in their native Los Angeles, and in 1965 they recorded the first Sonny & Cher hit single, "Baby Don't Go." Of course, they're best known for "I Got You Babe."

10. **The Crystals**. This girl group comprised Barbara Alston, Mary Thomas, Dee Dee Kennibrew, Lala Brooks, and Pat Wright, who were in high school in Brooklyn when they were signed to record for the legendary producer Phil Spector in 1961. Some of their hits included "There's No Other (Like My Baby)," "Uptown," "He's a Rebel," and "Da Doo Ron Ron."

11. **Dion**. This legendary rock singer was born in 1939. Early in 1958, Dion, with a group of his neighborhood friends, formed a group called the Belmonts, whose second single, "I Wonder Why," was a hit, almost making the Top Twenty. "No

One Knows" and "Don't Pity Me" followed, but the Belmonts' big break-out hit came in the spring of 1959 with "A Teenager in Love."

12. **Maurice and Robin Gibb.** They were both 18 when the Bee Gees, along with their older brother Barry, recorded their first hit song, "Spicks and Specks," in 1967. Their many accomplishments include the sale of more than 110 million records worldwide, 7 Grammy Awards and 16 nominations, and induction into the Rock and Roll Hall of Fame. They're the only songwriters to have five simultaneous Top 10 singles; *Saturday Night Fever* is the best-selling movie soundtrack ever.

13. **George Harrison.** The famous Beatle was born on February 25, 1943, in Liverpool, England. By the age of 15, he was allowed to sit in with the Quarry Men, the Liverpool group founded by John Lennon, of which Paul McCartney was a member; by 16 he was a full-fledged member of the Beatles. Some of his most noted compositions are "Taxman," "While My Guitar Gently Weeps," "Here Comes the Sun," and "Something." Sadly, he passed away in 2001.

14. **Ice Cube** (of the group N.W.A.), also known as O'Shea Jackson, was born in Crenshaw, south-central Los Angeles, California, on June 15, 1969. At 16, Cube sold his first rap song, "Boyz 'N the Hood," to the rapper Easy-E. Ice Cube's talents as a lyricist earned him a spot in CIA, a fledgling rap music production company that was run by Dr. Dre.

15. **The Jackson 5** comprised Jackie, Tito, Jermaine, Marlon, and Michael. Their first single, in 1970, "I Want You Back," sold 2 million copies. At the time, Jackie was 18, Tito was 16, Jermaine was 15, Marlon was 12, and Michael was 11.

16. **LL Cool J** was born on January 14, 1969, and had his first hit single when he was only 18. Called "I Need Love," it hit the Black Single Chart at #1.

17. **Frankie Lymon** was born in New York City in 1942. At 14, Frankie and his group the Teenagers recorded "Why Do Fools Fall in Love?" which went to the top 10 in the U.S. Other hit songs they recorded were "ABC's of Love," "I'm Not a Juvenile Delinquent," and "Goody, Goody."

18. **Keith Moon** of the legendary band the Who was born on

August 23, 1947, in London. Renowned for his offbeat drum playing, his style helped set the Who apart from the other bands of the era. Moon's wild and zany antics off the stage endeared him to his fans.

19. Ricky Nelson was born Eric Hilliard Nelson on May 8, 1940, in Teaneck, New Jersey. In 1957, during an episode of the popular sitcom *The Adventures of Ozzie and Harriet* (Ricky's parents), Ricky, age 16, sang and performed the Fats Domino tune "I'm Walkin'," which was then recorded and went to #17 on the charts. The flip side, "Teenagers Romance," reached #2. In 1987 Ricky was inducted into the Rock and Roll Hall of Fame.

20. New Edition, made up of Ronnie DeVoe, Bobby Brown, Ricky Bell, Michael Bivins, Ralph Tresvant, and Johnny Gill, was a teen R&B singing group. Its hits included "Cool It Now," "Mr. Telephone Man," "A Little Bit of Love (Is All It Takes)," "With You All the Way," and "Earth Angel."

21. New Kids on the Block, composed of Donnie Wahlberg, Jordan Knight, Jon Knight, Danny Wood, and Joey McIntyre, all came from music or theatrical backgrounds. In 1989 both the Pop and R&B charts were absolutely dominated by these teens from Boston.

22. Britney Spears was born on December 2, 1981. On January 12, 1999, her first album, *Baby, One More Time,* debuted at the #1 spot on the Billboard charts. It featured "Sometimes," "(You Drive Me) Crazy," and "From the Bottom of My Broken Heart." *Oops! . . . I Did It Again* came out in May 2000 and sold 1.3 million copies during its first week, beating Mariah Carey's record for the highest first-week sales by a female solo artist.

23. Ritchie Valens was only 17 when he recorded his classic version of "La Bamba" and his own song "Donna." The result was a double-sided smash that is the foundation of the Valens legend. His other notable songs include "Come On Let's Go," "That's My Little Suzie," "Little Girl," and "Ooh My Head."

24. Steve Winwood was born on May 12, 1948. He joined the Spencer Davis Group when he was 15 as an accomplished musician: he sang and played guitar and keyboards. In 1967 he formed his own band, Traffic, and also became a member of Blind Faith, both legendary and highly influential rock bands.

His hits include "Gimme Some Lovin'" and "I'm a Man."

25. **Stevie Wonder** was born as Steveland Judkins on May 13, 1950. Blind from birth, Wonder learned the piano at the age of 7 and mastered the drums and harmonica by the age of 9. In 1963, the release of his live recording "Fingertips (Part 2)" made him a star. In 1965 he had a worldwide hit with the dance-oriented "Uptight (Everything's Alright)." This began a run of U.S. Top 40 hits that continued for over six years. He is now considered one of the most gifted performers and songwriters in the history of music.

157 Censored Rock Songs

Censorship is not always called censorship. Sometimes people censor things by claiming that they are protecting you. The fact that you may be mature enough to make up your own mind does not enter into their argument.

For example, after the tragedy of September 11, 2001, Clear Channel, a radio network with hundreds of stations throughout the country, sent a list of 157 songs to its stations and suggested that playing them on the air was "in bad taste." There was an immediate outcry. Thousands of people pointed out that many of these songs were anthems whose lyrics and ideas had been enjoyed for decades and that "censors" were using the occasion to rid the airwaves, not only of any songs with antiwar sentiments, but also any others that the censors might find offensive. Should you have the right to decide which music you listen to and which you ignore? We think so.

The list is reprinted here both as a record of Clear Channel's action and because we believe that these songs, taken together, represent a great history of what rock 'n' roll has been about for over 50 years.

1. AC/DC, "Dirty Deeds"
2. AC/DC, "Hell's Bells"
3. AC/DC, "Highway to Hell"
4. AC/DC, "Safe in New York City"
5. AC/DC, "Shoot to Thrill"
6. AC/DC, "Shot Down in Flames"

7. AC/DC, "TNT"
8. Ad Libs, "The Boy from New York City"
9. Alice in Chains, "Down in a Hole"
10. Alice in Chains, "Rooster"
11. Alice in Chains, "Sea of Sorrow"
12. Alice in Chains, "Them Bone"
13. Alien Ant Farm, "Smooth Criminal"
14. All Rage Against the Machine songs
15. Animals, "We Gotta Get out of This Place"
16. Louis Armstrong, "What a Wonderful World"
17. Bangles, "Walk Like an Egyptian"
18. Barenaked Ladies, "Falling for the First Time"
19. Barry McGuire, "Eve of Destruction"
20. Beastie Boys, "Sabotage"
21. Beastie Boys, "Sure Shot"
22. The Beatles, "A Day in the Life"
23. The Beatles, "Lucy in the Sky with Diamonds"
24. The Beatles, "Obla de Obla Da"
25. The Beatles, "Ticket to Ride"
26. Pat Benatar, "Hit Me with Your Best Shot"
27. Pat Benatar, "Love Is a Battlefield"
28. Black Sabbath, "Sabbath Bloody Sabbath"
29. Black Sabbath, "Suicide Solution"
30. Black Sabbath, "War Pigs"
31. Blood, Sweat, and Tears, "And When I Die"
32. Blue Oyster Cult, "Burnin' for You"
33. Boston, "Smokin"
34. Brooklyn Bridge, "Worst That Could Happen"
35. Arthur Brown, "Fire"
36. Jackson Brown, "Doctor My Eyes"
37. Bush, "Speed Kills"
38. Chi-Lites, "Have You Seen Her"
39. Petula Clark, "Sign of the Times"
40. The Clash, "Rock the Casbah"
41. Sam Cooke/Herman's Hermits, "Wonderful World"
42. Phil Collins, "In the Air Tonight"
43. The Cult, "Fire Woman"
44. Creedence Clearwater Revival, "Travelin' Band"
45. Bobby Darin, "Mack the Knife"

46. Dave Clark Five, "Bits and Pieces"
47. Dave Matthews Band, "Crash into Me"
48. Skeeter Davis, "End of the World"
49. Neil Diamond, "America"
50. Dio, "Holy Diver"
51. The Doors, "The End"
52. The Drifters, "On Broadway"
53. Drowning Pool, "Bodies"
54. Bob Dylan/Guns 'N Roses, "Knockin' on Heaven's Door"
55. Everclear, "Santa Monica"
56. Shelley Fabares, "Johnny Angel"
57. Filter, "Hey Man, Nice Shot"
58. Fontella Bass, "Rescue Me"
59. Foo Fighters, "Learn to Fly"
60. Fuel, "Bad Day"
61. Peter Gabriel, "When You're Falling"
62. The Gap Band, "You Dropped a Bomb on Me"
63. Godsmack, "Bad Religion"
64. Norman Greenbaum, "Spirit in the Sky"
65. Green Day, "Brain Stew"
66. Happenings, "See You in Septemeber"
67. Jimi Hendrix, "Hey Joe"
68. The Hollies, "He Ain't Heavy, He's My Brother"
69. Buddy Holly and the Crickets, "That'll Be the Day"
70. Jan and Dean, "Dead Man's Curve"
71. Billy Joel, "Only the Good Die Young"
72. Elton John, "Benny & the Jets"
73. Elton John, "Daniel"
74. Elton John, "Rocket Man"
75. Kansas, "Dust in the Wind"
76. Carole King, "I Feel the Earth Move"
77. Korn, "Falling Away from Me"
78. Lenny Kravitz, "Fly Away"
79. Led Zeppelin, "Stairway to Heaven"
80. John Lennon, "Imagine"
81. Jerry Lee Lewis, "Great Balls of Fire"
82. Limp Bizkit, "Break Stuff"
83. Local H, "Bound for the Floor"
84. Los Bravos, "Black Is Black"

85. Lynyrd Skynyrd, "Tuesday's Gone"
86. Martha and the Vandellas, "Nowhere to Run"
87. Martha and the Vandellas/Van Halen, "Dancing in the Streets"
88. Paul McCartney & Wings, "Live and Let Die"
89. Don McLean, "American Pie"
90. Megadeth, "Dread and the Fugitive"
91. Megadeth, "Sweating Bullets"
92. John Mellencamp, "Crumbling Down"
93. John Mellencamp, "I'm on Fire"
94. Metallica, "Enter Sandman"
95. Metallica, "Fade to Black"
96. Metallica, "Harvester or Sorrow"
97. Metallica, "Seek and Destroy"
98. Steve Miller, "Jet Airliner"
99. Alanis Morissette, "Ironic"
100. Mudvayne, "Death Blooms"
101. Ricky Nelson, "Travelin' Man"
102. Nina, "99 Luft Balloons/99 Red Balloons"
103. Nine Inch Nails, "Head Like a Hole"
104. Oingo Boingo, "Dead Man's Party"
105. P.O., "Boom"
106. Paper Lace, "The Night Chicago Died"
107. John Parr, "Elmo's Fire"
108. Peter and Gordon, "A World Without Love"
109. Peter and Gordon, "I Go to Pieces"
110. Peter, Paul and Mary, "Blowin' in the Wind"
111. Peter, Paul and Mary, "Leavin' on a Jet Plane"
112. Tom Petty, "Free Fallin'"
113. Pink Floyd, "Mother"
114. Pink Floyd, "Run Like Hell"
115. Elvis, "(You're the) Devil in Disguise"
116. The Pretenders, "My City Was Gone"
117. Queen, "Another One Bites the Dust"
118. Queen, "Killer Queen"
119. Red Hot Chili Peppers, "Aeroplane"
120. Red Hot Chili Peppers, "Under the Bridge"
121. REM, "It's the End of the World as We Know It"
122. The Rolling Stones, "Ruby Tuesday"

123. Mitch Ryder and the Detroit Wheels, "Devil with the Blue Dress"

124. Saliva, "Click Click Boom"

125. Santana, "Evil Ways"

126. Savage Garden, "Crash and Burn"

127. Simon and Garfunkel, "Bridge over Troubled Water"

128. Frank Sinatra, "New York, New York"

129. Slipknot, "Left Behind You"

130. Smashing Pumpkins, "Bullet with Butterfly Wings"

131. Soundgarden, "Blow Up the Outside World"

132. Soundgarden, "Fell on Black Days"

133. Bruce Springsteen, "I'm Goin' Down"

134. Bruce Springsteen, "I'm on Fire"

135. Edwin Starr/Bruce Springsteen, "War"

136. Steam, "Na Na Na Na Hey Hey"

137. Cat Stevens, "Morning Has Broken"

138. Cat Stevens, "Peace Train"

139. Stone Temple Pilots, "Big Bang Baby, Dead and Bloated"

140. Sugar Ray, "Fly"

141. Surfaris, "Wipeout"

142. System of a Down, "Chop Suey!"

143. Talking Heads, "Burning Down the House"

144. James Taylor, "Fire and Rain"

145. Temple of the Dog, "Say Hello to Heaven"

146. Third Eye Blind, "Jumper"

147. Three Degrees, "When Will I See You Again"

148. 3 Doors Down, "Duck and Run"

149. 311, "Down"

150. Tool, "Intolerance"

151. The Tramps, "Disco Inferno"

152. U2, "Sunday Bloody Sunday"

153. Van Halen, "Jump"

154. Frank Wilson, "Last Kiss"

155. Yager and Evans, "In the Year 2525"

156. The Youngbloods, "Get Together"

157. The Zombies, "She's Not There"

Teen Opinions About Free Music Downloads

Copyright law states that it's illegal to copy information, art, music, or ideas without getting permission from the owners. When you download music off the Internet, the copyright owner gets no compensation. On the other hand, some argue that people have been taping music off the radio forever and that this "free helping" is no different. They also say that the music on the Internet encourages people to buy the CD, so it's really advertising. Some rock groups say they were actually discovered on the Internet through their downloads. Here's the range of popular opinion. What do you think?

Wrong to download	25%
Wrong to stop downloading	17%
Not wrong either way	53%
Not sure	5%

Teen Opinions About the Effect of the Entertainment Media on Morals and Values

The Horatio Alger Association reports the following:

Negative effect	46%
Positive effect	11%
No effect	36%
Not sure	7%

18 Great Rock 'n' Roll Soundtracks

You may not be old enough to remember some of them, but they are more than worth listening to.

1. *American Graffiti* (1973). The film has a classic rock 'n' roll soundtrack composed of more than 40 hits (emanating from cruising car radios and sometimes serving as background music to define the emotions, dreams, and frustrations of the characters) ranging over almost a decade (1955–1962). Each of the 41 songs is a classic.

2. *Boyz 'N the Hood* (1991). The soundtrack features a powerful compilation of performances from Ice Cube, 2 Live Crew, Too Short, Tony! Toni! Tone!, Quincy Jones, and many others. The original score for the film was composed by Stanley Clarke, one of R&B's legendary bassists.

3. *Do the Right Thing* (1989). Features Take 6, Al Jarreau, Steel Pulse, Ruben Blades, and Public Enemy. The film received two 1990 Oscar nominations: for Best Original Screenplay (Spike Lee) and Best Supporting Actor (Danny Aiello).

4. *Easy Rider* (1969). This legendary film's soundtrack includes Steppenwolf's "Born to Be Wild" and "The Weight," written by Robbie Robertson of the Band, and Bob Dylan's "Its Alright Ma (I'm Only Bleeding)."

5. *The Graduate* (1967). Songs written by Paul Simon and sung by Simon & Garfunkel. The tunes include "Mrs. Robinson" and "The Sound of Silence." This is the first time a soundtrack was used to help tell the story.

6. *A Hard Day's Night* (1964). The first and best of the Beatles' films, the soundtrack featured "A Hard Day's Night," "Tell Me Why," "If I Needed Someone," "I Should Have Known Better," and "Can't Buy Me Love." If you buy only one soundtrack album in your life, this is the one to get.

7. *The Harder They Come* (1973). Introduced reggae music to America and features the music of Jimmy Cliff. It included the now-classic "You Can Get It if You Really Want," "Rivers of Babylon," "Many Rivers to Cross," and "The Harder They Come."

8. *High Fidelity* (2000). This Grammy-nominated soundtrack features 15 cuts, from the classic rock 'n' rollers Bob Dylan, the Kinks, and the Velvet Underground to relatively new artists—the Beta Band, Tenacious D, and 13th Floor Elevators.

9. *Jailhouse Rock* (1957). Perhaps Elvis's best movie, it featured the songs "Jailhouse Rock," "Treat Me Nice," "Young and Beautiful," "I Wanna Be Free," and "Don't Leave Me Now."

10. *The Last Waltz* (1978). Directed by Martin Scorsese, this film is the last performance of the legendary group the Band. A list of the songs and artists featured on the soundtrack would be a Who's Who of rock 'n' roll. There are 30 songs performed by over 30 artists.

11. *Pat Garret & Billy the Kid* (1973). Music by Bob Dylan. He wrote "Billy" and the masterful "Knockin' on Heaven's Door" as well as all the incidental music.

12. *Pump Up the Volume* (1990). Featured music by Concrete Blonde, Liquid Jesus, the Pixies, Bad Brains with Henry Rollins, Soundgarden, Sonic Youth, and Cowboy Junkies.

13. *Purple Rain* (1984). Features the music of Prince. Songs include "Purple Rain," "Let's Go Crazy," and "When Doves Cry."

14. *Quadrophenia* (1979). Pete Townshend and the Who's follow-up to the classic rock opera *Tommy,* it includes "I've Had Enough," "Helpless Dancer," and the hit single "Love Reign O'er Me."

15. *Saturday Night Fever* (1977). Features a string of #1 hits for the Bee Gees, including "Night Fever," "How Deep Is Your Love," and "Stayin' Alive." *Saturday Night Fever* sold over 30 million copies and was the best-selling album of all time until Michael Jackson released *Thriller.*

16. *Single* (1992). Arguably the best compilation from the Seattle scene. Led off by Alice in Chains' "Would?" and featuring very strong work from Pearl Jam, Soundgarden, and Screaming Trees, not to mention the immortal Jimi Hendrix.

17. *Superfly* (1972). Curtis Mayfield wrote the soundtrack, which was an immediate success and contained two hit songs: "Freddie's Dead" and "Superfly." The album stayed on the U.S. Pop Chart for 4 weeks.

18. *Woodstock* (1970). The film chronicles 400,000 fans celebrating three days of music and mud, then cuts to the stage for some of the finest concert footage from '60s mainstays the Who, Sly and the Family Stone, Santana, Jefferson Airplane, Janis Joplin, Canned Heat, and other luminaries.

10 Definitive Hip-Hop Albums

Here is about.com's list of the 10 albums released since 1990 that are undoubtedly destined to be true classics.

1. *Black Sunday*–Cypress Hill. This amazing album offers the classic Cypress Hill cuts "Insane in the Brain," "Lick a Shot," and "Hand on the Glock."

2. *Do You Want More?*—The Roots. This straight-up classic features "Mellow My Man," "I Remain Calm," and "Silent Treatment."

3. *Don Killuminati: The 7 Day Theory*—Makavelli. This Tupac Shakur album released under the alias Makavelli showcased a darker, almost prophetic side of the late artist.

4. *Enter the 36 Chambers*—Wu Tang Clan. This first album by *the* hip-hop supergroup knocked the music world on its ear and forever changed hip-hop.

5. *Illamatic*—Nas. This instant classic established Nas Escobar as an unrivaled poet.

6. *Like Water for Chocolate*—Common. Released in 2000, this album introduced the commercial world to an emcee who had reigned in the underground for years. It's relatively new to be considered a classic, but we bet it'll still be hot in 10 years.

7. *Miseducation of Lauryn Hill*—Lauryn Hill. This wildly successful debut from the Fugees' front woman established Hill as a hip-hop genius.

8. *The Score*—Fugees. Moody and atmospheric, this features Lauryn Hill's "Killing Me Softly" and the magnificent "Fu-Gee-La."

9. *Southernplayalisticadillacmuzik*—Outkast. This album helped establish the prowess of one of the most eccentric hip-hop groups ever.

10. *Straight Outta Compton*—NWA. This album ushered in an era of West Coast gangster rap: street reality, misogyny, and hardcore lyrics laced with old-school funked-out beats.

10 Albums That Define Alternative Music

For many, the following 10 albums define alternative music, which entered the music scene in the early '90s. Linked with classic rock, grunge, punk, techno, and even hip-hop, it is an evolving genre, ever changing as artists push the limits of the "alternative" label applied to them and their music. Thanks for this one to Pagewise, Inc.; www.pagewise.com.

1. *August and Everything After,* by the Counting Crows. It's difficult to classify the Counting Crows' sound. The band supplements the usual guitar-driven alternative sound with a folk influence. They are the best storytellers in the alternative genre, as exemplified by songs like "Mr. Jones" and "Round Here." The Counting Crows have followed the success of their debut album with two more excellent studio recordings and have solidified their place as one of alternative music's most talented bands.

2. *Automatic for the People,* by REM. REM is without a doubt one of the most significant alternative bands. Their myriad albums have helped define the alternative sound, and the band has been at the forefront of the alternative scene since the word existed. Of their albums, *Automatic for the People* stands out. It is one of the more relaxed REM albums, with an almost sleepy mood and a soft quality. But its two singles, "Man on the Moon" and "Everybody Hurts," are among the best songs of the last decade, and the rest of the album does not trail far behind. "Everybody Hurts" is one of the most emotional alternative songs ever, and one can only speculate about Michael Stipe's inspiration for writing it.

3. *Blood Sugar Sex Magik,* by the Red Hot Chili Peppers. The Red Hot Chili Peppers was the most important early '90s alternative band outside Seattle. It was around five years before any of the Seattle bands, but it wasn't until their 1991 *Blood Sugar Sex Magik* that they really saw commercial success. The Chili Peppers continues to be one of the most energetic and exciting bands on the alternative music scene they helped create.

4. *Freedom,* by Neil Young. Despite what some Nirvana fans might say, this is the album that started it all. Neil Young is the grandfather of grunge. *Freedom,* which Young released in 1989, was the first true alternative album. "Rockin' in the Free World" is the first true alternative song.

5. *Garbage,* by Garbage. Garbage broke all the rules for its first album, and the result was an album that pushed the limits of the alternative genre and blurred the lines between electronica, pop, techno, and alternative. Garbage definitely does not fit the mold. Its sound is almost impossible to describe. It carries the synthesized, produced quality of techno but adds a distinctly alternative vocal part. The members of Garbage are some of the most talented musicians in alternative music today, but they are also among the best producers. Their mouthpiece is the beautiful lead singer Shirley Manson, whose haunting, enchanting voice brings to mind the Fleetwood Mac vocalist Stevie Nicks.

6. *The Joshua Tree,* by U2. With *The Joshua Tree,* U2 proved that melody and popularity are not mutually exclusive in an album. Thanks to them, groups like the Dave Matthews Band, whose sound does not fit any mold, can be accommodated under the umbrella of alternative music. *The Joshua Tree* contains some of the best of what could be called soft alternative: "Where the Streets Have No Name," "With or Without You," and "Still Haven't Found What I'm Looking For."

7. *Nevermind,* by Nirvana. "Smells Like Teen Spirit." These might be the four most significant words in the history of alternative music. Without this one song, we might not even have heard of it. The "Seattle sound" might have fizzled out in Seattle clubs. "Smells Like Teen Spirit" somehow captured the mood of the early '90s youth. With his apathetic chorus of "Here we are now, entertain us," Cobain puts into words a discontented, disconnected, and disinterested youth culture. This album alone makes Nirvana one of the most important bands and *Nevermind* one of the most important albums in alternative music history.

8. *Purple,* by the Stone Temple Pilots. The Stone Temple Pilots would have been one of the most successful bands of the '90s if Scott Weyland could have stayed out of rehab for three months. Their studio albums are among the best work put forth by an alternative group in the last decade, and their MTV *Unplugged* show highlights their overwhelming musical ability. *Purple* covers the widest range of styles and best shows STP's ability. It fits into the classic mold of guitar-driven alternative music, but Weyland's vocals shine through and add a richness to STP's sound that is not found on many alternative albums.

9. *Temple of the Dog,* by Temple of the Dog. Never has a group of more talented musicians come together to make an album. After the tragic death of Mother Love Bone lead singer Andrew Wood, a few members of the budding Seattle alternative music scene decided to come together and make a recording dedicated to Wood. These musicians included former Mother Love Bone members and future Pearl Jam members Jeff Ament and Stone Gossard, Soundgarden members Chris Cornell and Matt Cameron, and longtime Seattle guitarist

Mike McCready. The quintet invited the little-known lead singer Eddie Vedder, who went on to become Pearl Jam's lead singer.

10. *Ten,* by Pearl Jam. This is far and away the best album of the alternative genre. In 10 songs, it encompasses the extremes of tempo, volume, and style of the genre. From the mellow "Release" to the contemplative "Black" to the powerful "Even Flow," this album has it all. More than any other quality, true emotion makes *Ten* the best album of its genre. No lead singer has ever poured his soul out like Eddie Vedder does on *Ten.*

The 10 Essential World Music Albums

"World music" is a way of describing music from around the globe that's not in English (and some that is). Though this ethnic and pop music has been available since the dawn of recorded music, the world music genre didn't emerge until the mid-1980s, when significant numbers of Americans and Europeans began to prick up their ears for the very first time. The following is a list of some of the most important world music records, as compiled by Tom Pryon, senior editor of CDNOW.

1. *Drums of Passion,* Babatunde Olatunji. Recorded in 1959, this was one of the first world music records ever, and it helped lead African music out of the anthropology textbook and onto the dance floor. Nigeria's Olatunji is still going strong today with international tours and a slew of records that showcase his powerful traditional Yoruba drumming. Every African artist to make it internationally—from Hugh Masekela to Youssou N'Dour—owes a small debt to him for paving the way.

2. *Foundation Ska,* the Skatalites. As the title implies, the Skatalites were the foundation of the modern Jamaican sound. Every Jamaican artist from Bob Marley to Buju Banton has been influenced by these illustrious graduates of Kingston's Alpha School for Boys. Fronted by such virtuoso horn players as Don Drummond and Roland Alphonso, the Skatalites made a frenetic, swing-based dance music called ska that introduced the characteristic "off" beat—later the hallmark of reggae—into Jamaican popular music.

3. *Gipsy Kings*, Gipsy Kings. Hailing from Montpelier and Arles, France, the Gipsy Kings have combined the prodigious talents of the Reyes and Baliardo families to form one of contemporary flamenco music's most profitable and enduring franchises. This 1988 classic was one of the best-selling world music albums ever. It introduced the world to their unique rumba catalana sound of massed guitars, wailing vocals, and subtle Latin percussion. Such hits as "Djobi Djoba," "Bamboleo," and "Bem Bem, Maria" had audiences around the globe singing along in the group's gitane dialect.

4. *The Girl from Ipanema: The Antonio Carlos Jobim Songbook*, Antonio Carlos Jobim. Chances are, you've heard one of Jobim's songs without even knowing it. From "The Girl from Ipanema" to "One Note Samba," his compositions—spanning 30 years—are a staple of both jazz and Brazilian pop and have been featured in such seminal reflections of the American subconscious as the Blues Brothers and Banana Republic commercials. Without question, it was Jobim's lush, wistful music that first introduced many Americans to the infinite pleasures of Brazilian music.

5. *Irish Heartbeat*, Van Morrison & the Chieftains. The Chieftains have been breathing new life into Ireland's traditional music since their mid-1960s apprenticeship with the brilliant composer and Irish musical scholar Sean O'Riada. Belfast's Van Morrison has been doing his own funky, mystical, blue-eyed Celtic soul thing for just as long. When these two musical titans finally got together for this 1988 masterpiece, Irish music fans from Dublin to Des Moines and Cork to Canberra stood up and cheered.

6. *Khaled*, Khaled. The Algerian singer Khaled—formerly Cheb Khaled—is the reigning king of rai, the gritty, soulful music that some call North African Blues. Forced to leave his homeland by both economic circumstances and Islamic militants, Khaled now lives in Paris, where he makes music for the millions of his fellow countrymen that also call the French capital their home. This 1991 album was a landmark that saw Khaled's blend of traditional rai with reggae and funk find a real international audience for the first time.

7. *Live Live Juju*, King Sunny Ade. Sunny Ade is the international face of Nigeria's juju music—popular Yoruba dance music heavy on sweet guitar rhythms and thundering drums. In the early '80s, his good looks and brilliant songcraft led Island Records to groom him as "the next Bob Marley" and the new standard-bearer for "tropical pop music." He never quite lived up to that, but he still performs and records today. This live recording from an early U.S. tour encapsulates some of his best work while perfectly capturing the sweaty communality and spontaneous improvisation of a live juju session.

8. *Must Must,* Nusrat Fateh Ali Khan. Pakistan's late, great Nusrat Fateh Ali Khan was one of the most gifted vocalists of the 20th century. His soaring, impassioned performances made him a sensation abroad and a legend at home. A Qawwali singer, Ali Khan performed the mystical, devotional music of Islam's Sufi sect. In the mid-'80s, he came to the attention of Peter Gabriel, who enthusiastically signed him to his Real World label. This 1990 Real World disk was the high water mark of Ali Khan's international popularity and caught him at the height of his considerable vocal powers.

9. *Mystère des Voix Bulgares,* Mystère des Voix Bulgares. This 1987 release came out of nowhere to take the nascent world music community by storm. Walled-off behind the Iron Curtain, this state choir of Bulgarian women (the National Television and Radio Chorus) was originally formed to preserve the folk traditions of the Bulgarian peasantry. When the French producer Marcel Cellier heard their incredible repertoire of otherworldly harmonies and soaring vocal acrobatics, he recorded them on the spot and initiated a successful cottage industry that thrives to this day.

10. *Ry Cooder Presents the Buena Vista Social Club.* As American blues is to jazz and rock, Cuba's venerable son is the granddaddy of everything from the mambo to salsa. When the American guitarist Ry Cooder went to Havana in 1996 to search out some authentic songs, little did he know that he would stumble into one of the most lucrative, if unlikely, Cuban pop crossovers in years. This 1997 Grammy winner assembled some near-forgotten leading lights from Havana's glamorous, pre-Castro past (Ibrahim Ferrer, Compay Segundo, Eliades Ochoa, etc.) and let them loose in the studio. The result reignited America's musical love affair with Cuba.

24 Pearls of Rock Wisdom

1. "When you ain't got nothin', you got nothing to lose."
   —Kris Kristofferson; Janis Joplin, "Me and Bobby Mc-
   Gee"
2. "All you need is love."—The Beatles
3. "Different strokes for different folks."—Sly and the Family Stone, "Everyday People"
4. "Fools we are, if hate's the gate to peace."—Dave Matthews Band, "The Last Stop"
5. "Love is a battlefield."—Pat Benatar
6. "Optimism is my best defense."—Rod Stewart, "Baby
   Jane"
7. "Rather die on our feet, than keep living on our knees."
   —James Brown, "Say It Loud (I'm Black and I'm Proud),
   Part I"
8. "A hungry mob is an angry mob."—Bob Marley and the
   Wailers, "Them Belly Full"
9. "The words of the prophets are written on the subway
   walls."—Simon and Garfunkel, "The Sounds of Silence"
10. "All things must pass, all things must pass away."
    —George Harrison, "All Things Must Pass"
11. "Thinking is the best way of traveling."—The Moody
    Blues, "The Best Way to Travel"
12. "War is not the answer, because only love can conquer
    hate."—Marvin Gaye, "What's Going On"
13. "You can't always get what you want, but if you try some-
    time you just might find you get what you need."
    —The Rolling Stones, "You Can't Always Get What You
    Want"
14. "Free your mind and your ass will follow."—Funkadelic,
    "Good Thoughts, Bad Thoughts"
15. "A pretty face don't make a pretty heart."—Robert
    Palmer, "Bad Case of Loving You"
16. "Fill your life with love and bravery, and you shall live a
    life uncommon."—Jewel, "Life Uncommon"
17. "He who forgets will be destined to remember."—Pearl
    Jam, "Nothingman"
18. "There ain't no way to hide your lyin' eyes."—The Ea-
    gles, "Lyin' Eyes"

19. "Kingdoms rise and kingdoms fall, but you go on." —U2, "October"
20. "Life is what happens when you're busy making other plans." —John Lennon, "Beautiful Boy"
21. "Poor man wanna be rich, rich man wanna be king, and a king ain't satisfied until he rules everything." —Bruce Springsteen, "Badlands"
22. "Every thought is a possibility." —The Indigo Girls, "Mystery"
23. "They don't gotta burn books, they just remove them." —Rage Against the Machine, "Bulls on Parade"
24. "The mistakes of each generation will just fade like a radio station." —Ani DiFranco, "Out of Range"

12 Ideas for Get-Togethers

1. Dinner for 12. Have everyone bring a dish to a formal dinner. Tell everyone to dress up.
2. Tell everyone to bring a camera and have a photo shoot of everyone taking pictures.
3. Have a fortune-telling party. Rent a psychic or get a ouiji board. Or get a deck of tarot cards and an instruction book.
4. Get multiple copies of the script to a play or movie and have people over for a dramatic reading.
5. Have a book party. Choose a book that you know all your friends are familiar with and invite them over to talk about it. Each person could be asked to rewrite the ending.
6. Hold a clothing swap. Everyone brings an item of clothing they don't wear much, and they all trade. Do this right after the holidays and trade all those red earmuffs for something you can actually use.
7. Get together with friends a few weeks before Halloween to work on costumes.
8. Have a craft party. Maybe you can invite some little kids who might enjoy the fun, too. The money you make babysitting will pay for your supplies.
9. Have a babysitters' New Year's Eve party. The babysitters and their charges can entertain one another at one person's house. Of course, all the parents must support the idea.

10. Appoint one night of the week (or month) game night, and hold the event at a different person's house each time.

11. Invite everyone over for a room-redecorating party. You can go the whole nine yards — paint everything, including the walls — or just rearrange the furniture.

12. Have a pity party! If someone's had bad luck, invite a few friends over for the sole purposes of cheering them up. Bring gag gifts. Guests can take turns talking about the worst things they've lived through.

12 Easy Halloween Costumes

1. There's always the traditional standby — the ghost. But does yours have to be traditional? How about some lipstick and eye makeup on the face along with some gaudy jewelry? Or wear a baseball cap and go as the ghost of Joe DiMaggio.

2. Go as an obnoxious tourist. Guys wear Hawaiian shirts and shorts; girls wear oversized loud sundresses, sunglasses, and large straw hats. Carry shopping bags and a camera. Ask everyone to take your picture.

3. Be a Wanted poster. Paint a Wanted poster on the front of a large carton and cut a hole where your face will go.

4. Wear a ratty wig and an oversize coat with a pillow stuck in the back of your neck. Poof! You're the Hunchback of Notre Dame.

5. Wear a solid color like black or white and, using safety pins, attach all sorts of small laundry items — socks, underwear, etc. Tell everyone you're Static Cling.

6. Go as Mother Nature. Wear an old bridal or bridesmaid dress (or just a very long bridal veil) and attach twigs, fake birds, leaves, and flowers all over.

7. Wear all black, including a black hood, and use white tape to attach a white strip from the top of your head all the way down to your butt. Add a tail. You're a skunk. (Use your imagination to create an "odorama" version of this costume.)

8. Wear anything you want, then just hold a bunch of purple balloons and go as a bunch of grapes. Use different-colored balloons and be a bunch of jellybeans.

9. An easy bat costume: wear black and carry an open black umbrella.

10. Paint on a milk mustache and go as a "Got Milk?" ad.

11. Great for anyone in a wheelchair: wear the costume of a king or queen and make the chair look like a throne. Act bossy.

12. A clever fellow named Sean Clancy once went to a Halloween party as Urban Sprawl. He wore boots, jeans, and a flannel shirt to represent the land. Then, to represent the destruction and commercialization that accompany urban sprawl, he decorated his costume with a street sign, a Coke can, a road atlas, and other symbols of "progress." The costume cost nothing yet made a powerful statement. Design a costume that tells people what you really think!

12 Nonalcoholic Cocktails

1. **The Goldfish.** Pour a cup of orange juice over ice. Fill the rest of the glass with club soda and add an orange slice. Serves 1.

2. **Mellow Yellow.** In a saucepan, combine $1^3/8$ cups sugar with $1^3/8$ cups water. Bring to a boil. Add $1^1/2$ cups grapefruit juice, $2^3/8$ cups pineapple juice, and $1^1/2$ cups lemon juice. Chill and serve. Serves 4.

3. **The Purple People Eater.** Combine $3^1/2$ cups lemonade with $1^1/2$ cups grapefruit juice. Serve over ice. A variation of this drink, called the Red Riding Hood, calls for $3^1/2$ cups cranberry juice mixed with $1^1/2$ cups orange juice, also served over ice. Serves 4.

4. **The Texas Cow.** Add a splash of grenadine to a glass of milk. To make a Heifer, add the grenadine to chocolate milk instead. Serves 1.

5. **Tutti-frutti Shake.** Blend $1^1/3$ cups chilled apricot or strawberry juice with $2/3$ cup cold milk. Serve over ice. Serves 4.

6. **Virgin Mary.** Combine 5 ounces tomato juice with 2 dashes Worcestershire sauce. Shake well. Fill a glass with ice and pour the juice into it. Add a dash of celery salt, a dash of pepper, and a celery stick for garnish. Serves 1.

7. **Cherry Bing.** Dilute 1 pint cherry juice and 4 ounces orange juice in 10 ounces water. Stir to blend. Add ice cubes. Makes 1 large drink or 2 smaller ones.

8. Florida Cocktail. In a shaker, combine $3^1/2$ ounces grapefruit juice, 1 tablespoon lemon juice, 2 ounces sugar syrup, and a pinch of salt. Fill the rest of the shaker with ice and shake well. Strain over crushed ice, then add 1 ounce of club soda to the glass and decorate with a mint leaf. Serves 1.

9. Ginger Peach Cocktail. Combine 8 ounces peach juice, 8 ounces orange juice, and 4 ounces lemon juice. Stir well. Add 1 pint ginger ale. Pour into 8 glasses and add a chunk of whole ginger to each. Serves 8.

10. Mock Manhattan. Start with a shaker containing a few ice cubes. Add 2 ounces orange juice, 2 ounces cranberry juice, a few drops lemon juice, a few drops maraschino cherry juice, and a dash of orange bitter. Shake well. Strain over ice and decorate with a cherry. Serves 1.

11. Raspberry Delight. Scoop 3 ounces raspberry sherbet into a glass. Add some ice and fill the rest of the glass with ginger ale. Garnish with a few fresh raspberries. Sip through a straw. Serves 1.

12. Shirley Temple. Fill a champagne glass with ginger ale. Add a few drops of grenadine. Stir. Add a cherry for garnish. Serves 1.

6.
FACTS
on
FILE

Your Legal Rights

Being young doesn't mean you don't have rights. The following are not all written laws, but based on judges' decisions in cases that have involved kids, this is pretty much what you can expect from the American judicial system. Keep in mind that legal attitudes change from state to state.

1. Within limits, you have the right to dress and wear your hair any way you and your parents wish when you go to school. If school authorities want to challenge you, they must show that your clothing or hairstyle interferes with the educational process or that it is disruptive.

2. You have the constitutional right to demonstrate in an orderly fashion at school as long as you are not disruptive or violent.

3. If you have a job, you are entitled to the same minimum wage as adults earn, but your salary can be limited based on your lack of experience.

4. Girls must receive the same salary as boys for doing the same work.

5. As a minor, no contract you sign is valid unless your parent or guardian signs it, too.

10 Reasons to Establish a Teen Court

Teen Court is a program that gives youth offenders the chance to clear their records. In order to participate, teens must admit to their guilt and agree to a sentence to be set by a community of their peers. The sentence is generally expressed in hours of community service. For more information, go to the official Teen Court Web site, library.thinkquest.org.

1. It can cut down the crime rate of teenagers.

2. Teens learn to take responsibility and be accountable for their actions because of early intervention.

3. The program does not require a great deal of funding.

4. It encourages parents or guardians to get involved in the process.

5. It allows young people to get involved in the community.

6. It wipes clean the juvenile court record of first offenders.

7. Cases are handled confidentially.

8. The program is totally voluntary and promotes volunteerism.

9. It gives teens an opportunity to learn about the judicial system.

10. It helps kids develop a healthy respect toward authority.

10 Important Federal Child Labor Laws to Know

For more information, contact the Child Labor Coalition, c/o National Consumers League, 1701 K St., NW, #1200, Washington, DC 20006; phone: 202-835-3323; fax: 202-835-0747; www.stopchildlabor.org. The figures here were valid in May 2002.

1. The minimum age for employment is 14 years old. There are some exceptions such as newspaper delivery; performing in radio, television, movie, or theatrical productions; and work for parents done in their solely owned nonfarm business.

2. Fourteen- and 15-year-olds may be employed outside of school hours for a maximum of 3 hours per day and 18 hours per week when school is in session and a maximum of 8 hours per day and 40 hours per week when school is not in session. This age group is prohibited from working before 7 A.M. and after 7 P.M., except during summers, when they may work until 9 P.M. (June 1–Labor Day).

3. Sixteen- and 17-year-olds may be employed for unlimited hours. There are no federal laws restricting the number of hours of work per day or per week.

4. There are 17 prohibited jobs for youth (under the age of 18) that are considered hazardous. Some of these include manufacturing or storing explosives, driving a motor vehicle and being an outside helper on a motor vehicle, and operating power-driven circular saws, band saws, and guillotine shears, etc.

5. Ten- and 11-year-olds may perform jobs on farms owned or operated by parents, or with a parent's written consent, outside of school hours in nonhazardous jobs on farms not covered by minimum wage requirements.

6. Twelve- and 13-year-olds may work outside of school hours in nonhazardous jobs, either with a parent's written consent or on the same farm as the parents.

7. Fourteen- and 15-year-olds may perform any nonhazardous farm job outside of school hours.

8. Beginning at 16, teens may perform any farm job, whether hazardous or not, for unlimited hours.

9. The federal minimum wage at the time of this writing is $5.15 per hour. Overtime pay at a rate of not less than one and a half times their regular rates of pay is required after 40 hours of work in a workweek (except in some agricultural employment).

10. A minimum wage of not less than $4.25 an hour (as of 2002) is permitted for employees under 20 years of age during their first 90 consecutive calendar days of employment with an employer.

The 5 Worst Jobs for Teens

The National Consumers League says that these jobs carry the most safety risks and are therefore dangerous to young people.

1. Delivery and other jobs that require driving, including farm vehicles and other motorized equipment.

2. Working alone in a cash-based business, such as a convenience store or a gas station where you might be responsible for lots of money.

3. Traveling in a youth crew selling candy, subscriptions, or other consumer goods in strange neighborhoods and distant cities.

4. "Under the table" jobs, where you are paid in cash so that someone can avoid paying taxes.

5. Construction, including all work that involves heights or contact with electrical power.

21 Legal Terms You Should Know

1. **Accomplice:** A person who voluntarily helps someone commit or attempt to commit a crime.

2. **Age of majority:** The age at which you are no longer considered a minor; you can make your own decisions and manage your own affairs. In most states the age of majority is 18.

3. **Bill of Rights:** The first 10 amendments to the Constitution.

4. **Capacity to sue:** The ability of a person to come into court under his or her own name. This right is available to adults and emancipated minors.

5. **Censorship:** The act of limiting access to material found by the censors to be objectionable.

6. **Child endangerment:** The intentional harming of a child, also known as child abuse. Specific definitions vary from state to state.

7. **Child protection laws:** State laws that provide for the protection of minors from abuse and neglect.

8. **Civil commitment laws:** The right to hospitalize people against their will who are a danger to themselves or others.

9. **Civil detention:** Detaining someone in order to protect them from hurting themselves or others.

10. **Corporal punishment:** Physical discipline such as swats, paddling, and spanking.

11. **Criminal detention:** Detaining a minor who has been charged with a crime in a juvenile facility. State laws determine the type and length of the confinement.

12. **Delinquent:** A minor who violates a criminal law. If found guilty, he or she is called a juvenile delinquent.

13. **Emancipation:** The process of becoming legally free of your parents or guardian. If you are emancipated, your parents are no longer responsible for you.

14. **Felony:** A classification of the criminal laws that carries the strictest penalties, usually a minimum of 1 year in jail. A felony is more serious than a misdemeanor or a petty offense.

15. **Guardian:** An individual with the legal power and duty to take care of another person.

16. **Judicial bypass procedure:** A procedure used when a minor seeks an abortion without her parents' knowledge or consent. The minor must show the court that she is mature enough to make this decision on her own and that the abortion is in her best interest.

17. **Minor:** Someone who is not legally an adult.

18. Probation: A program in which you are placed under the supervision of a court-appointed agency. Various probation terms can include detention, community service, restitution, counseling, or a fine.

19. Sexual harassment: Any unwelcome sexual advances, request for sexual favors, or other verbal or physical contact of a sexual nature that disrupts the victim's education, civil rights, or the ability to do his or her job.

20. Statutory rape: Sexual relations with a minor, even if the minor consents.

21. Transfer: The process by which a minor is charged with a crime and tried in adult rather than juvenile court because of the nature or severity of the crime. Under these circumstances, the juvenile is eligible for adult sentences, including life imprisonment and the death penalty.

The Rights You Will Have as an Adult

In most states, children are afforded the rights and responsibilities of an adult at the age of 18. Others consider you an adult when you get married, join the U.S. military, or are granted an order of emancipation by a court. Here are some of the privileges you can look forward to.

1. The right to stand trial in a criminal court.

2. The right to enter into enforceable contracts, including employment contracts and leases, without parental consent.

3. The right to apply for state assistance, such as welfare.

4. The right to sue and be sued in your own name.

5. The right to make a will.

6. The right to authorize health care, medical care, dental care, and mental health care without parental consent.

7. The right to marry without parental consent.

8. The right to join the military service without parental consent.

9. The right to enroll in college or technical school without parental consent.

10. The right to vote in state and local elections.

14 States in Which Men Under the Age of 18 May Marry with a Parent's Consent

Without the consent of a parent or guardian, most states require that men be at least 21 years old when they marry. If a parent or guardian signs, the requirements change to 18 in all states except the following:

State	Age	State	Age
Alabama	17	New York	16
California	16	Pennsylvania	16
Colorado	16	South Carolina	16
Connecticut	16	Tennessee	16
Mississippi	17	Texas	16
Missouri	15	Utah	16
New Hampshire	14	Washington	17

11 States in Which Women Under the Age of 18 May Marry with a Parent's Consent

Even with the consent of a parent or guardian, most states require that women be at least 18 years old in order to marry; some states even set 21 as the requirement. In Washington, the age is 17. But women can marry without parental consent in the following states at the ages shown.

State	Age	State	Age
Alabama	14	Oklahoma	15
Massachusetts	15	South Carolina	14
Missouri	15	Texas	14
New Hampshire	13	Utah	14
New York	14	Vermont	14
North Dakota	15		

4 Teens Who Challenged Laws and Won

1. In 1965, John Tinker, 15, and Beth Tinker, 13, decided that they wanted to protest the war in Vietnam by wearing black armbands despite the fact that their school district said that this would not be allowed because it would be disruptive. The Tinkers refused to take the armbands off and were suspended from school. John and Beth, with the support of their parents, sued the school district. The court ruled that the school was wrong because it violated the First Amendment to the Constitution, which gives all citizens the right to free speech.

2. In 1983, a 15-year-old boy named William Thompson, along with three friends, murdered his sister's abusive husband. All four were convicted of the crime and sentenced to death. William, however, was a minor, and with the aid of his attorney, he petitioned the U.S. Supreme Court stating that his sentence was cruel and unusual punishment for a minor. The Supreme Court reversed the decision by the lower court and reduced William's sentence to life in prison. It then ruled that anyone under 16 could not be given a death sentence.

3. In 1964, 15-year-old Gerald Gault, who was already on parole for a burglary conviction, placed an obscene phone call to his next-door neighbor. Gerald was arrested and was ordered to be placed in a reform school until he turned 21. However, his parents were never informed that he had been arrested, he didn't have the opportunity of questioning his accuser, and was not provided with an attorney. The Supreme Court ruled that as a juvenile his parents should have been notified, he should have had the right to confront his accuser, and that he had the right to a lawyer.

4. In 1998, a high school grad named Beth Faragher went to work as a part-time lifeguard at a city beach in Florida. During her employment she was sexually harassed by her supervisors and filed a lawsuit against the city of Boca Raton. She won her case because the city failed to set rules for the conduct of all its employees regarding sexual misconduct. This case was important because it helped establish the guidelines for conduct in the workplace.

7 Bad White House Kids

1. In 2001, Jenna Bush, 19, made the news for underage drinking and wild partying. She was photographed at clubs that serve liquor (she was underage) and violated her probation.

2. John Quincy Adams's son George was a drug addict who fathered a child out of wedlock. He eventually killed himself, just a month after his father left office.

3. Alan Arthur, the son of Chester A. Arthur, went skinny dipping in the White House fountain with the young prince of Siam and caused an international incident.

4. James Madison's stepson Payne was an alcoholic and a gambler who wound up in prison for not paying his debts. He also had a love affair with a Russian princess who disappeared mysteriously.

5. Alice Roosevelt, daughter of Theodore Roosevelt, raised eyebrows when she smoked cigarettes in public, way before this was socially acceptable. She also drank and threw wild parties for her friends in the White House. Her father issued this statement: "I can be President of the United States or I can control Alice. I can't possibly do both."

6. Franklin Roosevelt, Jr., was known for driving recklessly and throwing wild parties at Harvard, where he went to school. He was also known to punch out photographers who tried to take his picture.

7. Patti Davis had a number of ways of rebelling against her father, Ronald Reagan. She denounced his political policies, talked openly about her cocaine addiction, wrote a book that put down her parents, and in 1994 appeared nude in *Playboy*. She has since reconciled with her family.

The 10 Youngest British Monarchs

1.	Henry VI, 1422–61	8 months
2.	Henry III, 1216–72	9 years old
3.	Edward VI, 1547–53	9 years old
4.	Richard II, 1377–99	10 years old
5.	Edward V, 1483	12 years old
6.	Edward III, 1327–77	14 years old
7.	Jane, 1553	15 years old

8. Henry VIII, 1509–47   17 years old
9. Victoria, 1837–1901   18 years old
10. Charles II, 1660–85   18 years old

Teens Who Started Internet Companies

Far from the afterschool jobs of the past, business ventures today allow teens to explore skills that once were reserved for adults. Find out more about how to start an Internet company at www.teentechmag.com. Here is a list of some teens in whose footsteps you may want to follow.

1. Canadians Michael Furdyk, 16, and Albert Lai, 20, teamed with Australian Michael Hayman, 18, to develop a network of seven Web sites that offered advice, news, and views about computer software and hardware. In 2001, they sold their company, Mydesktop.com, to the Web publishing company Internet.com for an undisclosed figure in the millions.

2. Toronto's Jennifer Corriero, 19, completing a business degree at York University, is a Microsoft consultant who advises the software giant and develops Web sites for McDonald's and Swatch.

3. Rishi Bhat, a 15-year-old student from Chicago, sold his anonymous Web-surfing software to a Vancouver Internet company for $3 million.

4. Shazad Mohamed, a 14-year-old freshman at Hebron High School in Carrollton, Texas, is the founder of the Internet firm GlobalTek Solutions. His company develops interactive Web sites for small businesses and designs sites for personal digital assistants and digital telephones to use with the wireless Web. It is not uncommon for Shazad to stay up until 2 A.M. on school nights and until 5 or 6 A.M. on the weekends trying to maintain his competitive edge, all the while maintaining a straight-A average.

5. Adam Smith, a 15-year-old sophomore high school honor student, got his first computer in 1994 and within two years, at the age of 11, began writing computer programs. He launched his software development company, Viratech Development, when he was 13. His company remains successful today.

6. Jud Bowman and Taylor Brockman, both 18, began an Internet startup company that builds search engines for Web sites. Since their graduation from boarding school in North Carolina, Bowman and Brockman have received financial backing for their venture, now known as Pinpoint Networks. The company has had some major successes. Terra Lycos agreed to integrate Pinpoint's search technology into its wireless application portal. And the telecommunications giant Verizon Wireless agreed to incorporate the company's search feature into its Net-enabled phones.

7. Brad Ogden, 17, created a company that designs Web pages and sets up computer networks for small businesses. As a kid Brad played "office," carrying his dad's briefcase to 1st grade. He took up Web design at 13 and is quoted as saying, "If you go into a meeting thinking you're handicapped because you're young, you'll leave the meeting with people thinking you're handicapped."

8. Melissa Sconyers's Ativity is a hip and unique Web design studio in Austin, Texas, the home of the high-tech hippies. Founded by Melissa in 1994, Ativity now offers a colorful palette of services including Web design, graphic design, videography, photography, public speaking, and more. She founded her company when she was 16. Internationally known as a top designer, she has earned much acclaim for her work.

6 Successful Teen Entrepreneurs

1. Andrew Schneider began doing magic at an early age. By the time he was 14, he had started a company called Mystifying Magic. He is experienced in the art of magical illusions and close-up magic. He specializes in corporate events, trade shows, walk around magic, private shows, and birthday parties. His Web address is www.mystifyingmagic.com.

2. Deanna and Jana Thies, 18 and 15, respectively, founded a company called the Veggie Patch, begun as part of an FFA project. Today they sell fruits, vegetables, and flowers at the Columbia Farmers Market in Glasgow, Missouri, and take in over $25,000 a year.

3. Amanda Lujan, 15, founded the Rocky Mountain Horse

Resort in Cleveland, New Mexico. She began the resort as a sideline to her parents' business, which offers guided hunting and fishing trips on horseback. One year, an outdoorsman from Texas brought two horses to her parents to take on hunting and fishing expeditions. When he discovered how much experience Amanda had with horses, he asked her to train them. "They had been ridden two or three times but still liked to buck," she explains. "It took me about a month to train them." Now, Amanda offers boarding and training services, riding lessons, and also guides fishing and riding trips into the mountains.

4. Melissa Goolick was only 9 when she started her computer graphics firm, MelMaps. Now, at 17, she produces location, vicinity, site, and floor maps for real estate agents and banks. Melissa was actually following in the footsteps of her sister Mallory, who also went into business at age 9. Her business, Jungle Beans, sells an average of 88 pounds of gourmet coffee each week.

5. Randy Meissen, at 18, began the Meissen Entomology Company, an entrepreneurship that started as part of a Supervised Agricultural Experience program—a requirement for FFA and his agricultural science class. He had collected insects for years but now sells them to schools and individuals. He was named the January/February 1999 Young Entrepreneur Magazine Business All-Star.

6. James Anderson started his Athletic Dance Studio International when he was 17. Although he never took dance lessons he mastered the art of hip-hop dancing by watching performers on TV. He now choreographs routines for cheerleading squads and dance teams, as well as giving individual and group dance lessons. His new goal is to start an athletic dance studio for kids.

22 Highly Visual, Multidimensional Thinkers

That's because they all share a special gift: dyslexia! Why a gift? Because dyslexic people are typically highly creative, imaginative, and great at hands-on learning. Because they think in pictures (most people think in words), they have problems understanding letters, symbols, numbers, and written words. But they can learn to read, write, and study using any of the many special teaching methods that are available. To find out more, check out www.dyslexia.com.

1. Muhammad Ali, boxer
2. Hans Christian Andersen, writer
3. Erin Brockovich, political activist
4. Cher, pop singer
5. Winston Churchill, statesman
6. Tom Cruise, actor
7. Leonardo da Vinci, artist
8. Walt Disney, entertainment mogul
9. Thomas Edison, inventor
10. Albert Einstein, scientist
11. Harrison Ford, actor
12. Henry Ford, inventor
13. Whoopi Goldberg, actress
14. Thomas Jefferson, statesman
15. Magic Johnson, basketball player
16. John Lennon, musician
17. Pablo Picasso, artist
18. Nolan Ryan, baseball player
19. Ted Turner, media mogul
20. George Washington, statesman
21. Robin Williams, actor
22. Woodrow Wilson, statesman

12 Left-handed Musicians

Life as a lefty can be difficult, since the whole world seems to be built for right-handed people. To make matters worse, there was a time when lefties were told they'd never learn to write properly or play musical instruments. Here are 12 rockers who proved them wrong.

1. Kurt Cobain
2. Natalie Cole
3. Phil Collins
4. Bob Dylan
5. Albert King
6. Mark Knopfler
7. Annie Lennox
8. Paul McCartney

9. George Michael   11. Carly Simon
10. Robert Plant   12. Sting

18 Actual but Totally Bizarre Newspaper Headlines

1. "Include Your Children When Baking Cookies"
2. "Drunk Gets Nine Months in Violin Case"
3. "Iraqi Head Seeks Arms"
4. "Eye Drops Off Shelf"
5. "Squad Helps Dog Bite Victim"
6. "Killer Sentenced to Die for Second Time in Ten Years"
7. "Kids Make Nutritious Snacks"
8. "Local High School Dropouts Cut in Half"
9. "Miners Refuse to Work After Death"
10. "Juvenile Court to Try Shooting Defendant"
11. "If Strike Isn't Settled Quickly, It May Last a While"
12. "Red Tape Holds Up New Bridge"
13. "Typhoon Rips Through Cemetery; Hundreds Dead"
14. "Astronaut Takes Blame for Gas in Spacecraft"
15. "Steals Clock, Faces Time"
16. "Hospitals Are Sued by 7 Foot Doctors"
17. "Sex Education Delayed, Teachers Request Training"
18. "Arson Suspect Is Held in Fire"

10 Teen Inventors

The National Gallery for America's Young Inventors (www.princeton.edu/~kmendels/inventors.html) is a program that was established in 1996 to demonstrate that valuable inventions can be created by America's youth. Here are some of the teens that have been inducted into the National Inventor's Hall of Fame.

1. At 16, Christina Adams of Bartlesville, Oklahoma, invented a wheel chair that allows the user to control pressure and moisture, which are the two biggest causes of sores among wheelchair users.

2. When Lindsey E. Clement of Longview, Texas, was 12, she observed that a big problem for people who live in the southern U.S. was cleaning up the "gumballs" that are dropped by the sweet gum trees that grow throughout the region. They are a nuisance to anyone who has a sweet gum tree in or near their yard. So she invented something that resembles a small lawnmower that picks up the gumballs and deposits them in a special container.

3. Chester Greenwood was born in Farmington, Maine. It gets mighty cold there in the winter, so he invented earmuffs when he was only 15. He accumulated more than 100 patents in his lifetime.

4. Hans Christiansen Lee, 18, of Carmel, California, invented a Differential Torque Control System to improve a car's controllability when a driver is faced with radical steering maneuvers or begins to skid or spin out of control.

5. Krysta Morlan of Vacaville, California, was 13 when she invented a device that relieves the irritation caused by wearing a cast.

6. Elina Onitskansky of Lyndhurst, Ohio, was 17 when she invented a revolutionary sensor that detects certain elements in polluted water — a microelectrochemical sensor and plating system to detect and remove cadmium, copper, iron, lead, nickel, and zinc ions from polluted water, if you must know.

7. Becky Schroeder received a patent at the age of 14 for creating a way of reading and writing in the dark. She used phosphorescent paint on paper under her paper so that she could write in the dark. Doctors now use it in hospitals to read patients' charts at night without waking them. Astronauts use this same technology when their electrical systems are turned down for recharging. Becky was named an Ohio Inventor of the Year and was inducted into its Hall of Fame.

8. Kavita M. Shukla of Woodstock, Maryland, invented a process that coats food packaging materials such as paper with a botanical extract in order to help preserve and extend the food's shelf life. She was 16.

9. Eric Van Paris, from Belgium, was 14 when he invented a "cooling fork" that blew air onto hot food so that kids could eat more easily.

10. Rishi S. Vasudeva, 17, of Roswell, Georgia, invented an eco-friendly, biodegradable diaper made of a corn-based polymer lining and an absorbent cellulosic inner padding. It is capable of biodegradation within days after use and is thus healthier for the environment than the polyethylene-lined disposable diapers currently on the market.

52 Famous Short People Who Proved Once and for All That Big Things Do Come in Small Packages

Someone has to be the shortest person in the class. If it's you, consider the advantages: you fit into smaller places, you can get into the movies for the price of a child's ticket, and everyone thinks you're adorable, even on your worst hair days. Here are some "small" people who made it big.

1. Michael Ain, b. 1962, 4'3": surgeon
2. Gracie Allen, 1902–64, 5'0": actress
3. Tammy Faye Bakker, b. 1942, 4'11": spiritual leader
4. Clara Barton, 1821–1912, 5'0": activist
5. Billy Barty, 1924–2000, 3'9": actor and activist
6. Ludwig van Beethoven, 1770–1827, 5'4": composer
7. David Ben-Gurion, 1886–1973, 5'0": political leader
8. Pat Benatar, b. 1953, 5'0": musician
9. Thomas Hart Benton, 1889–1975, 5'0": artist
10. Charlotte Brontë, 1816–1855, 4'10": writer
11. Mel Brooks, b. 1926, 5'4": director and actor
12. Truman Capote, 1924–84, 5'3": writer and actor
13. Andrew Carnegie, 1835–1919, 5'0": entrepreneur
14. Nell Carter, b. 1948, 4'11": actress and musician
15. Gary Coleman, b. 1968, 4'10": actor
16. Lou Costello, 1906–59, 5'3": actor
17. Sammy Davis Jr., 1925–90, 5'3": musician and actor
18. Danny DeVito, b. 1944, 5'0": actor and director
19. Patty Duke, b. 1946, 5'0": actress
20. Michael J. Fox, b. 1961, 5'4": actor
21. Judy Garland, 1922–69, 4'11^1/$_2$": actress and musician

22. Estelle Getty, b. 1923, 4'9": actress
23. Harry Houdini, 1874–1926, 5'4": magician
24. Davy Jones, b. 1945, 5'3": musician
25. Nikita S. Khrushchev, 1894–1971, 5'3": political leader
26. Olga Korbut, b. 1955, 4'11": athlete
27. Irving (Swifty) Lazar, 1907–93, 5'2": agent
28. Emmanuel Lewis, b. 1971, 3'4": actor and musician
29. Shari Lewis, 1933–98, 5'0": ventriloquist
30. Margaret Mitchell, 1900–49, 4'10": writer
31. Dudley Moore, 1935–2002, 5'2^1/$_2$": actor
32. Rick Moranis, b. 1954, 5'4": actor
33. Annie Oakley, 1860–1926, 5'0": athlete
34. Bonnie Parker, 1911–34, 4'10": criminal
35. Dolly Parton, b. 1946, 5'0": musician
36. Edith Piaf, 1915–63, 4'8": musician
37. Alexander Pope, 1688–1744, 4'6": poet
38. Mary Lou Retton, b. 1968, 4'9^1/$_2$": athlete
39. Cathy Rigby, b. 1952, 4'11": athlete
40. Rod Serling, 1924–75, 5'4": producer and writer
41. Willie Shoemaker, b. 1931, 4'11": athlete
42. Paul Simon, b. 1941, 5'3": musician
43. Harriet Beecher Stowe, 1811–96, 4'11": writer
44. Mother Teresa, 1910–97, 5'0": spiritual leader
45. General Tom Thumb, 1838–83, 2'9": circus performer
46. Henri de Toulouse-Lautrec, 1864–1901, 4'11": artist
47. Queen Victoria, 1819–1901, 5'0": political leader
48. Hervé Villechaize, 1943–93, 3'11": actor
49. Mae West, 1893–1980, 5'0": actress and playwright
50. Dr. Ruth Westheimer, b. 1928, 4'7": psychologist
51. Paul Williams, b. 1940, 5'0": composer and actor
52. Natalie Wood, 1938–81, 5'0": actress

The 9 Top Sources of Social Pressure Among Teens

This list (and the two that follow) is based on studies conducted by the Horatio Alger Association of Distinguished Americans (www.horatioalger.com), whose purpose is to celebrate the lives of Americans who have overcome adversity. They publish *The State of our Nation's Youth Report,* which collects the results of surveys that help people show more sensitivity to the concerns of young people. The survey was conducted by phone and included 1,014 students aged 14 through 18 across the country.

	Problem	Not a Problem
Pressure to get good grades	62%	38%
Pressure to look a certain way	46%	53%*
Family pressures	46%	54%
Financial pressures	42%	57%
Pressure to do drugs or drink	36%	64%
Loneliness or feeling left out	33%	67%
Pressure to have sex	30%	69%

* All students did not respond to all questions.

High School Students Choose the Most Important Definitions of Success in Life

Of the 1,014 students polled, the following percentages named these characteristics as being among the most important ingredients for success in life.

Having close family relationships	84%
Having a close group of friends	60%
Making a contribution to society	49%
Having an active religious/spiritual life	44%
Making a lot of money	35%
Being famous or respected in your field	27%
Being attractive/popular	8%

6 Ways Teens Get Money

According to Teenage Research Unlimited (www.teenresearch.com), if all the teens (aged 12–19) in America pooled their earnings, they would have a combined income of $124 billion. They'd be richer than Bill Gates! Where does the money come from?

1. 53% receive money from parents.
2. 46% do odd jobs.
3. 46% have gift accounts.
4. 32% have part-time jobs.
5. 26% receive allowances regularly
6. 13% have full-time jobs.

34 Weird Phobias

If you really don't want to go to Aunt Whosis's house for Thanksgiving, try telling your parents you've suddenly developed a bad case of syngenesophobia. Or try convincing them that it's unfair to ground you, given your poinephobia. Those excuses probably won't work, but you might get "extra credit" for your improved vocabulary.

1. Ablutophobia: The fear of bathing
2. Achluphobia: . . . the dark
3. Arachiutyrophobia: . . . peanut butter sticking to the roof of your mouth
4. Atelophobia: . . . being imperfect
5. Bibliophobia: . . . books
6. Blennophobia: . . . slime
7. Bogyphobia: . . . the bogeyman
8. Ceraunophobia: . . . thunder
9. Chionophobia: . . . snow
10. Chrometophobia: . . . money
11. Chronomentrophobia: . . . clocks
12. Clinophobia: . . . going to bed
13. Coulrophobia: . . . clowns
14. Didaskakeinophobia: . . . school
15. Emetophobia: . . . vomiting
16. Ergophobia: . . . work
17. Glossophobia: . . . speaking in public
18. Gymnophobia: . . . being naked
19. Hypegiaphobia: . . . responsibility

20. Lachanophobia: . . . vegetables
21. Melophobia: . . . music
22. Novercaphobia: . . . stepmothers
23. Numerophobia: . . . numbers
24. Odynophobia: . . . pain
25. Pantophobia: . . . everything
26. Papyrophobia: . . . paper
27. Pediophobia: . . . dolls
28. Philemaphobia: . . . kissing
29. Poinephobia: . . . punishment
30. Samhainophobia: . . . Halloween
31. Scholiophobia: . . . school
32. Syngenesophobia: . . . relatives
33. Testophobia: . . . taking tests
34. Triskaidekaphobia: . . . the number 13

Statistics About Teens and Violence

All of these figures are based on annual U.S. statistics.

3,500	Average number of people under 18 killed by handguns
9,700	Average number of kids wounded by guns
87,715	Average number of kids arrested for violent crimes
62,650	Average number of students assaulted at school
2.19 million	Average number of reports of abused or neglected children
4,000	Average number of suicides among people aged 15–24
9,300	Average number of acts of violence seen on TV by the average teen

11 Things You Should Know About Tobacco

For more information or for help with quitting smoking, contact the Office on Smoking and Health, Centers for Disease Control and Prevention: 1-800-CDC-1311 or www.cdc.gov/tobacco.

1. All nicotine in cigarettes, cigars, and spit tobacco is addictive.

2. Smoking can wreck your lungs and reduce oxygen available for muscles used during sports. Smokers run slower and can't run as far, affecting overall athletic performance.

3. Tobacco smoke can make hair and clothes stink, stain your teeth, and cause bad breath. Short-term use of spit tobacco can cause cracked lips, white spots, sores, and bleeding in the mouth.

4. Surgery to remove oral cancers caused by tobacco can lead to serious changes in the face.

5. Among young people, the short-term health effects of smoking include damage to the respiratory system, addiction to nicotine, and the associated risk of other drug use.

6. Smoking among youth can hamper the rate of lung growth and the level of maximum lung function.

7. The resting heart rates of young adult smokers are 2–3 beats per minute faster than those of nonsmokers.

8. The younger people start smoking cigarettes, the more likely they are to become strongly addicted to nicotine.

9. Teens who smoke are 3 times more likely than nonsmokers to use alcohol, 8 times more likely to use marijuana, and 22 times more likely to use cocaine. Smoking is associated with a host of other risky behaviors, such as fighting and engaging in unprotected sex.

10. Smoking is associated with poor overall health and a variety of short-term adverse health effects in young people and may also be a marker for underlying mental health problems, such as depression, among adolescents. (High school seniors who are regular smokers and began smoking by grade 9 are 2.4 times more likely than their nonsmoking peers to report poorer overall health; 2.4–2.7 times more likely to report cough with phlegm or blood, shortness of breath when not exercising, and wheezing or gasping; and 3.0 times more likely to have seen a doctor or other health professional for an emotional or psychological complaint.

11. Some 70% of adolescent smokers wish they'd never started smoking in the first place.

Why D.A.R.E. Didn't Work

The D.A.R.E. program was created in 1983 by Los Angeles police chief Daryl Gates. The program involves uniformed police officers going to schools and talking to students about the dangers of drug use in seventeen weekly sessions, after which students "graduate" from the program. D.A.R.E. was widely adopted by school systems throughout the United States. But in recent years, parents and teachers have begun to question whether the program really works, and even the D.A.R.E. administrators themselves admitted that maybe they need to go back to the drawing board. Here are some of the problems they need to tackle.

1. **It isn't necessarily effective in preventing drug use.** Although D.A.R.E. is present in almost half the schools in the country, government studies indicate that the program has "little or no" effect on whether kids use drugs. The D.A.R.E. people claim that even if just one kid is prevented from using drugs, the program works. (If the reading program at school taught only one kid to read, would that be considered effective?)

2. **It sends the wrong messages.** Parents have complained that the D.A.R.E. teaching materials, specifically the video called "The Land of Decisions and Choices," depict all adults —other than the uniformed officer—as senile drunks and drug abusers, implying that only the officers can be trusted. They also emphasize resistance to illegal drugs, when statistics clearly show that the greater risk for kids has to do with alcohol and tobacco. Finally, critics say that they don't really teach kids about drug abuse and what it is. Instead, they adopt a "just say no" stance, which doesn't always work. Maybe "just say *know*" would have been a better slogan.

3. **It confuses kids about the true role of the police.** Citizens expect the police to protect the population and respond to emergencies. Having officers in the classrooms in a teaching capacity communicates unrealistic priorities to kids.

4. **It takes too much time.** The program takes 17 hours. Considering the fact that it hasn't been proven effective, there's a good chance that time would have been better spent learning math or science.

5. **It gives people the impression that the war on drugs is under control.** People who don't know much about the program get the idea that it's being handled and they need do nothing more. So D.A.R.E. is actually keeping people from finding effective ways to fight drug abuse.

6. **It costs $750,000,000 a year.** That's a lot to spend on something we're not sure really works.

The 5 Top Causes of Death Among Teens

These figures break down the average annual mortality rate among teens.

1. Accidents: 39%
2. Murders: 26%
3. Suicide: 18%
4. Cancer: 15%
5. Other: 2%

12 Great Contests to Enter

1. **The American History Essay Contest.** The Daughters of the American Revolution (descendants of soldiers in the Revolutionary War), known as the DAR, hold an annual contest for 5th- through 8th-graders. Local contest winners receive certificates and pins, but national winners get cash prizes, and their essays are published in *DAR Magazine*. Contact your DAR chapter online to find out more: www.dar.org.

2. **The American Mathematics Competitions.** Each year, every high school in the country is invited to participate in this program. In 2000, over 5,000 schools were involved, so you can imagine how tough the competition is. Winners on the local levels go onto prestigious finals, and scholarships are awarded to the winners. The national winner goes on to represent the country at the International Mathematics Olympiad. For information, go to www.unl.edu/amc/.

3. **Ann Arlys Bowler Poetry Prize.** Every year, *READ Magazine* sponsors a contest for students in grades 6–12. Poems can be about anything and up to one page long. The winner gets $100, a medal, national publicity, and publication in the magazine. Find out more at www.weeklyreader.com.

4. **The Craftsman/NSTA Young Inventors Awards Program.** Students in grades 2–8 are challenged to use their creativity and imagination to invent or modify a tool that can be used in a practical way. Entrants have to create the tool and submit a diagram of it along with a photograph of the tool being used. Two national winners each receive a $10,000 U.S. savings bond. Twelve second-place winners receive $500 bonds, and third-place winners receive $250 bonds. Sign up at www.nsta.org.

5. **Intel International Science and Engineering Fair.** This is the world series of science competitions. Winners of local science fairs are invited to compete internationally for scholarships, tuition grants, and internships. The winner of the grand prize receives a trip to Stockholm, Sweden, to attend the Nobel Prize ceremonies. Find out more at www.sciserv.org/isef/.

6. **Let's Get Real.** This competition gives teams of 6th- through 12th-graders an opportunity to solve real-life issues faced by the sponsoring corporations, such as Hershey's. Teams must comprise between 2 and 6 members, and an adult coordinator is required. If you're interested in this contest, it would be a good idea to get your school involved. To learn how, go to www.lgreal.org.

7. **The National Geographic Bee.** Sponsored by the National Geographic Society, this contest involves answering oral and written questions about geography. Students compete on local levels. The winners go on to state championships and finally the national level. A $25,000 college scholarship awaits. Visit www.nationalgeographic.com.

8. **The National Spelling Bee.** Local winners of spelling bees, which are typically sponsored by newspapers, go on to the Scripps Howard National Spelling Bee in Washington, D.C. If your school doesn't participate in the program, go to www.spellingbee.com for more information.

9. **The Newscurrents Student Editorial Cartoon Contest.** Students up through high school are invited to enter as many cartoons as they wish. The 100 best cartoons are published in a book, and the winners receive U.S. savings bonds. To enter, go to www.knowledgeunlimited.com.

10. **The Rube Goldberg Machine Contests.** There's a great scene in the film *Edward Scissorhands* in which Vincent Price, Edward's creator, demonstrates a giant machine that takes up a whole room yet accomplishes nothing more than a huge cookie-cutter. They got the idea for that from Rube Goldberg, a Pulitzer Prize–winning artist who built complicated machinery that did simple tasks—like a giant pencil sharpener or a toaster with about 300 moving parts. Each year, Purdue University in Indiana sponsors a contest in which students are invited to build something that's much more complicated than it needs to be. That contest is only for college students, but they sponsor high school events, too. Log on to www.rube-goldberg.com.

11. **Teen Ink Contests.** *Teen Ink* magazine is written completely by teens. Each month they have contests in various areas, and many of the essays submitted get published in the magazine. You have to be between 13 and 19 to enter. Example of contests are the Educator of the Year Contest (describe the most amazing teacher you ever had), the Cover Photo Contest (take a great photo of a friend and get it on the cover of *Teen Ink*), the Interview Contest (write a great interview and win a chance to interview a celebrity), the Environmental Solutions Contest (solve an environmental problem and win $25), and the Community Service Award Contest (write an essay about how you would make the world a better place). Prizes vary, and if your work is published, you'll get a free copy of the magazine in which your work appears. Go to www.teenink.com.

12. **The ThinkQuest Internet Challenge.** Teams of students have a chance to create Internet learning materials. The contest is open to students around the world and is sponsored by

ThinkQuest, which is an internet community of students and educators dedicated to developing online learning. Contest winners receive substantial scholarships. Find out more at www.thinkquest.com.

The 20 Languages Most Commonly Spoken in American Households

Language	Number of Households
1. English	198,601,000
2. Spanish	17,339,000
3. French	1,702,000
4. German	1,547,000
5. Italian	1,309,000
6. Chinese	1,249,000
7. Tagalog	843,000
8. Polish	723,000
9. Korean	626,000
10. Vietnamese	507,000
11. Portuguese	430,000
12. Japanese	428,000
13. Greek	388,000
14. Arabic	355,000
15. Hindi, Urdu, and related languages	331,000
16. Russian	242,000
17. Yiddish	213,000
18. Thai	206,000
19. Persian	202,000
20. French Creole	188,000

11 Physical Traits You are Most Likely to Inherit from Your Parents

Ever fear that you're becoming just like your parents? Well, sometimes you just can't help it. Especially when you've inherited their traits. Here are some of the most common dominant traits that are passed down by your parents.

1. Dimples (on your cheeks or chin)
2. Freckles
3. A pointed hairline forming a "V"
4. Brown eyes
5. Brown hair
6. Tallness
7. A bent pinky finger. (Hold your hands together as if you are covering your face. If the tips of the pinkies point away from one another, the pinkies are *bent*.)
8. Detached earlobe (an earlobe that hangs from the side of your face)
9. Long eyelashes
10. Round face
11. Prominent chin

The Most Common Plastic Surgeries for Teens

It's normal for teens to feel frustrated and self-conscious about their appearance. Plastic surgery may help, but it's not for everyone. If you are considering plastic surgery, remember that it is a huge decision that must be discussed with your parents and your doctor first. There are also a few important things to bear in mind. First of all, you should only do it if *you're* the one who wants it done; don't be convinced by others that a feature you're totally comfortable with has to go. Second, be realistic and know that all of life's problems are not going to magically disappear with surgery. Third, plastic surgery is not recommended for teens who are prone to mood swings or erratic behavior, are addicted to drugs and/or alcohol, or are being treated for clinical depression or other mental illnesses. You must be able to mentally tolerate the temporary disfigurement and discomfort that accompany surgery. Remember, this is a mature decision that will affect your life. If you don't feel that surgery is right for you but you're upset about your appearance to the point where it affects your everyday life, get help by talking it out with a parent or a professional.

1. Rhinoplasty. Nose reshaping is one of the most common procedures for teenagers. It may straighten the bridge, remove an unsightly bump, reshape the tip, or open breathing passages. Ordinarily, rhinoplasty is not performed until the nose finishes growth, which is 13 or 14 years for girls and 15 or 16 for boys.

2. Breast reduction for girls. Surgical reduction can help relieve both physical and emotional pain for girls with large breasts. Even though this procedure can be done on girls as young as 15, it is best to do it when the breasts are fully developed. Insurance reimbursement is often possible for this procedure.

3. Breast reduction for boys. Girls are not the only ones that can feel self-conscious about their breast size. Gynecomastia, or large breast size in boys, may be corrected through surgery. Insurance companies will often reimburse the cost of this procedure.

4. Otoplasty. Surgical correction of protruding ears, in which the ears are "pinned back," may be performed any time after the age of five.

5. Acne and acne scar treatments. Certain prescription drugs such as Retin-A can reduce or eliminate the appearance of acne and their scars. In addition to supervising the use of these drugs, doctors may smooth or "refinish" the skin with a laser or with a sanding technique called dermabrasion.

6. Chin augmentation. Chin implants that give your face more structure are often inserted at the same time that a rhinoplasty is performed and may be suitable for teenagers after the age of 15.

The 8 Worst Fashion Trends of the 1990s

Every decade has its best and worst fashions. But usually, when you look back, almost all of them seem to be the worst. Listed here are some of the weirdest, funniest, and most awful fashion trends of the '90s. If you're wearing any of them now, you may want to head for the closet.

1. Baggy pants. Remember when guys wore their pants so low that their boxers showed?

2. Backwards jeans. Inspired by the young rap duo Kris Kross, people used to wear their jeans backwards. That didn't last long, of course.

3. Pacifier necklaces. Yep. People actually wore pacifiers around their necks.

4. The Rachel haircut. When Rachel from TV's *Friends* got that irresistible layered look, nearly every female had to have it.

5. Baby doll dresses. To enhance that grunge punk-rocker look, women like Courtney Love wore adorable little dresses that made them look like they were on their way to a play date.

6. Caps with the price tags still on. There was a fashion statement here, but we can't figure out what it was.

7. Flannel shirts. Grungy flannel shirts from dad's closet worn over concert T-shirts like Wayne and Garth from *Wayne's World.* Comfy!

8. Canvas shoes. Worn in the early '90s with tapered pants and scrunch socks. The most popular were Keds.

The World's 5 Fastest Roller Coasters

1. Millennium Force, Sandusky, Ohio, 92 mph
2. Fujiyama, Yamanashi, Japan, 86 mph
3. Desperado, Primm, Nevada, 85 mph
4. Goliath, Valencia, California, 85 mph
5. Steel Phantom, West Mifflin, Pennsylvania, 80 mph

The World's 5 Longest Roller Coasters

1. The Ultimate, North Yorkshire, England, 7,498 feet
2. The Beast, Cincinnati, Ohio, 7,392 feet
3. Son of Beast, Cincinnati, Ohio, 7,032 feet
4. Millennium Force, Sandusky, Ohio, 6,595 feet
5. Desperado, Primm, Nevada, 5,843 feet

The World's 4 Tallest Roller Coasters

1. Millennium Force, Sandusky, Ohio, 310 feet
2. Fujiyama, Yamanashi, Japan, 259 feet
3. Son of Beast, Cincinnati, Ohio, 218 feet
4. Pepsi Max Big One, Lancashire, England, 214 feet

23 Foods That Further Flatulence

Also known as farting, passing gas, cutting the cheese. If you do "let one rip," excuse yourself and get on with what you were doing. Or blame the dog.

Although most farts go unnoticed, those of Joseph Pujol did not. He turned the fart into an art and, in the 1930s, toured Europe with his awesome feats of flatulence, which included blowing out candles and playing music with his posterior. He died rich and happy in 1945.

These foods should especially be avoided on dates.

1. Apples
2. Avocados
3. Beans
4. Brussel sprouts
5. Cantaloupe
6. Cabbage
7. High-fiber cereals
8. Chewing gum. (It's not the gum that gives you gas, it's the air you swallow when you chew the gum.).
9. Corn
10. Cucumbers
11. Dairy products
12. Eggs
13. Fried foods
14. Lima beans
15. Melons
16. Nuts
17. Peas
18. Prune juice
19. Raisins
20. Radishes
21. Sauerkraut
22. Soda (or any carbonated beverage)
23. Turnips

8 Snack Food Preferences Among Teens

The general population of snack food lovers breaks down like this:

1. Popcorn: 23%
2. Potato chips: 21%
3. Pretzels: 16%
4. Nuts: 15%
5. Tortilla chips: 12%
6. Cheese curls: 6%
7. Meat snacks: 4%
8. Snack crackers: 3%

9 Safe Snacks

Do you really need a list?

1. Air-popped or low-fat microwave popcorn
2. Raw vegetables and low-fat dip
3. Nonfat yogurt with fresh fruit
4. Pretzels
5. Frozen fruit juice bars (but read the labels)
6. Mini-pizzas made with English muffins (or pita bread or bagels), tomato sauce, and low-fat cheese.
7. Granola bars
8. Rice cakes with peanut butter and fruit spread
9. Quesadillas made with salsa and low-fat cheese

Eating Healthfully at 9 Fast-Food Restaurants

Here's bad news, good news, and something in between.

1. Boston Market

BAD	Meatloaf Sandwich with Cheese	860 calories
BETTER	Meatloaf with Brown Gravy	390 calories
BEST	1/4 Chicken (white meat with skin)	330 calories

2. Burger King

BAD	Double Whopper Cheese Sandwich	920 calories
BETTER	BK Broiler Chicken Sandwich (no mayo)	390 calories
BEST	Chicken Tenders	170 calories

3. Hardee's

BAD	Frisco Sandwich	720 calories
BETTER	Mushroom 'N' Swiss Burger	490 calories
BEST	Hamburger	270 calories

4. KFC

BAD	Honey Barbeque Wings	607 calories
BETTER	Honey BBQ Flavored Chicken Sandwich (with sauce)	310 calories

5. McDonald's

BAD	Quarter Pounder with Cheese	530 calories
BETTER	Chicken McGrill (no mayo)	340 calories
BEST	Grilled Chicken Salad Deluxe (reduced calorie dressing)	230 calories

6. Pizza Hut

REALLY BAD	Pepperoni Lover's Stuffed Crust Pizza, 2 slices	1,150 calories
BETTER	Chicken Supreme Thin 'n' Crispy Pizza, 2 slices	400 calories
BEST	Ham Thin 'n' Crispy Pizza, 2 slices	340 calories

7. Subway

BAD	Spicy Italian Sandwich on Wheat Bread	482 calories
BETTER	Seafood and Crab Sandwich on Wheat Bread	430 calories
BEST	Veggie Delight on White Bread	222 calories

8. Taco Bell

BAD	Taco Salad with Salsa	840 calories
BETTER	Mexican Pizza	570 calories
BEST	Steak Taco	200 calories

9. Wendy's

BAD	Big Bacon Classic	580 calories
BETTER	Junior Cheeseburger	320 calories
BEST	Junior Hamburger	280 calories

3 Ways to Tell if Chocolate Is Fresh

Here are some ways to make sure you're not wasting all those calories on bad chocolate.

1. The chocolate should smell chocolatey. If there's not a strong, pleasant odor or if there's a chemical smell, it might have been stored improperly.

2. The surface should be smooth and shiny. That dull coating you sometimes see on chocolate, called bloom, tells you that the chocolate isn't fresh.

3. If it's a filled chocolate and the bottom has become concave, the chocolate has dried and shrunk. The cream inside should be smooth.

Candy Is Not So Dandy After All: Calorie & Fat Contents of 11 Candy Bars

	Calories	Fat Grams
1. Almond Joy (1.76 oz)	250	14
2. Good & Plenty (1.8 oz)	191	0
3. Hershey's Milk Chocolate (1.55 oz)	240	14
4. Junior Mints (1.6 oz)	192	5
5. Kit Kat (1.5 oz)	230	12
6. Life Savers (.9 oz)	88	0
7. M&M's peanut (1.74 oz)	250	13
8. Mr. Goodbar (1.65 oz)	240	15
9. Sugar Daddy (2 oz.)	218	1
10. Tootsie Roll (2.25 oz)	252	6
11. York Peppermint Pattie (1.5 oz)	180	4

A Candy Timeline

You'll find lots more mouth-watering factoids at www.candyusa.org. Yum.

1868 Richard Cadbury introduces the Valentine's Day box of chocolates.

1893 William Wrigley, Jr., introduces Juicy Fruit gum and Wrigley's Spearmint gum.

1896 Tootsie Rolls debut, introduced by Leo Hirshfield of New York who named them after his daughter, whose nickname was Tootsie.

1900 Milton S. Hershey of Lancaster, Pa., introduces the Hershey milk chocolate bar.

1906 Hershey's Kisses chocolates first appear in their familiar foil wraps.

1912 Life Savers are introduced in peppermint flavor. It will be 22 years before the popular five-flavor roll is offered.

1913 Goo Goo Clusters, a southern favorite, is the first bar to combine milk chocolate, caramel, marshmallow, and peanuts.

1920 The Baby Ruth candy bar appears, named for President Grover Cleveland's daughter, not the famous baseball player.

1921 Chuckles are introduced.

1922 Goldenberg's Peanut Chews are first made in Philadelphia and soon become popular on the East Coast.

1923 Mounds, the double candy bar, offers a coconut filling covered in chocolate.

1923 The Milky Way Bar is the first of many candies made by the Mars family.

1925 Bit-O-Honey debuts, the honey-flavored taffy bar made with bits of almond.

1926 Milk Duds are introduced.

1928 Heath Bars appear, offering chocolate-covered toffee.

1928 Reese's Peanut Butter Cups, named for the man who created them, are among the most popular candy bars today.

1930 The Snickers Bar is introduced, named for a favorite horse owned by the Mars family. It is the top-selling candy bar in the U.S. today.

1931 Tootsie Roll Pops appear and are widely advertised as the lollipop that offers "two candies in one—flavored hard candy on the outside and chewy Tootsie Roll center inside."

1932 Red Hots, those fiery little candy pellets flavored with cinnamon, are introduced by the Ferrara Pan Candy Company.

1932 M&M/Mars debuts the 3 Musketeers Bar, originally a three-flavor bar, with chocolate, vanilla, and strawberry nougat. In 1945, it became all chocolate .

1936 The 5th Avenue Bar is originated by the man perhaps best known for his cough drops — William H. Luden. It is made from layers of peanut butter crunch coated in milk chocolate.

1939 Hershey's Miniatures chocolate bars debut.

1941 M&M's are introduced in response to slack chocolate sales in summer months.

1949 We get the first Junior Mints.

1954 Marshmallow Peeps are introduced by Just Born, Inc., in the shape of Easter chicks. Today, Peeps come in a variety of seasonal shapes.

1960 Starburst Fruit Chews are introduced and later fortified with 50% of the daily value for Vitamin C.

1960 Blammo becomes the first sugar-free soft bubble gum, made by Amurol Confections.

1978 Hershey's Reese's Pieces bite-size candies are introduced. Four years later they are made widely popular by the blockbuster movie *E.T.*

1979 Twix Caramel Cookie Bars are introduced in the U.S.

1980 Goelitz introduces the first American gummy bears and gummy worms. Formerly, these candies were imported from Europe.

1981 A European favorite since 1974, Skittles Bite Size Candies are sold in the U.S.

1998 Holopops become the first hologram lollipops, developed by Light Vision Confections. The design on their etched surface appears to change as you move the pop.

1999 Sound Bites Lollipops from Cap Candies is the first radio-lollipop combination in the growing interactive candy segment, first developed in Japan. (We're not kidding.)

2001 M&M's Dulce de Leche Caramel Chocolate Candies are introduced in the U.S. to tap a growing Latino market.

Some Words About Words

1. "Typewriter" is the longest word that can be made using the letters on only one row of the keyboard.

2. "Go" is the shortest complete sentence in the English language.

3. No word in the English language rhymes with "orange," "silver," "purple," or "month."

4. "Stewardesses" is the longest word typed with only the left hand.

5. The sentence "The quick brown fox jumps over the lazy dog" uses every letter in the alphabet.

6. The only 15-letter word that can be spelled without repeating a letter is "uncopyrightable."

7. "Dreamt" is the only English word that ends in "mt."

8. Only 4 words in the English language end in "dous": "tremendous," "horrendous," "stupendous," and "hazardous."

9. The letters of the alphabet in order of frequency of use are: ETAISONHRDLUCMFWYPGVBKJQXZ

10. Five words begin with "dw": dwarf, dwell, dwelling, dwindle, dwy.

11. The 3 longest words without using a vowel are: "crwth" (pronounced *krooth*), which is a type of stringed instrument, "llwchwr," a city district in Wales, and "rhythms."

12. The longest one-syllable word in the English language is "screeched."

42 Absolutely Useless Facts

1. Rubber bands last longer when refrigerated.

2. Peanuts are one of the ingredients of dynamite.

3. The national anthem of Greece has 158 verses. No one in Greece has memorized all of them.

4. There are 293 ways to make change for a dollar.

5. The average person's left hand does 56% of the typing.

6. The venom in Daddy Longlegs spiders is more poisonous than a Black Widow's or a Brown Recluse's, but they cannot bite humans because their jaws won't open wide enough.

7. Mel Blanc (the voice of Bugs Bunny) was allergic to carrots.

8. A shark is the only fish that can blink with both eyes.

9. There are more chickens than people in the world.

10. Two-thirds of the world's eggplants are grown in New Jersey.

11. On a Canadian $2 bill, an American flag is flying over the Parliament Building.

12. Women blink nearly twice as much as men.

13. Shakespeare invented the words "assassination" and "bump."

14. Marilyn Monroe had six toes on one foot.

15. If you keep a goldfish in the darkroom, it will eventually turn white.

16. All 50 states are listed across the top of the Lincoln Memorial on the back of the $5 bill.

17. Winston Churchill was born in a ladies' room during a dance.

18. Maine is the only state whose name is just one syllable.

19. Los Angeles's full name is El Pueblo de Nuestra Senora la Reina de los Angeles de Porciuncula and can be abbreviated to 3.63% of its size: L.A.

20. A cat has 32 muscles in each ear.

21. An ostrich's eye is bigger than its brain.

22. Tigers have striped skin, not just striped fur.

23. The names of all the continents end with the same letters they start with.

24. In most ads, including those in newspapers, the time displayed on a watch is 10:10.

25. The only real person ever to be a Pez head was Betsy Ross.

26. The *Sesame Street* characters Bert and Ernie were named after Bert the cop and Ernie the taxi driver in the film *It's a Wonderful Life*.

27. If you toss a penny 10,000 times, it will be heads not 5,000 times but more like 4,950. The heads picture weighs more.

28. A dragonfly has a lifespan of 24 hours.

29. American Airlines saved $40,000 in 1987 by eliminating one olive from each salad served in first-class.

30. China has more people who speak English than the U.S.

31. You share your birthday with at least 9 million other people in the world.

32. The electric chair was invented by a dentist.

33. A goldfish has a memory span of 3 seconds.

34. A dime has 118 ridges around the edge.

35. On an American $1 bill, an owl is in the upper-left-hand corner of the "1," encased in the "shield," and a spider is hidden in the front upper-right-hand corner.

36. It's impossible to sneeze with your eyes open.

37. The winter of 1932 was so cold that Niagara Falls froze completely solid.

38. Polar bears are left-handed.

39. A cockroach will live for 9 days without its head before it starves to death.

40. In England, the Speaker of the House is not allowed to speak.

41. Donald Duck comics were banned in Finland because Donald doesn't wear pants.

42. Mister Rogers is an ordained minister.

18 Palindromes

These read the same backward and forward.

1. A dog, a plan, a canal: pagoda.

2. Rats live on no evil star.

3. Dennis, Nell, Edna, Leon, Nedra, Anita, Rolf, Nora, Alice, Carol, Leo, Jane, Reed, Dena, Dale, Basil, Rae, Penny, Lana, Dave, Denny, Lena, Ida, Bernadette, Ben, Ray, Lila, Nina, Jo, Ira, Mara, Sara, Mario, Jan, Ina, Lily, Arne, Bette, Dan, Reba, Diane, Lynn, Ed, Eva, Dana, Lynne, Pearl, Isabel, Ada, Ned, Dee, Rena, Joel, Lora, Cecil, Aaron, Flora, Tina, Arden, Noel, and Ellen sinned.

4. A man, a plan, a cat, a canal; Panama?

5. A man, a plan, a cat, a ham, a yak, a yam, a hat, a canal—Panama!

6. Doc note, I dissent. A fast never prevents a fatness. I diet on cod.

7. If I had a hi-fi.

8. A man, a plan, a canoe, pasta, hero's, rajahs, a coloratura, maps, snipe, percale, macaroni, a gag, a banana bag, a tan, a tag, a banana bag again, or: a camel, a crepe, pins, spam, a rut, a Rolo, cash, a jar, sore hats, a peon, a canal, Panama!

9. Rise to vote sir.
10. Madam I'm Adam.
11. A Toyota! Race fast, safe car. A Toyota.
12. You can cage a swallow, can't you, but you can't swallow a cage, can you?
13. Cigar? Toss it in a can, it is so tragic.
14. Oh, no! Don Ho!
15. No, Mel Gibson is a casino's big lemon.
16. Kay, a red nude, peeped under a yak.
17. Never odd or even.
18. No lemons, no melon.

BIBLIOGRAPHY

Books

Anthony, Carl. *America's First Families* (New York: Simon & Schuster, 2000).

Bailly, Sharon. *Pass It On* (Brookfield, Conn.: Millbrook Press, 1995).

Collier, Peter. *The Roosevelts: An American Saga* (New York: Simon & Schuster, 1994).

Collins, Yvonne, and Sandy Rodeout. *Totally Me* (Minneapolis: Free Spirit, 2000).

Fox, Annie. *Can You Relate* (Minneapolis: Free Spirit, 2000).

Godek, Gregory. *1001 Ways to Be Romantic* (New York: Sourcebooks, 1999).

Hample, Zack. *How to Shag Major League Baseballs* (New York: Aladdin, 1999).

Handler, Stacey. *The Body Burden: Living in the Shadow of Barbie* (Cape Canaveral, Fla.: Blue Note, 2000).

Hirsch, Alan. *What Flavor Is Your Personality* (New York: Sourcebooks, 2000).

Israel, Elaine, ed. *The World Almanac for Kids, 2001* (New York: World Almanac Education, 2001).

Jacobs, Thomas A. *What Are My Rights?* (Minneapolis: Free Spirit, 1997).

Nelson, Richard E., and Judith Galas. *The Power to Prevent Suicide* (Minneapolis: Free Spirit, 1994).

Packer, Alex J. *Highs!* (Minneapolis: Free Spirit, 2000).

Rees, Dafydd, and Luke Crampton. *The DK Encyclopedia of Rock Stars* (London: Dorling Kindersley, 1996).

Tyler, Suzette. *Been There Should've Done That II* (Haslett, Mich.: Front Porch Press, 1997).

Periodicals

Bervera, Sara Xochitl, et al. "When Perceptions Are Not Reality: Youth Role in Crime Exaggerated," *San Francisco Chronicle*, Oct. 9, 1998.

Cauchon, Dennis. "Why DARE Didn't Work," *USA Today*, Oct. 11, 1994.

"The Classroom of the Future." *Newsweek*, Oct. 29, 2001.

Doliver, Mark. "Seeing Beyond the Stereotype of the Defiant Teen," *Adweek*, Dec. 14, 1998.

"The Dominator." *Newsweek*, June 18, 2001.

Handler, Stacey. "Barbie Doll Blues," *Jump*, March 2001.

Katz, Jon. "The Kids Are All Right," *Hotwired*, Feb. 26, 1997.

Kluger, Jeffrey. "Fear Not," *Time*, Apr. 2, 2001.

Males, Mike. "Bashing Youth: Media Myths about Teenagers," *Extra!*, March/April 1994.

Mary Ann, "How to Start Your Very Own Band," *Sassy*, April 1994.

Various issues

The Enquirer
Jump
Seventeen
Sweet 16.com Magazine

Miscellaneous

"Close the Book on Hate: 101 Ways to Combat Prejudice." Barnes and Noble, 2000.

Hirsch, Alan. "Avocation as an Indication of Snack Food Hedonics," unpublished paper, 2001.

———. "Ice Cream Hedonics and Personality," unpublished paper, 2001.

———. "Snack Food Hedonics and Personality," unpublished paper, 2000.

Horatio Alger Association. "State of Our Nation's Youth, 2001–2002," 2001.

U.S. Department of Education, National Center for Education Statistics, "The Comparison of Teens International," *Outcomes of Learning: Results From the 2000 Program for International Student Assessment of 15-Year-Olds in Reading, Mathematics, and Science Literacy*, 2001.

Web sites

About.com: www.about.com

Camp Supplies: www.campsupplies.com

Career Builder: www.careerbuilders.com

City of Orlando Police Department: www.cityoforlando.net

DRCNet: www.drc.net

Dream Moods: www.dreammoods.com

Entertainment Earth: www.entertainmentearth.com

Glowport: www.jokes.glowport.com

IHigh.com: www.iHigh.com

In the '80s: www.inthe80s.com

In the '90s: www.inthe90s.com

Jon Sandy's Movie Mistakes: www.moviemistakes.com

Karaoke Scene magazine: www.karaokescene.com

KidsHealth: www.kidshealth.org

Marylaine.com: www.marylaine.com

National Institute on Media and the Family: www.mediafamily.org

Project Happy Child: www.happychild.org.uk

Recovering Racists Network (RRN): www.jmckenzie.com

The Self-Esteem Institute: www.theselfesteeminstitute.com

Teen Central: www.teencentral.net

Teen Outreach: www.teenoutreach.com

Theft Talk: www.thefttalk.com

Tom Mazza/LCT: www.lctmag.com

USA Weekend: www.usaweekend.com

INDEX

Mental health, signs of depression in, 20

Merlyn's Pen (magazine), 207

Mickey Mouse Club, former members of, 203–4

Middle child, best and worst things about being, 115–16

Misconceptions on sex, 144–45

Misery, 197

Mohamed, Shazad, 278

Moms, 185–88
best television, 185–88

Monarchs, British, 277–78

Money
getting, for college, 180–81
managing, 81
sources of, for teens, 286–87
things to sell to raise, 84–85

Morals, effect of entertainment media on, 255

Morlan, Krysta, 283

Movie kiss, giving perfect, 136

Movies
coming-of-age, 199–200
high school, 201–3
mistakes in favorite, 193–96
questions for videoshop assistant, 203
scariest, 196–99

Moving, friends and, 123–24

Mr. Holland's Opus, 202

Music. *See also* Songs
alternative, 258–61
censorship and, 60–62
essential world albums, 261–63
free downloads, 255
hip-hop albums, 257–58
most demented, 237–39
party dance songs, 236–37
rock 'n' roll soundtracks in, 255–57
starting band, 243–46
staying safe at concerts, 79–80

teenage pop stars and, 246–50
tips for buying stereo, 242–43
Weird Al songs, 240–42

Musicians, left-handed, 281–82

My Bodyguard, 202

N

National Association of Anorexia Nervosa and Associated Disorders, 27

National Child Abuse Hotline, 25

National Clearinghouse for Alcohol and Drug Information (NCADI), 25

National Coalition Against Domestic Violence, 56

National Council on Child Abuse and Family Violence, 56

National Crime Prevention Council, 47–48, 56

National Domestic Violence Hotline, 25–26

National Information Center for Children and Youth with Disabilities, 56

National Jewish Council for the Disabled, 57

National organizations
supporting, 46–49
youth, 53–58

National Runaway 24-Hour Switchboard, 27

National Safety Council, 74

National School Safety Center, 57

National Sexually Transmitted Disease Hotline, 27

National Suicide Prevention Directory (NSPD), 26

National Wildlife Federation, 48

National Youth Crisis Hotline, 27

Nerds, 16

Nervousness, about public speaking, 177–78